T0219844

Lecture Notes in Computer Science 10825

Commenced Publication in 1973
Founding and Former Series Editors:
Gerhard Goos, Juris Hartmanis, and Jan van Leeuwen

More information about this series at http://www.springer.com/series/7409

Heide Karen Lukosch · Geertje Bekebrede
Rens Kortmann (Eds.)

Simulation Gaming

Applications for Sustainable Cities and Smart Infrastructures

48th International Simulation and Gaming
Association Conference, ISAGA 2017
Delft, The Netherlands, July 10–14, 2017
Revised Selected Papers

 Springer

Editors
Heide Karen Lukosch 🆔
Faculty of Technology, Policy
   and Management
Delft University of Technology
Delft
The Netherlands

Rens Kortmann
Faculty of Technology, Policy
   and Management
Delft University of Technology
Delft
The Netherlands

Geertje Bekebrede
Faculty of Technology, Policy
   and Management
Delft University of Technology
Delft
The Netherlands

ISSN 0302-9743   ISSN 1611-3349 (electronic)
Lecture Notes in Computer Science
ISBN 978-3-319-91901-0   ISBN 978-3-319-91902-7 (eBook)
https://doi.org/10.1007/978-3-319-91902-7

Library of Congress Control Number: 2018944310

LNCS Sublibrary: SL3 – Information Systems and Applications, incl. Internet/Web, and HCI

Printed on acid-free paper

This Springer imprint is published by the registered company Springer International Publishing AG
part of Springer Nature
The registered company address is: Gewerbestrasse 11, 6330 Cham, Switzerland

Simulation Games for Sustainable Cities and Smart Infrastructures – Foreword

Simulation and gaming have proven their value in contributing to the analysis and design of so-called complex systems, such as the development of sustainable cities and smart infrastructures. Numerous examples of games about urban planning, intelligent transport systems, social cohesion, and other related themes have been developed, played, and studied in the past years. In the International Simulation and Gaming Association (ISAGA) Conference 2017, we aimed at taking the current state of affairs one step further and move toward a comprehensive theory of simulation games for sustainable cities and smart infrastructures. During the conference, which was held jointly by ISAGA and SAGANET (Simulation and Gaming Association The Netherlands), hosted by Delft University of Technology, science met practice, and many academic as well as practice-based games and concepts were presented and discussed. The result of the scientific contributions is presented in this LNCS book.

The contributions to this book range from design thinking related to simulation gaming, the analysis of the consequences of design choices in games, to games for decision-making, examples of games for business, climate change, maritime spatial planning, sustainable city development, supply chain, and team work factors, up to games that facilitate (organizational) learning processes or are used for attitude measurement, and the use of VR technologies in games, not to forget the role of de-briefing in the game process.

In the section "Design and Development," the focus is on the design process of simulation games. The articles show the importance of design choices and the influences of these choices on the game's effectiveness. They also highlight the role of the designer as well as the use of accepted design concepts and approaches. In the section "Planning and Policy," games are presented that serve as support tool for policy-making processes. The articles describe how stakeholders can be engaged in a decision-making process, and how games can facilitate the participation of and discourse between them. The perception of games as well as their use for (organizational) learning processes is discussed in the contributions in the section "Games and Simulations." Learner activation and individual value of games in learning processes are topics discussed along with concrete examples of games facilitating, e.g., knowledge development in the field of supply chain management. In the next section, we give room to the relatively new and yet underexplored field of "Games as Research Instruments." The contributions show how games can serve as research instruments themselves, and how they can be combined with other research measures in order to provide both a rich feedback to participants and researchers and a rigid research set-up for measurement of, e.g.. participants' attitudes in the transportation domain. Games that are used for learning processes are discussed in the last section, "Learning." The authors introduce theoretical concepts of games as a learning instrument, from assessment to conditions for learning, up to the role of de-briefing.

Thus, the 20 selected articles discuss game methodologies for the design and research of and with games, applications of gaming to tackle the grand challenges of our society as well as to support learning processes and policy development, new insights in interface and interaction designs for games, and evaluated applications of games in real-world settings.

The present collection of articles represents current advances in the field of simulation and gaming, which were presented and discussed at a very constructive and energetic conference in Delft, the Netherlands. The editors wish to thank all contributors to this book, reviewers of the articles, as well as all participants of the ISAGA 2017 conference for adding to this important and still-growing field of research that is strongly related to its application domains. We also want to thank Maria Freese and Shalini Kurapati, who helped us process all contributions to the conference. We look forward to future exchanges and further advancements of our exciting field of research and design of simulation games!

April 2018

Heide K. Lukosch
Geertje Bekebrede
Rens Kortmann

Organization

48th International Gaming and Simulation Association (ISAGA) Conference, Delft, July 10–14, 2017

ISAGA 2017 was organized by Delft University of Technology in collaboration with ISAGA and Saganet (Simulation and Gaming Association, The Netherlands).

General Chairs

Heide Karen Lukosch	Delft University of Technology, The Netherlands
Geertje Bekebrede	Delft University of Technology, The Netherlands
Rens Kortmann	Delft University of Technology, The Netherlands

Organizing Committee

Geertje Bekebrede	Delft University of Technology, The Netherlands
Maria Freese	German Aerospace Center, Germany
Rens Kortmann	Delft University of Technology, The Netherlands
Shalini Kurapati	Delft University of Technology, The Netherlands
Heide Lukosch	Delft University of Technology, The Netherlands
Simon Tiemersma	Delft University of Technology, The Netherlands
Linda van Veen	Delft University of Technology, The Netherlands
Alexander Verbraeck	Delft University of Technology, The Netherlands

Scientific Committee

Gabriele Hoeborn	University of Wuppertal, Germany
Maria-Eugenia Iacob	University of Twente, The Netherlands
Michal Jakubowski	Kozminski University, Poland
Toshiko Kikkawa	Keio University, Japan
Jan Klabbers	KPMG, The Netherlands
Martijn Koops	Hogeschool Utrecht, The Netherlands
Willy C. Kriz	FH Vorarlberg, Austria
Shalini Kurapati	Delft University of Technology, The Netherlands
Elyssebeth Ellen Leigh	FutureSearch, Australia
Maria Freese	German Aerospace Center, Germany
Sebastiaan Meijer	KTH Stockholm, Sweden
Kirsten de Ries	NHTV Breda, The Netherlands
Rolf Nohr	HBK Hochschule für Bildende Künste, Germany
Vincent Peters	Hogeschool van Arnhem en Nijmegen, The Netherlands
Jayanth Raghothama	KTH Stockholm, Sweden

Riitta Smeds   Aalto University, Finland
Luiz Antonio Titton   Universidade de Sao Paulo, Brazil
Eric Treske   intrestik Organisation & Planspiel, Germany
Shigehisa Tsuchiya   Chiba Institute of Technology, Japan
Alexander Verbraeck   Delft University of Technology, The Netherlands
Marcin Wardaszko   Kozminski University, Poland
Harald Warmelink   NHTV Breda, The Netherlands
Birgit Zürn   DHBW Hochschule Baden-Württemberg, Germany

Award Committee

Geertje Bekebrede   Delft University of Technology, The Netherlands
Maria Freese   German Aerospace Center, Germany
Michael Jakubowski   Kozminski University, Poland
Rolf Nohr   HBK Hochschule für Bildende Künste, Germany

Sponsors

Honey Highway
InThere
Saganet
Sagsaga
The Barn
The Conference Game
TU Delft

Contents

Games as Research Instrument

Learning

Design and Development

Design Thinking: Project Portfolio Management and Simulation – A Creative Mix for Research

Saeed Shalbafan[✉] and Elyssebeth Leigh

University of Technology Sydney, Ultimo, Australia
saeed.shalbafan@gmail.com

Abstract. This paper takes de Bono's explanation of 'design thinking' as the starting point for a report on a doctoral research project that began with a conventional 'why?' question, and then, instead of looking for an 'explanation', chose to look forward in time to establish an understanding of 'how to' think differently about a recurring problem. The catalyst for this work was observation of otherwise competent managers making desperately wrong decisions when good decision making was crucial to their company's future. The initial choice to 'look forward' when designing the research strategy was made well before there was a clear understanding of what was being observed. Given that trajectory, this paper explores the process by which a simulation was created and then used in conjunction with a comparatively new approach to data collection (Explanation looks backwards and design looks forward [1].).

Keywords: Design thinking · Project portfolio management
Cynefin knowledge domains · Sense making in complex contexts

1 Introduction

It all began with a series of increasingly worrying decisions that seemed to be at odds with what was otherwise known about the capabilities of the decision makers. The context was a project portfolio management (PPM) office which was thrown into chaos as the events of the Global Financial Crisis (GFC) began impacting on the rate of business growth in Australia. A comparatively new member of the PPM team was expecting to see considered and thoughtful attention being given to the quality of decision making as conditions worsened. Instead attention to decision making seemed to be haphazard and lacking in the kind of thoughtful focus needed in times of stress.

As time passed the idea of researching the nature of what had happened emerged as a doctoral research proposal. The initial questions were focused on why things were not better managed and the research began with that in mind. At first the intention was to conduct research directly within the context of what had been observed. However, those poor decisions had proved costly enough that the observer, along with other staff, was eventually out of work, as the number of projects dwindled and there was no longer a project portfolio office to research. Although that seemed a death knell for the research, it took it in an entirely new and creative direction. Instead of asking 'why' the

© Springer International Publishing AG, part of Springer Nature 2018
H. K. Lukosch et al. (Eds.): ISAGA 2017, LNCS 10825, pp. 3–14, 2018.
https://doi.org/10.1007/978-3-319-91902-7_1

decision making was not of a better quality, the research focus shifted towards understanding how to help others, facing similar situations in future, make better decisions by looking forward rather than back. de Bono [1] noted that 'explanation looks backwards and design looks forward', and since it had become impossible to seek explanations about those past events, the opportunity was emerging to apply the painfully garnered observations to the task of developing an understanding of 'how to' think differently about a recurring problem.

This paper reports what happened when the focus of the question changed. Design thinking came to the fore, and a unique simulation was designed to assist in researching the process of thinking differently about an unfamiliar situation. The initial thought had been to use an existing simulation game to simulate the context of PPM decision making. The simulation was to be the replacement for an organisationally based case study. As organisational life cycles are becoming shorter and less certain, it made sense to create a similar environment that would remain under the researcher's control for studying decision making. Lack of access to confidential information about those prior strategic decisions was another issue supporting the idea of using simulation. The aim was to create opportunities for participants to act 'as if' decision makers in a role play context while allowing the observer to understand how decision makers make decisions. Key challenges emerging from these initial thoughts, included the extent to which existing designs would be a fit with the context of decision making in PPM, while providing sufficient relevant rich data for analysis. Each of these concerns were addressed in the process of developing a more creative view of the presenting problem which, in turn, led to the design of a unique simulation for use as the research instrument.

2 The Background

The observer/researcher had started working as a skilled migrant in a new country. The homeland with its rich history for addressing complexity and uncertainty was a place where, to survive, people must be forward thinking in their day-to-day life. During the observer's social learning in childhood each plan was understood to need a plan B to respond to unexpected events. Having arrived in a country famous for its luck in policy making and blessings for its rich natural resources, this approach did not seem to be much of importance for senior managers. Observation of local management practice began to reveal indicators of an absence of a holistic view about resources utilisation, as well as poor/delayed responses to the need for setting strategic direction – both indicators of problems in senior management decision making.

The crisis occurred for the observer's employer when funding limits were suddenly imposed on a major project. The corporation was derailed from its flourishing practice, and the business unit absorbed into other units. The company vanished from the market within three years. The observer's initial re-action had been a desire to help senior management teams avoid further such crashes arising from poor decision making. The lack of a holistic view, and an absence of tools to promote its benefits, had been identified as two factors indicating the need to work on a framework for implementing a better approach to PPM in the corporation.

Discussion with senior managers, and reviews of publications, created a project portfolio road map focusing on resource utilisation and timelines as the core of an exercise to improve efficiency in regard to selecting and prioritising projects to align with available resources [2]. This was to support a single case study for the PhD project and had, indeed, begun to show its value. The sudden, unexpected market changes, coupled with growing competition and side effects of the GFC in 2008 [12], forced the company board to re-shuffle the organisation chart, downsize and eventually sell the business within a very short period. The observer was a new comer to Australia, and the employer had been the only reliable source of research data, as well as a good context for researching use of a multiple projects structure. However, as the changes took effect the research shifted from a case-study to an entirely new approach. The resulting journey let to the design of Hooshmand-1 – a bespoke simulation designed for the purpose of researching the problem, which has now been adopted for use in education programs in Australia and overseas. The research also changed focus, producing a forward-looking, rather than a backward-facing research dissertation, as well as a number of intermediate research papers (e.g. Shalbafan, Leigh et al. 2015).

3   Design Process

While design thinking, as a term and a method, is still somewhat contested, it is generally considered to be method allowing practical, creative exploration of problems leading to solutions that are 'emergent' rather than pre-defined. Its use encourages consideration of both present conditions and future needs and interests. Design thinking may produce a number of alternate solutions, rather than a single 'first best fit' outcome. In this regard it is fair to say that there were several options available at the beginning of the research, yet none of them were so obvious as to automatically rule out any of the others. This led to a time-consuming, and at times painful, series of action learning cycles. Each of these had three distinct goals. The first was to identify key features needed in a simulation to serve the emerging purpose of the research. The second was to identify whether any existing designs might meet these criteria. The third was to work out the logistics for making use of whatever design proved to be most suitable. Two key underlying assumption were, first that the data-collection aspect of the research would use decision makers already employed in senior levels of management with experiences in a number of different industries; and second, that the action would explore how they made decisions when facing the kind of unexpected events commonly called 'Black Swan' episodes [19].

3.1   Trialling Existing Designs

A number of diverse designs were identified and some were trialled with volunteer participants. Key and essential features needed for developing a successful research tool, were unclear at the beginning, and each iteration brought only a very rough approximation by the end of each trial. Fragments and evidence to support the ideal simulation were collected and analysed throughout the cycle of trials as the process began helping to uncover what an effective simulation design - that would be fit for purpose – could look like.

Each trial took two to three months for completion beginning with identification through to enactment, examination of outcomes and conclusions about what needed to be sought next. There was a clear 'tipping point' that shaped much of the ensuing process during the first trial of a role-play simulation which had been originally designed for exploring communication and decision making in academic settings. This was called *WipWap* and was the outcome of a Master research project [11, 12].

WipWap was re-crafted to compress time to create a learning environment for volunteers to assess pre/post knowledge of decision making in PPM. The game provided a good model of a setting in which to engage participants in group decision making, a factor which informed the final design of Hooshmand-1, but was otherwise deemed not fit for purpose. Key lessons emerging from enactment this simulation, included the observation that cause-and-effect relationships and linear/non-linear behaviour could not be understood by participants at the same time as their activity was causing the process to slip into chaos. This was the tipping point that changed the research question from 'why?' to 'how?'

Keeping in mind that the research aim was to study PPM decision making in complex situations, with the goal of supporting effective strategic direction setting, the intention was to explore how to implement PPM as a vital contributory mechanism. An anticipated outcome would be to provide corporations with guidelines to reduce the chance of failures in executive decision making. After this first challenging simulation, conducted with volunteer participants, it became obvious that many were unable to make a connection between their knowledge of PPM and their performance in the simulation. This was interpreted as an indicator of the absence of consensus on a definition of PPM as included in organisational structures. This led to abandoning the intended pre-test/post-test strategy for assessing participants' understanding of the Project Management body of knowledge. Instead, the focus shifted to a consideration of whether self-proclaimed 'rational decision makers' are making decisions based on their emotions. Thus emerged the second tipping point contributing to the final design of the new simulation and its associated research questions.

After observing the first iteration of this simulation, the observer/researcher realised that many beliefs and assumptions about the linear behaviour of decision makers, and the timing of associated actions, were not working well. It became clear that a different approach would be needed to create meaningful results for the research project. Analysis of these observations resulted in a shift to a research method that would involve moderating factors such as facilitation processes in the design of a simulation to help form a research study that would have some degree of control over the outcomes of participants' actions.

The second iteration was a simulation game – AirPower2100 - developed for use in re-shaping decision making in regard to flight and maintenance schedules on a military air base [7]. Its design was diametrically opposed to that of the first trial. In this design, every action was followed by an instructor's permission to take the next action, so participants had far less freedom of action. It was played for one cycle of activity (the full simulation involves two cycles) to develop a sense of whether a conversion could be made from the original design for air force training, to an executive decision making simulation. The immediate conclusion was that the existing design could not support the kind of communications and freedom of decision making familiar to those working in the context of a PPM office. However, observing this enactment showed the value of including strict rules in the role play to achieve desired the objectives. This finding was central to the design of the facilitation process for use in managing Hooshmand-1.

3.2 Encountering Cynefin

Both simulations thus failed to provide an effective context for referencing theories relevant to PPM. Both also demonstrated aspects of the non-linear nature of decision making in complex problems. An additional problem was also emerging at this time - the recruitment of volunteers was becoming more difficult than had been expected. This triggered a curiosity leading to investigation of the Cynefin framework [10] as a tool for studying decision making in complex situations.

The Cynefin model proposes that we encounter knowledge in three modes across five domains. Knowledge modes are either 'Ordered' (systematic and structured), 'Unordered' (complex, without pre-determined form) or 'Disordered' (without form or knowable structure). Within these modes the Domains are 'Obvious' and 'Complicated', in the Ordered mode, 'Complex' and 'Chaos' in Unordered mode, and 'Disorder' stands alone. Each Domain represents a way in which knowledge is received and responded to; individual capacity for awareness to context, impacts responsiveness to conditions in which we find ourselves.

The Obvious domain is the most familiar of the knowledge domains. We are usually comforted by the *appearance* of the orderliness of things, and prefer not to depart from it. Unless there is reassuring guidance. Such guidance usually comes in the form of 'expert help' to introduce us to the 'hidden order' - which is knowable and accessible – in the Complicated domain.

The comfort of these ordered modes is very different from the uncertainties of the 'Un-ordered' knowledge domains, where there are no absolute certainties. Knowledge in the Complex domain can be sought but is not readily evident. So there is much 'shuffling of feet' when conditions seem to be sliding away from our 'comfort zones'. However, if we plunge in, we become adept at the essential tasks of checking assumptions, and learning to 'probe' for meaning, developing a capacity for 'making sense of' what confronts us, and finding ways to manage unfolding events. There will be time, later, for reflecting on the quality of responses. The Complex domain necessitates reducing dependency on experts, and increasing proficiency at designing our own strategies and actions. Taleb's 'Black Swans' (ibid) may be found here, and also in the 'Chaos' domain – depending on their severity and impact.

The Chaos domain is evidenced by an absence of causes, rules or guidelines for action. While, in truth there may be, they may not ever be fully understood - so we have a choice – flee, or take action to reduce the confusion. Life is often going to be chaotic, so becoming able to take action and make sense of what happens reduces the need to rely on someone else rescuing us from uncertainty. When we confuse Chaos and its opportunities with Disorder we may flee into denial and attack others (things and people) who seem to be causing the 'chaos'.

Finally there is the pivotal domain of 'Disorder' around which the other four are arrayed. As Cynefin is a conceptual model for thinking about knowledge, the positioning of 'Disorder' as the central pivot is not so much a tribute to its importance, as an indication of its potential for destruction. Disorder is to be feared. It is the name of all those nameless dreads that induce fear and cause individuals to flee to the known and 'safe' context of the Obvious, while failing to realise that uncertainty and 'Chaos' are merely learning tools with which to tackle a future that is forever unknown but always coming. An idea was forming about the possibility of creating case-based scenarios to replicate features of the chosen Cynefin domains. Of the five, the 'Complicated' and 'Complex' domains became central to creating a design incorporating two scenarios.

3.3   Establishing Realism and Setting Parameters

The process of developing a theoretical framework for a simulation is always challenging and the context needs to be finely tuned, if it is to be realistic. As part of the search for a framework the researcher interviewed a professor in PPM who had completed research using multiple case studies on the nature of uncertainty in PPM decision making. An exchange of ideas and information, with professor Yvan Pettit, provided great insight into existing research work on uncertainties and mechanisms for managing their impacts on decision making processes [14]. Discussion of those case studies helped to create fictional scenarios and refine the research questions into a more precise format.

The final design elements emerged through the opportunity to attend a classroom exercise for postgraduate students enabling observation of several factors allowing integration of key theoretical components into a simulation game. The exercise occurred after a lecture about PPM tools and their application [15].

On the first occasion the researcher attended the event to observe its operation. On the second occasion, the chance to participate with the students was taken up. The game included an embedded decision making process for project selection and introduced different methods of presenting data and the participants' judgements of the data [9]. This simulation included a short pilot to help participants become familiar with the objectives; while the main session was intended for individual participants to work out their solutions. All this was followed by a group discussion about the final agreed solution/s.

Participating with the students illuminated key aspects of theory in PPM decision making - including decision criteria, objective setting, and how individual judgements can be influenced by the presentation of information. This triggered the researcher/ observer to extend this aspect of the design to the emerging simulation as an index with which to measure the dynamics of peoples' judgements while the decision-making environment is changing.

These experiences provided the features that together showed how to develop a promising design for a new game. This final step, enabling the transition from sense making of fragmented observations and cues, to use creative thinking and relying on intuition, proved necessary to achieve a successful outcome. Table 1 summarises the results of these experiences in relation to the development of the simulation Hooshmand-1.

Table 1. Summary of thinking for different components of the simulation Hooshmand-1

Data description	Stream	Step	Collection/presentation tools
Warm up game and briefing	Input	1	A short game to make participants familiar with each other
Facilitated Simulation	Input	2	Timer on Wall, Roles and Scenarios (Papers)
Time of Completion, Value of Decision, process of decision making	Output	3	Report Sheet 1/Data for Time/value/ Consequences of decisions, consensus on final decision
Facilitated Simulation + Real Time Events	Input	4	Timer on Wall, Roles and Scenarios (Papers), Emergency Letters
Time of Completion, Value of Decision, process of decision making	Output	5	Report Sheet 2/Data for Time/value/ Consequences of decisions, consensus on final decision
Short stories if individual/group reflection	Input	6	Flip chart and sticky notes
Recorded Audio - Video	Output	7	Facilitated Reflection
Emerging Patterns	Output	8	Narrative analysis by using sense-maker

3.4   Assembling the Components

Having decided to use Cynefin as a framework, the contexts for scenarios 1 and 2 of the simulation were constructed so as to resemble a Complicated and a Complex world. At this stage, the concept of a 'sense making process' was becoming available as a tool to understand complex problems and it was agreed that the SenseMaker software [17] was a suitable tool with which to analyse participant post-event narratives.

3.5   Trials, Tribulations and Changes

Table 1 summarises the thinking behind the different components of Hooshmand-1. Once these elements were in place, a set of draft materials was prepared for an initial pilot session. This first session had an estimated length of 4 h - however it actually lasted 7 h. The key lesson learned at this point, was about the essence of having a strong and clear – but short – verbal briefing to provide essential background information. On this first occasion everything was in writing, which proved to be a time-consuming mistake. The second observation was that participants enjoyed the interactive session at the end where they were asked to prepare a group presentation to the other teams, however this too, was very time consuming. As the aim was to engage senior executive managers in the simulation process, and it is self-evident that their time is scarce, there was a clear indication of the need to improve the design to ensure it held its sense of realism but was more time efficient.

The second pilot session began with a verbal presentation, but participants completed only one scenario because they ignored all the alerts for finishing on time and could not arrive at agreed solutions. A key improvement gained from this experience concerned the importance of enforcing good time management via the facilitation process. A bell alarm and countdown calendar were added to the space of the simulation to make time more tangible and create a sense of urgency in participants during the decision-making process. It was also decided to create a road map – as a source of key information – to give to the team leaders for use as they saw fit with their team members, so that all individuals could better grasp the information.

By this time, the facilitation process had been standardised through use of a simulation protocol, which was helping the researcher ensure there was minimum variation between multiple simulations, from a process perspective. The members per group was set at a minimum of three people per group, to ensure a balanced, but minimum level of, communications channels in favour of process efficiency. Introduction of a 'role rotation' was recognised as a valuable addition and included during the final stage of the design. This was introduced as an additional element and put into action between the two scenarios to avoid any sense of a negative bias on role performances. Figure 1 illustrates the completed simulation design for Hooshmand-1.

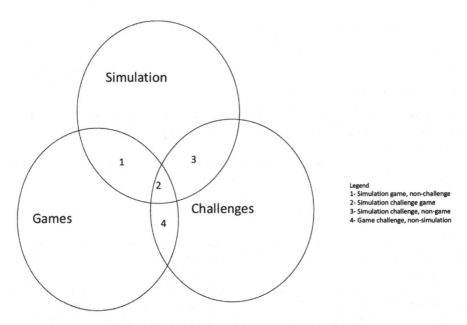

Fig. 1. Simulation, challenges and games relationships (Sa. Silva, Pedrosa et al. 2011, p. 66)

Recruiting for participants was the next challenge, as professional people were only available after working hours and persuading them to participate was difficult. The key message emerging from this aspect of the research process was the importance of providing the opportunity for self-imposed challenges on individuals' decision making capabilities in uncertain conditions. The growth of complexity in business was a key driver encouraging people to come to the assessment lab and explore how they deal with unexpected and changing conditions. Hooshmand-1 has a number of embedded components including communications processes, group decision making and interactive dialogue to facilitate the process of sense making in two increasingly difficult scenarios where participants have only limited information available for arriving at final decisions.

4 Applying Hooshmand-1 to Research PPM Decision Making

Silva et al. [15] state that simulations, games and challenges have common areas as shown in Fig. 1. Their Venn diagram shows that depending on the designer's desire to use each/any of these three concepts, four additional areas may be identified in the common/overlapping areas between each pair of the three components.

Simulation game, non-challenge engages participants to interact with an imitation of a system based on real world settings within defined rules of a game. According to Hussein [4] there is still little research on the use of simulation games for learning about/exploration of project leadership for individuals responsible for identification and execution strategies in relation to projects in the early planning phase. Hooshmand-1 can be categorised as a 'simulation challenge game' in this model, since it generates an open-ended simulation of project portfolio management for research purposes, in which participants play designated roles without there being a defined resolution at the end [17].

Four runs of Simulation Hooshmand-1 with 33 participants has proved this to be a successful design that creates space and time for participants to learn through an interactive process of decision making. It also exposes individuals to deeper awareness of their sense making skills as well as factors influencing group decision making.

As the research process evolved it became evident that the concept of 'Groupthink' [5, 6] could contribute an explanation of the causes for misjudgements and poor decision outcomes. Figure 2 presents an analysis using aspects of the concept of 'Groupthink' and its impact on decision (especially defective ones) based on evidence observed in four simulations. Antecedent conditions are listed at A, B1 and B2. Decision makers were from different group without any joint experience prior to the simulation. A key organisational fault emerged in the form of the insular way in which groups worked in isolation from each other, although this was not forbidden by the rules of the simulation. An absence of pre-agreed norms meant that participants had to decide how to work together and make decisions. None chose to do so. Conflicts arose because of (a) imposed time pressures, (b) increasing complexities and difficulties of working in an unfamiliar (although representative) context, and (c) the PPM tools introduced in Context 1 and Context 2.

Symptoms of Groupthink indicate problems can arise such categories as – (1) overestimation of capability, with an illusion of invulnerability, (II) closemindedness that can suffocate critics of an apparently, group-collective position, and (III) pressure to uniformity - manifesting as self-censorship [19]. The symptoms of Groupthink manifested during the simulation showed up as type II and type III - especially rationalisation and stereotyping of the PPM process.

Participants' feedback, from the four completed events, has confirmed that the design of Hooshmand-1 provides a context 'close enough' to their real-world experiences (Figs. 3 and 4).

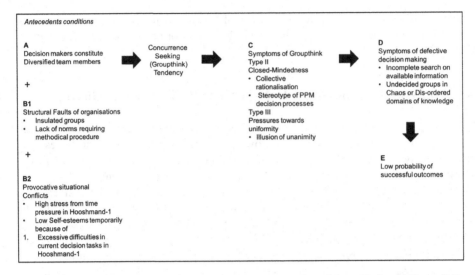

Fig. 2. An application of Groupthink to Hooshmand-1 (adapted from Yetive 2003, p. 421)

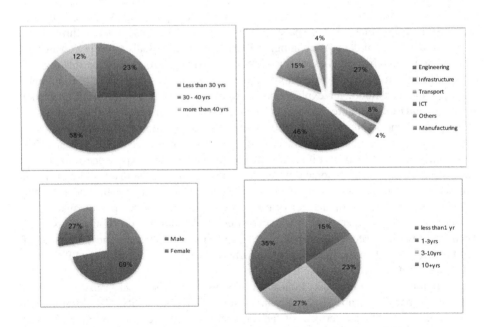

Fig. 3. Demography of participants in 4 trials of Hooshmand-1

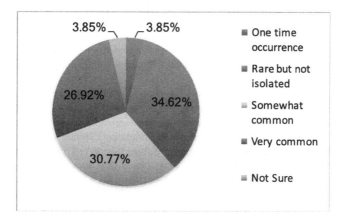

Fig. 4. Participants responses about the 'familiarity' of Hooshmand-1 experiences

5 Recommendations and Conclusions

The design of this unique simulation game has contributed to ways of learning how to make sense of complex situations and improve the decision-making of senior managers. Although an examination of project portfolio management (PPM) as a function of corporate strategic decision making was a core goal in developing Hooshmand-1, the activity can be applied to many kinds of decision-making situations in which there are high level of uncertainty and persistent complexity. Such contexts include urban planning, sustainable energy strategies, capital transport and infrastructure projects, and macro-economic strategies. All these areas have some things in common with the environment created in Hooshmand-1 - including the impact of social factors linked to decision makers' emotions, unintended consequences of inadequate decisions arising from poor use of limited information, confusion about how to handle unknown factors, and variations in technical knowledge occurring during the early stages of planning for mega projects.

The development of Hooshmand-1 demonstrated the application of a positivist approach to learning from failure, rather than merely seeking to identify causes of failure points. The design process embraced creative thinking in its early stages to develop alternatives and collect cues from testing in order to develop a simulation that could be used for research purposes. Such an approach can help designers achieve a robust outcome from their design process. Hooshmand-1 is an environment within which difficult issues concerning decision making are created and framed for discussions which lead to fresh understanding for further analysis. Such discussion can become tools for exploring the kinds of early warnings which can prevent disaster occurring during complex workplace situations. Hooshmand-1 illustrates how emergence of 'Groupthink' can contribute to ill-formed decisions that created failure for corporations. Hooshmand-1 also demonstrates that identification and acknowledgement of decision makers' emotions, along with effective resolution of them, can help to reduce the negative impact of biased views, and reduce the risk of defective decisions.

References

1. De Bono, E.: I Am Right and You Are Wrong. Penguin Books, London (1991)
2. Archer, N.P., Ghasemzadeh, F.: An integrated framework for project portfolio selection. Int. J. Proj. Manag. **17**(4), 207–216 (1999)
3. Engwall, M., Jerbrant, A.: The resource allocation syndrome: the prime challenge of multi-project management. Int. J. Proj. Manag. **21**, 403–409 (2003)
4. Hussein, B.A.: On using simulation games as a research tool in project management. In: Organizing and Learning Through Gaming and Simulation, Trondheim (2007)
5. Janis, I.L.: Victims of Groupthink. Houghton Mifflin, Boston (1972)
6. Janis, I.L.: Groupthink-Psychological-Studies-of-Policy-Decisions-and-Fiascoes (2016)
7. Kearney, J.W., Heffernan, M., McLuckie, J.: Fleet Doctor To Airpower 2100 - from Tailored Solution to Learning Environment (2013)
8. Killen, C.P.: Evaluation of project interdependency visualizations through decision scenario experimentation. Int. J. Proj. Manag. **31**, 804–816 (2013)
9. Kurtz, C.F., Snowden, D.J.: The new dynamics of strategy: Sense-making in a complex and complicated world. IBM Syst. J. **42**(3), 462 (2003)
10. Leigh, E.: Short Description of WipWap1 and Airpower2100. S. Shalbafan. Sydney: 1 (2012)
11. Naber, T., van Oort, M.: Master thesis, University of Tilburg (2005)
12. Perković, G.: Global crisis effects on financial position and business efficiency of B&H's industrial companies. Sarajevo Bus. Econ. Rev. **33**, 11 (2014)
13. Petit, Y., Hobbs, B.: Project portfolios in dynamic environments: sources of uncertainty and sensing mechanisms. Proj. Manag. J. **41**(4), 46–58 (2010)
14. Project Management Institute: The Standard for Project Portfolio Management. 3rd Edition, Project Management Institute (2012)
15. Sá Silva, P., Pedrosa, D., Trigo, A., Varajão, J.: Simulation, games and challenges: from schools to enterprises. In: Barjis, J., Eldabi, T., Gupta, A. (eds.) EOMAS 2011. LNBIP, vol. 88, pp. 63–73. Springer, Heidelberg (2011). https://doi.org/10.1007/978-3-642-24175-8_5
16. Sardon, G., Wong, S.W.: Making sense of safety: a complexity-based approach to safety interventions. In: Association of Canadian Ergonomists 41st Annual Conference, Kelowna, BC (2010)
17. Shalbafan, S., Leigh, E., Pollack, J., Sankaran, S.: Using simulation to create a time-bound, space-constrained context for studying decision-making in project portfolio management using the Cynefin framework. APROS - EGOS 2015, Sydney (2015)
18. Taleb, N.N.: The Black Swan (2007)
19. Yetive, S.A.: Groupthink and the gulf crisis. Br. J. Polit. Sci. **33**, 419–442 (2003)

Analyzing the Implications of Design Choices in Existing Simulation-Games for Critical Infrastructure Resilience

Joeri van Laere[1]([⊠]), Osama Ibrahim[2], Aron Larsson[3], Leif Olsson[3], Björn Johansson[4], and Per Gustavsson[5]

[1] University of Skövde, Box 408, 54128 Skövde, Sweden
joeri.van.laere@his.se
[2] Stockholm University, Stockholm, Sweden
osama@dsv.su.se
[3] Mid Sweden University, Sundsvall, Sweden
{aron.larsson,leif.olsson}@miun.se
[4] Linköping University, Linköping, Sweden
bjorn.j.johansson@liu.se
[5] Combitech AB, Skövde, Sweden
per.m.gustavsson@combitech.se

Abstract. A literature study has identified the major impacts of important design choices in simulation models and simulation-games that model critical infrastructure resilience. The four major groups of design choices discussed in this article are: (1) the chosen learning goal (system understanding or collaboration training), (2) realism and time scale of the scenario, (3) design of player roles and communication rules, (4) number of action alternatives, replay-ability and richness of performance feedback while playing. Researchers and practitioners who build simulation-games for studying critical infrastructure resilience can use the accumulated insights on these four aspects to improve the quality of their game design and the quality of the simulation models the game participants interact with.

Keywords: Design choices · Critical infrastructures · Resilience
Gaming-simulation · Simulation

1 Introduction

Resilience of critical infrastructures is a complex problem area. Gaming-simulation can help us to understand this area. Building a simulation game involves many design choices. Depending on which choices are made, consciously or unconsciously, very different simulations or simulation-games can be created for studying the same problem. It is important to build simulation-games of good quality and to understand how crucial design choices impact simulation-game design and simulation-game outcomes. In the literature study presented in this article we have identified and analyzed two simulation models and four simulation games that each attacked this challenge in a different way. Lessons learnt in the analysis have already influenced our own design

© Springer International Publishing AG, part of Springer Nature 2018
H. K. Lukosch et al. (Eds.): ISAGA 2017, LNCS 10825, pp. 15–23, 2018.
https://doi.org/10.1007/978-3-319-91902-7_2

process where we create a simulation-game for critical infrastructure resilience, focusing on cascading effects of payment system disruptions for the food, fuel and transport system. The analysis can also inspire other practitioners and researchers to reflect on the impact of their design choices. The aim of this study is not to advocate certain design choices, but rather to show what alternatives there are, and how they differ in their impact on the nature and outcomes of a simulation-game.

2 Background

2.1 Critical Infrastructures

Societies rely on well-functioning critical infrastructures such as Energy, Information and Communication technology, Water supply, Food and Agriculture, Healthcare, Financial systems, Transportation systems, Public Order and Safety, Chemical Industry, Nuclear Industry, Commerce, Critical Manufacturing, and so on [1]. When one or more critical infrastructures break down or provide only limited service, large numbers of citizens, companies or government agencies can be severely affected [2, 3]. Breakdowns can be caused by internal factors (human or technical failure), external factors (nature catastrophes, terror attacks) or by failures of other infrastructures as there are many dependencies between critical infrastructures [3]. Energy and Information technology or Telecommunications are well-known event-originating infrastructures that generate cascading effects in many other infrastructures, as has been shown in different types of analyses [3].

Resilience of interdependent infrastructures increasingly depends on collaborative responses from actors with diverse backgrounds that may not be familiar with cascade effects into areas beyond and outside the own organisation or sector [4]. There is limited empirical evidence of cascading effects across many infrastructures, which makes it hard to foresee which interactions may occur across sectors [2, 3]. Risk analysis, business continuity management and crisis management training are often performed within the context of a single organisation or sector, and are seldom addressing the holistic analysis of multiple infrastructures [3].

2.2 Resilience

Studies such as [5, 6] have made efforts to review literature and describe what the term 'resilience' can refer to: bouncing back to a previous state, or bouncing forward to a new state, or both; absorbing variety and preserve functioning, or recovering from damage, or both; and being proactive and anticipating, or being reactive (when recovering during and after events), or both. The variety of interpretations of resilience that have been identified makes it difficult to operationalize resilience into measurable indicators [5]. The Systemic Resilience (SyRes) model was developed as a step towards better metrics and a more comprehensive understanding for determining the resilience of a system in crisis management [5]. Most systems in society, such as the payment system, depend on several other systems managed by different actors to function properly. Therefore, resilience must not only be approached with a systems perspective from researchers trying to understand them, but also from practitioners faced with the task of managing/controlling a complex system. A systems perspective demands deep knowledge about the system components and their interdependencies that ideally should have been acquired before a disruption takes place so that quick action for compensating for and controlling system dynamics is possible. As disruptions often demand simultaneous response by several actors, there is a risk that these responses counteract each other. A simulation-game that is created with the intention of strengthening resilience must reflect the complexity and interdependencies of a real world system. At the same time, the simulation-game must provide well-structured and accessible feedback to allow the participants in the simulation-game to explore the consequences of different actions of themselves and others, as well as to understand the consequences of not acting.

2.3   Design Choices in Gaming-Simulation

Gaming-simulation is defined as a specific form of simulation. Simulation in general aims at designing a model of a system in a complex problem area in other to be able to experiment with the model. Deeper insight in the behavior of the system is created by evaluating various operating strategies against each other in one ore multiple scenarios. Gaming-simulation differs from other forms of simulation in that it incorporates roles to be played by participants and game administrators, implying that people and their (goal-directed) interactions become part of the simulation. In addition to role descriptions and interaction formats, simulation-games can also include a physical simulation model (a board game, a mock-up, a computer simulation, or any other representation of a physical reality) which the game participants need to interact with. It is important to understand that both the changes and impacts of changes to the physical simulation model in the simulation-game and the interaction between the participants (often negotiation processes about what to change and how to interpret changes in the physical simulation model) are part of the simulation-game and object of study [7]. Gaming-simulation is especially relevant when the "*how and why*" of the interaction processes between the participants are of interest and when these interactions cannot easily be incorporated in computer simulation models. In addition, it creates a deeper learning opportunity, as simulation-game participants literally are active participants in the simulation, rather than passive observers of a computer simulation.

To design a high quality simulation-game, many design choices have to be taken into account, which often are not self-evident, but rather involve tricky cost-benefit analyses ending up with a dilemma (is the benefit worth the extra cost?). Examples of such design choices are for example [8, 9]: defining a limited number of research or learning objectives, defining the number and content of roles, defining the scope of the modelled situation/problem, guaranteeing the validity of the simulation, defining rules and constraints, defining the load (difficulty), choosing the location/environment where the game will be played, selecting the type of participants to be invited, design of qualitative and quantitative data collection during the game, degree of realism of the scenario, degree of complexity of the game (often phrased as modelling internal complexity of the system to be modelled, but creating external simplicity, i.e. an easy to understand and easy to play game for the participants), degree of competition, degree of dynamics, macro cycle (preparation, playing, debriefing, follow-up), micro-cycle (number of playing rounds) and real-time or symbolic-time.

3 Method: Identify and Analyze Existing (Gaming-) Simulations

The literature study started with a broad search in databases like EBSCO, Emerald, Google Scholar, IEEE, ScienceDirect, Springer and Wiley. Search terms included: critical infrastructure, simulation, gaming, gaming-simulation, payment, banking, food, fuel, energy, transport. Search results were narrowed down in several steps by reading abstracts and parts of the articles. Identified studies were rated as more attractive the more they resembled our envisioned project i.e.: when they used computer simulations as part of multiple actor games; when their problem area covered multiple critical infrastructures; when design choices and their impacts were discussed extensively; and when the included critical infrastructures covered finance, food, energy and/or transport. Table 1 below gives an overview of the two simulation models and the four simulation-games that were selected for in depth analysis.

Table 1. Overview of simulations and simulation-games analyzed

Name [references]	Type	Critical infrastructures addressed
SIPG [10, 11]	Gaming-simulation	Water, agriculture, energy
CI-dependencies [12, 13]	Simulation	Energy, ICT, water, food, health, financial, legal, civil-admin, transport, chemical/nuclear, space
ASFF [14]	Simulation	Food, population, natural resources, trade, water, energy, waste
CIPRTrainer [15]	Gaming-simulation	ICT, transport, electricity, sewer system
Seaport [16]	Gaming-simulation	Transport, (energy, food, healthcare, electronics, forestry, metal)
SimportMV2 [17, 18]	Gaming-simulation	None: (port area development)

SIPG [10, 11] is interesting as it explicitly deals with the interaction between multiple critical infrastructures that should be managed in concert, and because it involves different player roles that interact with a computer simulation model. The CI-dependencies model [12, 13] and the ASFF-model [14] are included because they both are complex simulation models that analyze interactions between many critical infrastructures. Although they do not include a gaming approach, their simulation models can be compared to the computer simulation of our envisioned simulation-game. CIPRTrainer [15] and Seaport [16] are simulation-games like SIPG [10, 11], but are less focused on interaction between critical infrastructures. They acknowledge that interaction between multiple infrastructures exists, but their actual game design is mainly focused on managing disruptions in one single infrastructure. SimportMV2 [17, 18] is not addressing critical infrastructures at all, but is interesting because their game-design strongly resembles our envisioned design, especially with respect to that 88 teams have played the same scenario and the game designers have analyzed how satisfying results can be obtained with rather different strategies. These 6 (gaming-)simulations were analyzed in detail by studying [10–18]. The analysis aimed at creating overview of important design choices and at revealing the motivations and the reflections of the authors/designers why these design choices were important and how they influenced the nature/quality of the gaming-simulation.

4   Design Choices and Their Implications

4.1   What Is the Learning Goal: System Understanding, Collaboration, or Both?

The six analyzed (gaming-)simulations differ with respect to what their main learning goal is. For some [12, 14, 17] the main purpose is to understand complex system behavior, for others it is training the participants [15, 16] and for one it is studying different forms of team collaboration [11]. Game design shall always aim at obtaining the learning goals in the most effective way. As such, [12, 14, 17] put much emphasis on realism of the scenario, whereas [16] chooses a fictive scenario to put focus on the collaboration process. Also, [11, 16] ponder much about how to limit communication between team members (to press participants being communication-effective when they have the opportunity). Sometimes multiple learning goals such as creating system understanding and training the participants can go hand in hand [15]. But when design choices favor one goal and inhibit the other, it is important for the game designer to know what the primary purpose of the gaming-simulation is.

4.2   Validity, Fidelity, Realism, Time Scale and Complexity of the Scenario

Many designers of the analyzed simulation-games discuss the challenge of getting hold of real data to increase the realism of the simulation-game [11, 12, 14, 15, 17]. As little is known about how critical infrastructures interact, and especially how they interact in case of single or multiple severe disruptions, there is little real data to compare the simulation results with. Therefore validation by experts is often used. In [14, 17] it is argued that the focus should be on mirroring "*general system behavior and dynamics*" rather than representing reality in detail, which means, as nicely phrased in [17], that there is a need for *realistic* data rather than *real* data. Combining real and fictive data can be preferable when real data is sensitive from a security perspective [15]. At the other hand (gaming-)simulation should not become too abstract and lose relevance from the perspective of learning complex system behavior [12, 14]. The current state of critical infrastructure models is criticized by [12, 14] for not opening the black box, limiting the analysis to too few infrastructures, focusing too much on single or short term disruptions, and not being able to analyze more long term and downstream risks.

To create models that can analyze interaction between infrastructures as well as the behavior of each specific infrastructure in detail, some argue for High Level Architectures (HLA) so already existing single-sector models can easily be included [11, 15]. Validation does not only matter for representing infrastructure behavior, but can also relate to how to operationalize the notion of resilience [15, 16]. When clear metrics for resilience are lacking it is hard for game designers to value performance and to direct learning. Finally, the analyzed simulations differ extremely in time scale. Some simulate 30 years [17], 30–60 years [11] or 150 years [14], while others simulate a scenario of only several hours or days [12, 15, 16]. Clearly, such choices can make a huge difference for the nature and outcomes of the learning experience, i.e. what impacts of disruptions are observed.

4.3 Number of Player Roles and Rules for Communication Between Them

All (gaming-)simulations acknowledge conflicting interests of different societal actors, but some put the need for addressing individual goals versus common goals, information sharing and negotiation more in focus as the main learning goal. Some games put players in isolated roles and limit communication possibilities [11, 16]. Others put players in collaboration teams where individual members need to monitor different goals, but where communication is free and the fact that you are a team rather than separate individuals through its structure promotes collaboration [15, 17].

4.4 Action Options, Re-Play Ability and Performance Feedback While Playing

Interaction between simulation model and players differs greatly. Some show only final outcomes [11, 12], some allow for choosing actions at fixed points from two alternatives [16], whereas some allow for continuous interaction with the simulation and have multiple choice alternatives [15, 17]. Too many options may hamper playability and learning [17], but too few options may harm realism and thus relevance of what is learnt [15]. A final interesting feature is the ability to play again, try out different scenarios and experience the consequences. Some do not allow this [17], some repeat the same work process, but each time with a new scenario [16] and some allow for unlimited re-play [11, 15]. In [15] re-play is a key element: different explored avenues are stored clearly to support the players in their learning.

5 Discussion

5.1 Lesson Learned for the Specific Case of Our Payment Disruptions Game

Learning Goals, Player Roles and Communication Rules: Our payment disruption game will focus stronger on system understanding and less on overcoming collaboration and information sharing challenges. Collaboration in crisis is a general problem that can be trained in many ways. The focus will be on **_how_** participants can help each other when they are cooperative, rather than learning to overcome hinders for collaboration. Still, awareness for collaboration will be raised as a by-effect, as participants will have uneven information and information sharing will be necessary to meet the overall goals. Therefore players will be grouped as crisis management teams (as in [17]), where members have to monitor different interests, but are not operating as isolated individuals. Communication will be unlimited.

Realism and Time Scale: Almost all designers in the analyzed studies struggled with balancing detailed realism versus a generally applicable, cost effective and understandable game design. It reminded us to put major attention to this early in the project. Our ambition is to design a scenario that pictures "*big and smaller cities surrounded by rural area, recognizable in many parts of Sweden*", without going into exactly mirroring a specific city or region. Regarding time scale our project will not only aim on short term scenarios (different types of problems under several days or several weeks), but look for at least one "*multiple years scenario*".

Replay-Ability, Action Options and Performance Feedback: Identification of vital actions and crucial performance indicators is ongoing. Our intention is to include an option for players to "*invent actions not prepared for by the simulation designers*", which will be evaluated by the game facilitators instantly and translated into impact on key variables in the simulation. Repeating the same steps in different scenarios [16] and free pause and re-play options [15] are very attractive from a pedagogical perspective. Such options have inspired us to consider a broader set of alternative game-session designs, besides only playing a single scenario once from start to end.

5.2 General Insights for Gaming-Simulations for Critical Infrastructures

As little is understood yet about critical infrastructure system behavior and interactions between infrastructures under stress, validity of our models should be a major concern. Interesting research avenues are for example: How can models be validated when they focus on seldom occurring crisis escalations or far away futures?; comparing different levels of realism and opening the black box: when are gaming-simulations too abstract and when do they become unplayable as players get lost in details?; how can the many definitions of resilience be operationalized in clear measures?; and finally, should we aim for one combined resilience measure that encapsulates different forms of resilience, or do we need multiple resilience measures picturing that resilience can be obtained in different ways?

6   Conclusions

A literature review of existing simulations and simulation-games that aim at understanding or training critical infrastructure resilience has revealed four groups of important design choices: (1) the chosen learning goal (system understanding or collaboration training), (2) realism and time scale of the scenario, (3) design of player roles and communication rules, (4) number of action alternatives, re-play ability and richness of performance feedback while playing.

The analysis informs our own process of designing a gaming-simulation for cascading effects payment disruptions for the food, fuel and transport system by reminding us of well-known issues (learning goals, degree of realism, choice of player roles) and by highlighting some new issues (time scale of scenario, re-play abilities). Identified challenges for the field of critical infrastructure simulation in general are: (1) models are often too abstract and not opening the black box sufficiently, (2) scenarios often limit themselves to single short term disruptions and do more seldom study slowly moving stressors over long time periods, and/or multiple interacting disruptions, (3) resilience is not specifically defined and thus it is hard for simulation-game designers to operationalize resilience in simple metrics.

Acknowledgments. This research was supported by Grant 2016-3046 of the Swedish Civil Contingencies Agency.

References

1. Alcaraz, C., Zeadally, S.: Critical infrastructure protection: requirements and challenges for the 21st century. Int. J. Crit. Infrastruct. Prot. **8**, 53–66 (2015)
2. Boin, A., McConnell, A.: Preparing for critical infrastructure breakdowns: the limits of crisis management and the need of resilience. J. Contingencies Crisis Manag. **15**(1), 50–59 (2007)
3. Van Eeten, M., Nieuwenhuis, A., Luijf, E., Klaver, M., Cruz, E.: The state and the threat of cascading failure across critical infrastructures: The implications of empirical evidence from media incident reports. Public Adm. **89**, 381–400 (2011)
4. Ansell, C., Boin, A., Keller, A.: Managing transboundary crises: identifying the building blocks of an effective response system. J. Contingencies Crisis Manag. **18**, 195–207 (2010)
5. Lundberg, J., Johansson, B.J.E.: Systemic resilience model. Reliab. Eng. Saf. Sci. **141**, 22–32 (2015)
6. Bergström, J., van Winsen, R., Henriqson, E.: On the rationale of resilience in the domain of safety: a literature review. Reliab. Eng. Syst. Saf. **141**, 131–141 (2015)
7. Mayer, I.S.: The gaming of policy and the politics of gaming: a review. Simul. Gaming **40**(6), 825–862 (2009)
8. van Laere, J.: Coordinating distributed work, exploring situated coordination with gaming-simulation. Doctoral dissertation, Delft University of Technology, Delft (2003)
9. Meijer, S.A.: The Organization of Transactions: Studying Supply Networks Using Gaming Simulation. Wageningen Academic Publishers, Wageningen (2009)
10. Grogan, P.T.: Interoperable simulation gaming for strategic infrastructure systems design. Ph.D. thesis, Massachusetts Institute of Technology, Cambridge, USA (2014)

11. Grogan, P.T., de Weck, O.L.: Collaborative design in the sustainable infrastructure planning game. In: Proceedings of the Annual Simulation Symposium (ANSS), Spring Simulation Conference (SpringSim16), Pasadena, CA, USA (2016)

12. Laugé, A., Hernantes, J., Sarriegi, J.M.: The role of critical infrastructures' interdependencies on the impacts caused by natural disasters. In: Luiijf, E., Hartel, P. (eds.) CRITIS 2013. LNCS, vol. 8328, pp. 50–61. Springer, Cham (2013). https://doi.org/10.1007/978-3-319-03964-0_5

13. Laugé, A., Hernantes, J., Sarriegi, J.M.: Critical infrastructure dependencies: a holistic, dynamic and quantitative approach. Int. J. Crit. Infrastruct. Prot. **8**, 16–23 (2015)

14. Candy, S., Biggs, C., Larsen, K., Turner, K.: Modelling food system resilience: a scenario-based simulation modelling approach to explore future shocks and adaptations in the Australian food system. J. Environ. Stud. Sci. **5**(4), 537–542 (2015)

15. Rome, E., Doll, T., Rilling, S., Sojeva, B., Voß, N., Xie, J.: The use of what-if analysis to improve the management of crisis situations. In: Setola, R., Rosato, V., Kyriakides, E., Rome, E. (eds.) Managing the Complexity of Critical Infrastructures: A Modelling and Simulation Approach, 233-276. Springer, Heidelberg (2016). https://doi.org/10.1007/978-3-319-51043-9_10

16. Kurapati, S., Lukosch, H., Verbraeck, A., Brazier, F.M.T.: Improving resilience in intermodal transport operations in seaports: a gaming approach. EURO J. Decis. Process. **3**, 375–396 (2015)

17. Bekebrede, G.: Experiencing complexity: a gaming approach for understanding infrastructure systems. Doctoral dissertation, Delft University of Technology, Delft (2010)

18. Bekebrede, G., Lo, J., Lukosch, H.K.: Understanding complex systems through mental models and shared experiences: a case study. Simul. Gaming **46**(5), 536–562 (2015)

Knowledge Management of Games
for Decision Making

Bill Roungas[1](✉), Sebastiaan Meijer[2], and Alexander Verbraeck[1]

[1] Delft University of Technology, Delft, The Netherlands
{v.roungas,a.verbraeck}@tudelft.nl
[2] KTH Royal Institute of Technology, Stockholm, Sweden
sebastiaan.meijer@sth.kth.se

Abstract. Games for decision making have developed into a powerful tool for corporations. Irrespective of their size, corporations have been increasingly using these games in order to evaluate and ascertain impactful business decisions and strategies. Despite their proven added value to the decision making process, there is still lack of research on whether, and if so how, these games can be used by researchers and practitioners to build evidents on systems' behavior, as part of a larger scheme. To this effect, this paper proposes a framework to determine the different artifacts of games that should be logged and stored for future use.

Keywords: Knowledge management system · Games · Simulations
Knowledge Elicitation · Game design · Debriefing

1 Introduction

All knowledge is not created equally [5]. The same applies to the knowledge gained from serious games. Serious games are a subgroup of simulations and are also known as simulators, human-in-the-loop, participatory simulations, or just games. Serious games have become a popular and effective tool for purposes like learning, training, and decision making [4]. As a result, research on serious games has dramatically increased over the last decade. A quick search of the term "serious games" in two of the most popular search engines for academic research, Google Scholar and Scopus, returned 17.900 and 4.418 results respectively for papers published between 2007 and 2016, but only 2.060 and 49 results for all the years up to 2007. These results might be skewed due to the adaptation of search engines in the past decade; yet, the differences are too large to ignore. Despite this boost in popularity and research, researchers have not as of today focused on how knowledge acquired through serious games can be retained and reused.

It has been observed that game artifacts reused in decision making processes often intertwine with artifacts reused in game development. The former are used in order to avoid iterations of the same games and apply, instead, prior knowledge to a current problem, whereas the latter are used in order to develop similar

© Springer International Publishing AG, part of Springer Nature 2018
H. K. Lukosch et al. (Eds.): ISAGA 2017, LNCS 10825, pp. 24–33, 2018.
https://doi.org/10.1007/978-3-319-91902-7_3

games in a faster and more cost-effective way, e.g. by reusing chunks of code. The present study, as suggested by the title, focuses on games for decision making (hereinafter referred to as games) and more specifically, on the respective artifacts that are used for knowledge reuse.

Knowledge management and reuse is not, and should not be, of academic interest only. The effectiveness of a corporation depends heavily on how it manages and reuses knowledge [11], or in layman terms, how in the first place it obtains and thereafter maintains the so-called "Know-how". As a corporation acquires and builds up on knowledge obtained through games, it improves its know-how, and thus sustains or even increases its competitive advantage [5].

In this paper, the first step towards the formalization of knowledge management and reuse of games is described. The different constituents of games are identified and ways to log and store them are proposed.

In Sect. 2, a representative sample of the body of work on knowledge management and reuse is identified and the lessons learned are discussed. In Sect. 4, the lessons learned in Sect. 2 are applied into games and a framework for formalizing knowledge management and reuse of games is proposed. In Sect. 5, the particularities of the proposed framework are analyzed and any potential threats towards its validity are identified. Finally, in Sect. 6, the future potential extensions of the framework are presented and final remarks are made.

2   Background Work

In this section, literature on knowledge management and reuse is reviewed. [8] first suggested that, even thought it may be complex, the collection of empirical data from game sessions can create a body of knowledge that can facilitate the researchers' understanding of systems' behavior.

Based on the literature reviewed and to the best of our knowledge, a methodology on management and reuse of knowledge derived from games has not yet been proposed. Hence, the aim of this section is first to present the state of the art in the field of knowledge management and reuse in general, and then to extract the techniques that can be applied into the games' field.

In principle, knowledge management and reuse requires some sort of documentation. [11] expands on the matter by making a distinction between documentation based on the author and the intended audience of these documents. He points three important factors that influence the successful management and reuse of knowledge, namely: (a) the costs involved, (b) the incentives knowledge producers have to contribute to a knowledge management system (hereinafter referred to as KMS) that can be used by others, and (c) the need to transform knowledge so that it is appropriate for use by others.

[20] propose a multi-theoretical model with the aim to tackle the problem of knowledge contribution and reuse. Their model, which is an extension of [9]'s model, addresses both the knowledge contribution to a KMS and the knowledge reuse. They further identify several factors that lead to increased contribution and reuse of knowledge, which include, inter alia, the reciprocal nature of contribution and the increased team performance. Further to the above, they assert

that reuse of knowledge is highly influenced by the ease with which someone can access the available knowledge, the trust towards the primary source of the knowledge, and undoubtedly the usefulness of this knowledge. Finally, the authors find a strong positive correlation between reuse and contribution.

By looking into management consulting firms, [7] distinguish two types of knowledge management and reuse - what they basically call *Codification* and *Personalization*. *Codification* stores and makes available for reuse any acquired knowledge, which is in reality isolated from its source. On the other hand, *Personalization* is the exchange of knowledge that has been acquired in the past through one-to-one conversations and brainstorming sessions; it is a way to promote discussion and exchange of ideas and knowledge between people in a more personal manner.

On a different level, [10] argue that when actually implementing a KMS, one shall prefer the use of Wikis to the traditional and conversational KMSs. Their study shows that Wikis, unlike the two other methods, address four of the most important challenges in knowledge management:

- The bottleneck of expertise, which refers to the limited number of experts that can contribute to a KMS [19].
- The lack of incentives, which refers to the lack of motivation from the experts in sharing their knowledge, either due to lack of rewards for sharing or due to the experts' tendency in maintaining expertise for themselves only, which in turn explains their unwillingness to share [15].
- Knowledge contextuality, which refers to the context required for the use of knowledge beyond narrow and well-structured tasks [6].
- The maintenance bottleneck, which refers to problems arising from maintaining a KMS against the backdrop of a system expansion, and especially, the possibility of knowledge sharing being impeded, or even ceased, due to the time required to just maintain the ever increasing knowledge [2].

While there is a lack of literature in the area of knowledge management and reuse of games, existing literature in the general areas of knowledge acquisition, contribution, management and reuse create a pathway towards knowledge management and reuse in games. The literature reviewed in this section shows that there are three distinct layers of knowledge management and reuse, while each of these layers influences one another in a sequential order. The first layer is the intended audience of this knowledge and their incentives. The second layer is the method pertaining to the management and reuse of knowledge, which is heavily influenced by the type of knowledge and the intended audience, in the sense that people who inquire on an expert's opinion but do not want to acquire his knowledge (expertise-seeking novices [11]) will most likely prefer to consult an expert in a one-to-one conversation (*Personalization*), whereas people that want to learn from past projects and apply this knowledge in the future (secondary knowledge miners [11]) will most probably prefer a documented and detailed record of these past projects (*Codification*). Finally, the third layer is the actual implementation of a KMS, which again is influenced by the knowledge management and reuse method, in the sense that a *Personalization* knowledge exchange method requires a simplistic system that can connect the interested party directly with an expert. On the other hand, a *Codification* knowledge exchange method requires a more complex and perhaps hybrid solution that can capture and store all the different elements of games for future use.

In the next section, the motivation for building a KMS for games is described; the analysis also provides an indirect answer to why a KMS for games can be an impactful contribution.

3   Motivation

Despite the fact that games have proven to be cost effective in multiple occasions, they still involve a substantial financial cost [13]. Depending on several factors, like the degree of realism or the intended audience, the cost of developing a game may vary significantly. For instance, board games are considered to be a low-cost solution, whereas high-fidelity military simulators usually bear a significant cost.

In addition to development costs, there are costs associated with game sessions which, more often than not, are not trivial. A game session might require expensive hardware, an appropriate space to take place, and most importantly participants, who are compensated for participating in the game.

Moreover, time is required to process the game outcomes and come with the best possible business decision. This additional time does not only increase the accrued costs but also delays decisions that sometimes are time-sensitive.

All of the above combined with the lack of a methodology for managing and reusing knowledge acquired through games, lead companies, researchers, and game practitioners to "reinvent the wheel" by conducting consecutive and (almost) identical game sessions, accompanied by data analysis.

The motivation for this study is therefore triggered by our strong belief that the acquisition, management and reuse of knowledge requires a methodology that will maximize the game outcomes concurrently with the minimization of the associating costs and risks.

4   Game Information

In this section, a framework for managing and reusing knowledge acquired from games is proposed. This framework aims at decomposing games into their core constituents, so as to give insight on the kind of knowledge a game produces and the way this knowledge can be stored and reused in the future.

4.1   Requirements

The development of a serious game starts by first eliciting the requirements. In regard to games, there are two sources from where requirements should be elicited, namely, the client and the real system the game imitates. The latter might be obsolete in case of open games, where there are (almost) no rules or restrictions.

In order for one to keep track of the progress and make sure that all the features are implemented as planned, eliciting and documenting the game requirements remains equally important throughout the development of the game. Although requirements are usually considered to be relevant only for the game they are elicited for, according to [21], requirements engineering is also concerned with the evolution of the relationships among the several factors of a system across software families. As such, requirements immediately become a tool for knowledge reuse, as they provide common ground for comparing different systems and pointing similarities. These similarities can be used either to improve future game development, as a domain specific knowledge [3], or in order to avoid building new games and reuse the outcome of previously created games to analyze a current issue.

4.2   Game Design Document

There have been several approaches towards the adaptation of game design documents from entertaining games to serious games as well as approaches towards structuring serious games in a model-driven way [16–18]. Regardless of the approach one chooses to adopt, there are certain game elements that need to be taken into account, as follows:

- Rules, which reveal information about the real system and the fidelity level of the game.
- Scenario, which shows the particular challenges and tasks of the game as well as its relevant setup details.
- Stakeholders/Actors, who are actively engaged with the game, such as participants, facilitator(s), game designer(s), and any other interested party.
- Purpose, which is the reason the client wants to build the game, e.g. for assisting decision makers.

The above indicated information shall be documented. On this basis, a comparison between a previously created game and a potential new game can determine whether the new game is actually required or not. In case the similarities between the two games are enough for the results of the old game to be used in the current occasion, the new game is obsolete.

4.3   Validation and Verification

Game validation deals with the assessment of behavioral or representational accuracy of the game and addresses the question of whether we are creating the "right game" [1]. On the other hand, game verification deals with the assessment of transformational accuracy of the game and addresses the question of whether we are creating the game in the right way [1].

Despite the fact that Validation & Verification (V&V) usually require formal methods and quantitative data, they are almost always subjective. Moreover, games cannot be absolutely validated [12] and verified, and successful V&V can only be claimed for an instantiation of a game (a specific game session) and for a specific use (purpose). Therefore, meticulously documenting every detail associated with V&V is of paramount importance; it can also reveal a twofold benefit to potential reusers: (i) they can ascertain, with rather minimal effort, whether the results of the game can be used for their intended purpose, and (ii) they can, again with much less effort than without the V&V details, perform their own V&V study and hence, use the game for slightly or completely different purposes.

A V&V study incorporates two types of data; (i) metadata associated with the V&V study, and (ii) information describing the V&V process along with raw data and final results.

The metadata that should be stored are:

- The date, time, & location (if relevant) of the V&V study.
- The version of the game, in case there are multiple versions available.
- The purpose for which the game has been used.

With regards to the actual V&V process, the information that should be stored is:

- The methods used for the V&V study and the justification on preferring these methods for the different phases of the game, like game requirements, game design, and game results [1].
- All the input and output data, both quantitative and qualitative ones, that were used during the V&V study (See how to store quantitative and qualitative data below in Sect. 4.4).

4.4 Game Sessions

A game session can also be seen as a game instantiation. In object oriented programming terms, the game can be seen as a class with the rules and general guidelines of how the game works, whereas the game session can be seen as an object of this class. A game is usually designed once (involving several iterations) but can be played multiple times with a similar or a completely different setup. In other words, a game session is the application of a game with a specific scenario, stakeholders, and purpose. Therefore, this characterization helps to understand how an actual KMS can be built to support a game.

Every game is different, hence it requires a different approach with regards to how the knowledge produced on it can be acquired and stored. Nevertheless, all games have the same main pillars; metadata, input and output data (quantitative & qualitative), and debriefing.

The metadata that should be stored are:

- The time, date, & location (if relevant) the game session took place.
- Detailed information regarding all stakeholders (participants, facilitator(s), and any other interested party.
  - Professional & educational background.

- • Age, sex, and any other relevant information.
- – The annotations to all the data (quantitative & qualitative), which can be in the form of textual description, path to figures and audiovisual material on a server etc.

Input data usually include the game design decisions captured in the requirements and documented in the game design document, and they are common (but not exactly the same) for every instantiation of the game. Some input data might differ for each game session, where variations on the rules or the scenarios can be introduced. Input data can be both quantitative and qualitative.

In turn, output data might include quantitative data produced during the gameplay, audiovisual material captured during the game session or the debriefing, notes from the participants and/or the facilitator(s), game-specific artifacts and a textual analysis of the lessons learned from the game. Same as with input data, output data can be both quantitative and qualitative.

With regards to quantitative data:

- – Raw datasets and any further quantitative analysis of these data should be stored in separate tables in a database, and any textual description or analysis should be included in the metadata.
- – Figures produced from quantitative data should be stored in the server, and the path and any other information associated with them should be included in the metadata.

With regards to qualitative data:

- – Audiovisual and any other relevant material should be stored in the server. Whilst the corresponding material should be annotated for ease of use in the future, these annotations should be included in the metadata.
- – Any quantification of qualitative variables should be stored in a database or a server, depending on their format. Similarly to the textual description and the quantification methodology, the relevant material shall contain annotations, which shall be included in the metadata.

5   The Knowledge Management System

In Sect. 4, a decomposition of games and game design into their core elements was made. This analysis serves as a road map towards defining and eventually implementing a KMS of games.

The analysis in Sect. 4 strongly indicates that on the basis of their structure, design, and required and produced data, games are multi-dimensional entities. As such, defining and implementing a one-dimensional KMS seems limited and thus restrictive. A one-dimensional KMS is a system that does not combine different KMS solutions into one but rather includes a single-solution KMS, like a Wiki or a conversational KMS.

In this section, we propose a hybrid KMS that combines the advantages of individual solutions and is able to store and facilitate the reuse of the complex information pertaining to games.

A KMS should have a server-side (backend) and a client-side (frontend). The backend of the proposed KMS for games incorporates three main components:

- A database, which should be designed so as to accommodate wiki's entries, and the quantitative data and metadata associated with the game.
- A filesystem, used as a repository of audiovisual material, figures, and any similar content.
- Analytical tools, like R or Python, for the quantitative analysis of data.

The frontend of the proposed KMS also incorporates three main components:

- A graphical user interface (GUI) for the wiki.
- Visualization tools for creating graphs and figures from the quantitative data.
- A search engine for querying all data.

The proposed framework bears similar validity threats to those of its individual components. A KMS can only be successful if people contribute and reuse knowledge; in fact a causal relationship between knowledge contribution and reuse has been identified [11]. Therefore, one of the most important goals of such a system should be the adaptation of a methodology for eliminating, or at least mitigating, knowledge bias that derives from human subjectivity, which is an inseparable part to knowledge contributed [14].

In the same spirit, the success of a KMS depends heavily on the credibility of the primary source of information. In this respect, a person who aims at using knowledge previously acquired shall be confident of the expertise of the knowledge contributors, and thus trust their respective findings [20].

Finally, in order for a KMS to be used in practice, it needs to be properly and consistently indexed [11]. It follows that Knowledge contributors need to feel confident that the time required to contribute to a KMS is not wasted-time and that their input has high chances to be easily accessible and used.

6   Conclusion and Future Work

The reviewed literature and the analysis in this paper indicate that a KMS for games is needed. To the best of our knowledge, a methodology for doing so does not todate exist. The greatest challenges for developing such a KMS is the wide nature of game requirements (the different types of knowledge and the diverse potential user-base of the KMS) and the threats towards the validity of the framework (described in Sect. 5).

Ergo, this study constitutes the first step towards that direction, by setting forth a framework for building a KMS for games. The proposed framework aims at maximizing knowledge acquisition and reuse from games, through the incorporation of the advantages of different technologies (wikis, databases, statistical scripting languages) in a hybrid system, which is platform, programming

·language and content agnostic and thus, easily adaptable to fit different needs. Moreover, due to its foreseen use, the framework is more *Codification*-oriented, as opposed to *Personalization*-oriented.

In the future, the actual implementation of this framework will test and fine-tune the theoretical concept, and consequently improve the derived KMS.

Acknowledgements. This research is supported and funded by ProRail; the Dutch governmental task organization that takes care of maintenance and extensions of the national railway network infrastructure, of allocating rail capacity, and of traffic control.

References

1. Balci, O.: Verification, validation, and certification of modeling and simulation applications. In: Proceedings of the 35th Conference on Winter Simulation, pp. 150–158 (2003). ISBN 0-7803-8132-7
2. Brooks Jr., F.P.: The Mythical Man-Month. Addison-Wesley, Boston (1975)
3. Callele, D., Neufeld, E., Schneider, K.: Requirements engineering and the creative process in the video game industry. In: RE 2005 Proceedings of the 13th IEEE International Conference on Requirements Engineering, pp. 240–252. IEEE (2005). https://doi.org/10.1109/RE.2005.58
4. Crookall, D.: Serious games, debriefing, and simulation/gaming as a discipline. Simul. Gaming **41**(6), 898–920 (2010). https://doi.org/10.1177/1046878110390784. ISSN 1046-8781
5. Dixon, N.M.: Common Knowledge: How Companies Thrive by Sharing What They Know. Harvard Business School Press, Brighton (2000). ISBN 0875849040
6. Feigenbaum, E.A.: Principles and practice, expert systems (1992)
7. Hansen, M.T., Nohria, N., Tierney, T.: What's your strategy for managing knowledge? In: Woods, J.A., James, C. (eds.) The Knowledge Management Yearbook 2000-2001, pp. 1–10. Butterworth-Heinemann (1999). ISBN 0-7506-7258-7
8. Hofstede, G.J., Meijer, S.: Collecting empirical data with games. In: Organisation and Learning Through Gaming and Simulation, Proceedings of ISAGA, pp. 111–121 (2007)
9. Kankanhalli, A., Tan, B.C.Y., Wei, K.-K.: Contributing knowledge to electronic knowledge repositories: an empirical investigation. MIS Q. Spec. Issue Inf. Technol. Knowl. Manag. **29**(1), 113–143 (2005)
10. Majchrzak, A., Wagner, C., Yates, D.: The impact of shaping on knowledge reuse for organizational Improvement with wikis. MIS Q. **37**(2), 455–469 (2012)
11. Markus, L.M.: Toward a theory of knowledge reuse: types of knowledge reuse situations and factors in reuse success. J. Manag. Inf. Syst. **18**(1), 57–93 (2001). https://doi.org/10.1080/07421222.2001.11045671
12. Martis, M.S.: Validation of simulation based models: a theoretical outlook. Electron. J. Bus. Res. Methods **4**(1), 39–46 (2006). ISSN 1477-7029
13. Michael, D.R., Chen, S.L.: Serious Games: Games that Educate, Train, and Inform. Thomson Course Technology PTR, Boston (2005). ISBN 1-59200-622-1
14. Musen, M.A.: Dimensions of knowledge sharing and reuse. Comput. Biomed. Res. **25**(5), 435–467 (1992). https://doi.org/10.1016/0010-4809(92)90003-S. ISSN 00104809

15. O'Dell, C., Grayson, C.J.: If only we knew what we know: identification and transfer of internal best practices. Calif. Manag. Rev. **40**(3), 154–174 (1998). https://doi.org/10.2307/41165948

16. Rocha, O.R., Faron-Zucker, C.: Ludo: an ontology to create linked data driven serious games. In: ISWC 2015-Workshop on LINKed EDucation, LINKED 2015, Bethlehem, Pennsylvania, United States (2015)

17. Roungas, B., Dalpiaz, F.: A model-driven framework for educational game design. In: de De Gloria, A., Veltkamp, R. (eds.) GALA 2015. LNCS, vol. 9599, pp. 1–11. Springer, Cham (2016). https://doi.org/10.1007/978-3-319-40216-1_1

18. Tang, S., Hanneghan, M.: Game content model: an ontology for documenting serious game design. In: Developments in E-systems Engineering (DeSE), 2011, pp. 431–436. IEEE, December 2011. https://doi.org/10.1109/DeSE.2011.68. ISBN 978-1-4577-2186-1

19. Wagner, C.: Breaking the knowledge acquisition bottleneck through conversational knowledge management. In: Knowledge Management, pp. 1262–1276. IGI Global (2008). https://doi.org/10.4018/978-1-59904-933-5.ch106

20. Watson, S., Hewett, K.: A multi-theoretical model of knowledge transfer in organizations: determinants of knowledge contribution and knowledge reuse. J. Manag. Stud. **43**(2), 141–173 (2006). https://doi.org/10.1111/j.1467-6486.2006.00586.x. ISSN 0022-2380

21. Zave, P.: Classification of research efforts in requirements engineering. ACM Comput. Surv. (CSUR) **29**(4), 315–321 (1997). https://doi.org/10.1145/267580.267581

Development of BASE Manufacturing Business Board Game

Ryoju Hamada[1(✉)], Tomomi Kaneko[2], and Masahiro Hiji[3]

[1] Sirindhorn International Institute of Technology, Thammasat University,
131 Moo 5, Tiwanont Road, Bangadi, Muang, Pathum Thani 12000, Thailand
hamada@siit.tu.ac.th
[2] Junior College, Hokkaido University of Science, 7-15-4-1, Maeda, Teine-Ku,
Sapporo, Hokkaido 0068585, Japan
kaneko@hus.ac.jp
[3] Graduate School of Economics and Management, Tohoku University, 2-1-1,
Katahira, Aoba-Ku, Sendai, Miyagi 9808577, Japan
hiji@tohoku.ac.jp

Abstract. The authors developed a board business game of manufacturing called BASE Manufacturing Game (BMG) to provide an opportunity to learn business for engineers. The purpose of development includes management, accounting, and to increase learner's motivation for further studies. By using Questionnaires, the authors proved incredible teaching effectiveness. BMG is a standard for following BASE business games and authors have been continuing board development in Japan and Thailand.

Keywords: Business game · Board game · Manufacture
Engineering education · Active learning · BASE

1 Introduction

Growing up high-quality engineers is an important requirement for higher education. In many universities, there are established curriculums to teach engineering. However, it is often biased on technological surfaces, often ignores social impacts. Engineers must have united knowledge across many topics, including a sense of Technology, Society, and Business.

To serve this purpose, the authors developed the business game which describes the most important ideas of manufacturing and business on tangible board in 2008. This game, BASE manufacturing game (BMG), was mostly used in Japanese and Thai universities and showed amazing performance to increase understandings and motivations of attendees. BMG became a standard and an origin of following BASE business games, and become famous in many conferences, workshops, and lectures.

2 Literature Review

Business Game and simulation has a long history. About the type of business games, Lean et al. [1] had a similar questionnaire based research and reported 35.9% of current users are using Role Play, 20.5% for non-computerized game, and 25.7% for

© Springer International Publishing AG, part of Springer Nature 2018
H. K. Lukosch et al. (Eds.): ISAGA 2017, LNCS 10825, pp. 34–40, 2018.
https://doi.org/10.1007/978-3-319-91902-7_4

computer-based simulations. Since there are quite a lot of business games, Greco et al. [2] tried to create a taxonomy of business games. However, this idea seems too complicated for most of the game developers who are not professional.

Let us examine how business simulation games are used in engineering education. Chapman and Martin [3] claimed that engineers should improve some other skills, not only technology. They tried "CRAC business game" for this purpose. Foss and Eikaas [4], based on strong reliance that students have good talent in computer games, created a computer-based learning system called "PIDstop." Hauge and Riedel [5] recognized the recent complexity of business and behavioral factors, and created two games, called "COSIGA" and "Beware". Kumar and Labib [6] explained the framework of "Next-Generation Manufacturing Simulation Game". There are few other references or popular business simulation board game which explicitly focuses on general manufacturing, to contribute engineering education. The Authors need more idea and experience of business games to grow up engineers.

3   Outlook of BASE Manufacture Business Board Game

3.1   Educational Policy

Before developing BMG, we defined the following educational policy. To say in briefly, BMG is a standard set of an easy business game with great fun for engineers.

(1) The target audience is students of engineering in a higher grade.
(2) Purpose: Learners will be able to do the followings with a relaxed environment with joy.
  (a) Understand basic of company management
  (b) Understand basic of accounting
  (c) Increase the further motivation to study business
(3) Avoid adding complicated rules or an exception to the rule.

3.2   BMG as Wooden, Tangible Board Game

BMG is the combination of wooden frame company board and market board, and cards. Figure 1 is the photograph of the whole set of BMG. There are four companies called (Red, Green, Blue, and Yellow) around the table. All companies are operated by two or three student groups. The company is designed as a combination of factory and office. Machines, Materials, Men and some optional pins are set on the board. Each company has a paper, pencil, eraser and calculator to manage operation and accounting. Toward the center of the table, there are five Markets (Town A to E). Companies will make a bidding in each market. There is a timer to control bidding. At the center, there are sets of "Action Card" turned inside out.

Fig. 1. Image of the whole set of TMG (Color figure online)

4   Flow of the BMG

4.1   Initiation

Two to three students form teams and manage a company. Each team must choose a CEO (Chief Executive Officer) and CFO (Chief Financial Officer). They receive a small share of capital (300,000 USD) and establish their company, which produces commodity products. The CFO records share capital as income. From the second year, there are no additional capital stocks. However, they can borrow money from the bank, based on their business strategy. Companies those last year's result was a surplus, have to pay tax in this period.

4.2   Monthly Role

Students must make a decision one manufacture action, and one management action except happening card appears.

Fig. 2. Samples of action cards (surface, standard, and happening (20%)).

1. The CEO draws an action card (Fig. 2). It includes 20% happening card to learn risk management.
2. The CEO makes a decision from the followings.
   (1) To buy new materials.
   (2) To compile existing materials to the products.
3. The CEO decides management action.
   (1) To hire new engineers or salesperson (Full time/ Part time with a six-month contract is selectable)
   (2) To buy a new machine
   (3) Other Options (Insurance, Loan, Advertisement, R&D etc.)
4. The CFO calculates all expenses and withdraws total cost from the cash at the end of last month.

4.3   Manufacturing

Players have a company board (See Fig. 3). From the players, on the left side, there are raw materials. In the middle, there are machines. On their right, they can see stockyard. They can see, touch, and move the items, in case they need, they can roll back to reconfirm whether their activity is correct. This is the great merit of the tangible game. The manufacturing process consists of two steps (One month for Input, another one month for Output, these processes are possible to complete at once). Throughout this rule, students learn the idea of lead time.

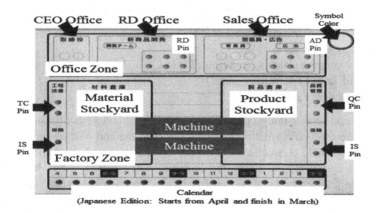

Fig. 3. Company board

4.4   Bidding

After the completion of manufacturing, Bidding is held on every three months.

(1) Students came up with the market with salesperson and items which they want to sell. They are allowed to bid, slide, or withdraw for two minutes.
(2) When the time is up, the dealer will start the judgment process.

(a) If the number of application is less than market capacity, all of them can sell at its maximum price.

(b) If the number of applications is more than market capacity, all of them must fight a price bidding.

(3) In a case of bidding, each participant must decide one price for their all products, type a price of the calculator, and following dealer's order, all teams open the price on the front.

(4) R&D and Advertisement have some advantage in bidding.

(5) Dealer declares the winner until the market will be full. Remained products must be brought back to their company.

(6) CFO will record the sales revenue and check the cash balance.

4.5   Closing Role, Accounting

At the end of the year, the CFO must finish workflow.

(1) Reconfirms all revenues.
(2) Recalculates all expenses and checks the cash flow integrity.
(3) Compiles other sheets (P/L, B/S).

Students must check their cash balance at any time, and at the end of the year, they create Profit and Loss Statement, and Balance Sheet. All process are required to complete by handwriting. Human being often makes errors, and the authors let students know this fact throughout their experiences. BMG has five different sheets, and they are proceeded by students, by handwriting, by following orders.

(1) Cash Flow Management Sheets (Table A)
(2) Product cost Calculation sheet (Table B)
(3) Depreciation cost Calculation Sheet (Table C)
(4) Profit and Loss Statement (Table D)
(5) Balance Sheet (Table E).

Table A represents a daily operation and horizontal and vertical proof ensures its integrity. Student gets a correct number and prices at the end of the year. In Table B, they calculate accurate product cost, to adjust raw material costs by adding carry-over from the previous year, deducting the loss and carry-over as assets to next year. Table C is the simple depreciation that fixed asset (machine) loses its value 10% per year. By getting those numbers, students complete Table D and E. Throughout this process, they can learn principles of accounting.

5   Teaching Effectiveness

BMG is used in Japan and Thailand. To verify the effectiveness of BMG, we conducted some surveys.

5.1   Survey on Understandings of Business Ideas

In June 2012, 20 students of Tohoku University joined a two-day program. The quiz was held on before and after the session, consists of 20 general business ideas and business ideas which the authors included in BMG. The Authors use five-point scale test (1 = Don't understand at all to 5 = Strongly Understand). They are from various faculties and are all freshmen. The Authors can regard there is no significant difference on their previous knowledge. 18 students answered both, so the authors compared these 18 students.

Table 1 shows its principal questions. In all 20 questions, after is higher than before and its average was 1.64. The Authors can point out three points as an evidence of its teaching effectiveness.

Table 1. Understanding survey in Tohoku University (2012)

No	Content of questions	Before	After	B/A
1	What is the management of company	2.59	3.94	1.52
2	What is the difficulty of company management	2.53	4.76	1.88
3	How to reduce fix cost ratio	1.29	4.53	3.50
4	Good company sometimes suddenly bankrupt	1.53	4.41	2.88
5	Effect of cash shortage	2.29	4.76	2.08
6	Outsourcing can reduce labor cost	2.29	4.53	1.97
7	Depreciation reduces benefits, but not reduce cash	1.82	3.59	1.97
8	Too hard price competition is harmful	2.06	3.94	1.91
9	Large Sales don't mean large surplus	3.82	3.88	1.02
10	Deflation suffers company	3.06	3.12	1.02
11	Education is necessary despite it takes a cost	3.41	4.35	1.28
12	Factors to obtain new job other than money	2.47	3.94	1.60

(1)   To understand management and difficulty as a real experience (Q1, Q2)
(2)   To learn importance of cash management and accounting (Q4, Q5, Q6)
(3)   To acquire new knowledge on accounting (Q3, Q7).

On the other hands, the authors have to mind BMG has not strong to increase understandings for commonly known ideas (Q9, Q10). However, it worked to improve understandings on general business ideas although it doesn't appear in BMG (Q11, Q12). Therefore, the authors can conclude BMG's teaching effectiveness is widely approved for beginners.

5.2   Satisfaction

The Authors conducted a survey of satisfaction and their motivation at after questionnaire. It is five-point scale questionnaire (1 = Very Negative to 5 = Very Positive). 19 students responded. Table 2 summarizes its result shows very high satisfaction of participants.

Table 2. Satisfaction survey in Tohoku University (2011)

No	Content of questions	Average	SD	Mode
1	Satisfaction of this program	4.67	0.58	5
2	Can you recommend this program to others?	4.47	0.94	5
3	If there is an advanced course, do you want to participate again?	4.21	0.95	4

6 Conclusion

Herein, the authors introduced our board game, BMG, to simulate traditional management. As a conclusion, the authors confirmed our work has enough teaching effectiveness and possible to provide opportunities to increase student's motivation.

6.1 Reconsidering Potential of Board Games

From the experience of creating BMG, the authors confirmed the potential educational power of board games. To adapt to physical limits and time limitations, the authors have to waive many important ideas bravely. Nevertheless, the authors were thereby able to create a very familiar game to beginners. Return to the origin of "Why we create a game?" is required.

6.2 BMG Afterwards

As we reported, the authors have been continuing development of tangible board game. SKG (Software Kaihatsu Game, Hamada et al. [7]), and SCC (Supply Chain Collaboration Game, Kaneko et al. [8]) are typical examples of the extension of BMG. Now the authors have seven categories, 17 games in BASE business game series and is expected to grow up in Japan and Thailand.

References

1. Lean, J., Moizer, J., Towler, M., Abbey, C.: Simulations and games: Use and barriers in higher education. Act. Learn. High Educ. **7**(3), 227–242 (2006)
2. Greco, M., Baldissin, N., Nonino, F.: An exploratory taxonomy of business games. Simul. Gaming **44**(5), 645–682 (2013)
3. Chapman, G.M., Martin, J.F.: Computerized business games in engineering education. Comput. Educ. **25**(1–2), 67–73 (1995)
4. Foss, B.A., Eikaas, T.: Game play in engineering education: concept and experimental results. Int. J. Eng. Educ. **22**(5), 1043–1052 (2006)
5. Hauge, J.B., Riedel, J.C.K.H.: Evaluation of simulation games for teaching engineering and manufacturing. Procedia Comput. Sci. **15**, 210–220 (2012)
6. Kumar, A., Labib, A.W.: Applying quality function deployment for the design of a next-generation manufacturing simulation game. Int. J. Eng. Educ. **20**(5), 787–800 (2004)
7. Hamada, R., Hiji, M., Kaneko, T.: Development of software engineering business board game. Dev. Bus. Simul. Exp. Learn. **41**, 292–299 (2014)
8. Kaneko, T., Hamada, R., Hiji, M.: Development of BASE supply chain collaboration game. Dev. Bus. Simul. Exp. Learn. **43**, 8–16 (2016)

Planning and Policy

Designing Disaster Diplomacy in the Context of a Climate Change Water Game

Abby Muricho Onencan$^{(\boxtimes)}$ and Bartel Van de Walle

Faculty of Technology, Policy, and Management,
Delft University of Technology, Delft, The Netherlands
{a.m.onencan, B.A.vandeWalle}@tudelft.nl

Abstract. In this paper, we explore how a climate change game can be designed to enhance trans-boundary water partnerships between governments and provide a window of opportunity to challenge the status quo, leading to change. The primary focus of the paper is to discuss a theoretical framework that utilizes "Disaster Diplomacy" as a pre-disaster capacity development tool for policymakers. The Nile Basin by 2050 scenarios, guided us in the design of the theoretical framework. The framework established a foundation for the design of the climate change game known as Nile WeShareIt. This game was played in October 2014, with policymakers from the Ministry of Water and Irrigation, in Nairobi, Kenya. Findings indicate that climate change games may challenge the current perceptions of normality and possibly lead to increased situation awareness, trust, and collaboration. Future work will entail redesigning the game, based on the initial outcomes and its application in the river Nzoia catchment, in West-Kenya.

Keywords: Climate change games · Disaster · Disaster diplomacy
Cooperation · Collaboration · Trust
Situation awareness and water resources management

1 Introduction

Disasters are a double-edged sword: they are catastrophic, but they can also lead to positive outcomes. A natural disaster causes extensive loss of human, environmental, economic and material resources. As a consequence of the severe loss, the affected community cannot survive under the circumstances and with the remaining resources [1, p. 17]. Examples of past natural disasters that have led to significant loss of life include the 2010 Haiti Earthquake (100,000 to 316,000 deaths), 2013 Typhoon Haiyan (6,343 deaths) and the 2004 Indian Ocean earthquake and tsunami (280,000 deaths). Some of the most expensive disasters in recent history include the 2011 Japanese earthquake and tsunami ($309 billion); the 2017 Hurricane Harvey ($125 billion) [2]; and the 2005 Hurricane Katrina ($81 billion) [3]. Despite the negative impacts of any disaster, a disaster could provide an opportunity for change. Since 2000, there has been an emerging area of research focusing on "disaster diplomacy" or disasters as "opportunities for change" [4–12]. Therefore, this paper seeks to contribute to this emerging area of research, with a focus on water management.

© Springer International Publishing AG, part of Springer Nature 2018
H. K. Lukosch et al. (Eds.): ISAGA 2017, LNCS 10825, pp. 43–57, 2018.
https://doi.org/10.1007/978-3-319-91902-7_5

The paper's scope is limited to "disaster diplomacy" in the area of future slow onset disasters. The paper relies on Kelman's definition of disaster diplomacy as a study that seeks to answer the question "Do natural disasters induce international cooperation amongst ... states that are not normally prone to cooperation? [13, p. 215]" The term disasters, in this paper, refers to future slow onset disasters. We define future disasters as the traditional disasters that may occur at a later date or "new distinctive class disasters and crises, not seen before [14, p. 16]." Slow onset disasters are disasters that cannot be easily detected because they slowly creep into the system, thus taking months, years or even decades, for the effects to be catastrophic. Though there are numerous studies on droughts and other slow-onset disasters, there is little research on assessing the impact of inaction due to the silent and deceptive nature of slow-onset disasters [15, p. 198]. Also, very few researchers have focused on the contribution of slow-onset disaster diplomacy in fostering water cooperation [8, 14]. Since disaster diplomacy is an emerging concept, there is a need for more in-depth action-based assessments, to examine its applicability, in water resources management.

To test whether the concept of "disaster diplomacy" can be applied to river basin management, we facilitated a participatory process of developing the Nile Basin by 2050 scenarios [11, 12, 16]. Scenarios are defined by Saritas as "narratives of alternative futures [17]." Scenario construction can be traced back to the works by Herman Kahn with his colleagues at the RAND and the Hudson Institute in the 1960s [17]. These scenarios were developed in Jinja, Uganda in February 2014 by a multi-disciplinary group of actors from the 11 Nile Basin riparian states and other international actors. The participants developed four scenarios, two under high climate variability and two under low climate variability [12], and their impacts on the Nile Basin, were assessed.

Based on an assessment of the four scenarios, the two scenarios (Miskeen – an Arabic word for poor, and Umoja – Swahili word for unity) developed under low climate variability led to future negative impacts and conversely, the two scenarios (EjoHeza and Kazuri) developed under high climate variability led to positive outcomes. In Miskeen (meaning poor), the countries managed the water resources unilaterally, and by 2050, depleted the water resources, and there was no water for any of the countries. Kazuri is a Swahili word that represents the phrase "small is beautiful." EjoHeza is a Kinyarwanda word for "a bright tomorrow." In Kazuri and EjoHeza, climate change induced disasters led to immense losses that challenged the status quo and triggered community (Kazuri) and inter-state (Ejo-Heza) collaboration, leading to positive outcomes [11, 12, 16]. Based on the scenario outcomes, we realized that absence of disasters might sustain the status quo leading to adverse outcomes and disasters may lead to positive change [12, 18]. Disasters may create a window of opportunity to challenge the status quo thus trigger positive changes. Hence, the need to investigate how this window of opportunity, created by disasters, can be utilized.

Undoubtedly, findings from some disaster diplomacy studies indicate that disasters, "do not create cooperation [13, p. 215]" but have the potential to catalyze a diplomacy process that may lead to collaboration [5, 7–9, 13]. A critical factor that led to positive change in the Kazuri and EjoHeza scenarios was the robust collaborative processes that led to the joint decision-making, planning and management. For example, in EjoHeza a basin commission was established to facilitate the process of jointly managing the scarce water resources and addressing the problems that had been caused by high climate variability. On the other hand, Kazuri established a citizen-led platform that connected all the basin citizens to facilitate the joint management of the water resources, by the citizens [11, 12, 16]. Therefore, in the two scenarios, disasters did not create cooperation but initiated a collaborative process that led to cooperation.

Similarly, recent research shows that disaster losses do not arise mainly from the extreme events but as a result of the complex interaction between the physical, social and built environments [19, p. 3]. Past research has heavily focused on how to make the physical and built environment more disaster resilient. However, little focus has been on the social environment and how it interacts with the physical and built environment to minimize or escalate disaster losses [20]. The social environment is responsible for steering the disrupted system toward the desired state. Hence, the social environment primarily determines whether the window of opportunity will be utilized efficiently [21].

Moreover, there are some pre-requisites that a social environment should have to enhance the collaborative process and eventually minimize losses during a particular disaster. They include increased situation awareness [22] and trust [23] (please refer to Fig. 1 for the definition of these terms). The evidence we derived from the Nile Basin by 2050 scenarios supports the argument that trust and situation awareness are essential social environment pre-requisites [12].

To assess whether a change in the social environment may steer the policy makers towards the desired state, we decided to design a game. Gaming simulates a pre, in and post-disaster situation [24]. It provides actors with an opportunity to test actions that they may take and their impacts [25]; increases their situation awareness [26]; increases their trust in other actors and institutions [27]; and helps them to agree on a collaborative process [28]. Also, gaming provides a safe learning environment [29] to prepare for future disasters [30].

We designed a game as a pre-disaster capacity development tool under the context of disaster diplomacy, incorporating the social environment pre-requisites (Fig. 1). In

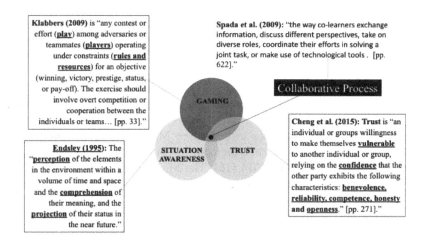

Fig. 1. Definition of the principal terms used in this paper: trust [31]; situation awareness [32]; gaming [33]; and collaborative process [34]

particular, we designed a climate change game known as Nile WeShareIt, to enhance the pre-disaster adaptive capacity of Nile Basin policymakers. We seek to answer the question: how can a climate change game be designed to enhance trans-boundary water partnerships between governments and provide a window of opportunity, through disaster diplomacy, to challenge the status quo, leading to change.

The paper outline is as follows. Section two explains the Nile by 2050 scenarios and discusses the main findings. Section three discusses the theoretical and methodological framework for the Nile WeShareIt game. Section four contains an assessment of existing games and an introduction to the Nile WeShareIt climate change game. The explanation of the initial findings is in Sect. 5, and our conclusion and further research are in Sect. 6.

2 Nile Basin by 2050 Climate Change Scenarios

As the supply of the Nile water resources declines, demand is steeply increasing, putting a strain on the shared resources. The Nile river traverses eleven countries in Africa. It is the source of life for 257 million people. The basin's aquifers, tributaries, lakes, rivers, and streams provide water for the environment, domestic use, energy production (hydro-electric power) and irrigation. High population growth, rapid urbanization, overexploitation and poor land practices pose a threat to the future of the Nile water resource [35]. Moreover, the Nile Basin is a highly complex basin with many uncertainties that compound decision-making [12, 36, 37]. Hence sound decision-making under deep uncertainty when there is no "clear print [37]" of what cause of action to take requires long-term thinking [36, 37]. The use of decision support tools like scenarios can support decision-making in complex basins such as the Nile, which face many challenges and profound uncertainty [11, 12].

A participatory scenario building exercise was held in Jinja Uganda in February 2014 [11, 12, 16]. We used the RAND methodology to develop four scenarios [16]. Figure 2 illustrates the three-step scenario development process and outcomes. At the foundation of every driving force[1] are contextual factors. We derived three key contextual factors from the 38 clusters that were identified by the participants during the scenario development workshop [11, 12, 16]. Notably, trust, situation awareness, and collaboration seemed to be critical factors that may shape the Nile Basin futures. Moreover, climate change was selected as a fundamental driving force and was a vital component of the scenario logic. After that, the scenarios were presented to stakeholders, to elicit views.

We explained the four scenarios to the eleven Ministers of water and over 400 participants during the 4th Nile Basin Development Forum (a bi-annual conference for the basin) on the 6th of October 2014 [16]. The Ministers of Water stated that they would like a future depicted in Ejo-Heza or Kazuri but fear Miskeen and Umoja [12].

---

[1] We define driving forces as the external factors that impact of the social, physical and built environments.

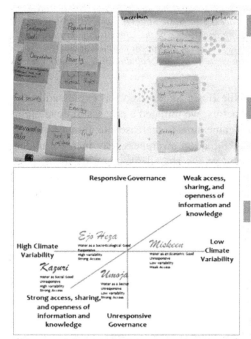

1. CLUSTER CONTEXTUAL FACTORS

Fig. 2.1 | Contextual factors were clustered into driving forces

The participants agreed the core question and from the core question they listed the contextual factors. We had 89 contextual factors that were grouped into 38 clusters. From the 38 clusters we finally agreed on 6 driving forces.

2. RANK DRIVING FORCES

Fig. 2.2 | Climate change is ranked as highly uncertain

The six driving forces were ranked in two categories, level of importance and level of uncertainty. The six driving forces were written on yellow stick notes and the participants voted with small round stickers for the driving force that they consider most uncertain and very important.

3. DESIGN SCENARIO LOGIC

Fig. 2.3 | Three axes scenario logic was constructed

From the six driving forces, three emerged as either the most important or the most uncertain. These three were climate change, governance and information access. First the participants had to agree on what the three terms mean to them. Once there was an agreement on the definition of terms, then the three axes were constructed as illustrated in Fig. 2.3. From these scenario logic, four scenarios emerged Ejo Heza (a bright tommorow), Miskeen (poor), Umoja (unity) and Kazuri (small but beautiful).

Fig. 2. In Fig. 2, we illustrate the Nile Basin scenario construction process. It emerged that climate change is a highly uncertain driving force that may shape the future of the Nile Basin. Figure 2.1: From the 89 contextual factors, we identified trust, collaboration and situation awareness as three factors that are relevant to this paper. In Fig. 2.1: Trust and Confidence are in green and yellow stick notes. Above the trust-sticky-note are many sticky notes that relate to situation awareness (degradation, population, food security and development needs). These sticky notes indicate that there is pressure on the resources but the system is not adjusting to these pressures. Finally, there are two sticky notes relating to cooperation: communication and CFA. Figure 2.2: The participants ranked climate change as one of the highly uncertain driving forces because it is highly uncertain. Figure 2.3: The scenario logic with three axes: climate change, governance, and access to information. Only the scenarios faced with high climate variability had positive outcomes. (CFA stands for Cooperative Framework Agreement. It is a draft legal framework to facilitate the joint management of the Basin.)

Surprisingly, the preferred scenarios were situated in a context of high climate variability, indicating a positive correlation between high climate variability and positive futures/scenarios.

As noted earlier, the stakeholders selected trust, situation awareness, and collaboration as crucial contextual factors and later confirmed their position, in the subsequent workshop held in Nairobi, Kenya. Furthermore, most of the Nile basin discussions confirm that these are the critical factors. For instance, after presenting the four scenarios, the Ministers of Water made a joint press statement, and the three contextual factors emerged, as illustrated in the press statement excerpt:

"Nile Basin States <u>have got no choice</u> (situation awareness) but to cooperate (collaborative process). Through cooperation (collaborative process), the Basin States are <u>able to harness the synergies</u> (trust and collaborative process), <u>taking cognizance of the comparative advantages</u> (situation awareness) presented by the <u>different development approaches</u> (situation awareness) and growing the pie for each individual Basin State (trust and collaborative process) [38, p. 2]."

To support the implementation of the Nile Basin States vision as expressed in the press statement, in collaboration with local actors, we initiated a process of developing a game known as Nile WeShareIt [36]. The game aims to increase situation awareness, trust and enhance the collaborative process. Situation awareness may increase understanding of the benefits of joint management of the shared river and the dangers of unilateral actions. Increased trust may be through the use of the benefit-sharing concept (trade in food, energy, and wood fuel). Improved collaboration process may be through identifying and utilizing the comparative advantage of each riparian state and new approaches for "growing the pie" together.

3   The Theoretical Framework

The objective of the theoretical framework (Fig. 3) is to provide a structure that describes the significant variables, elements, and constructs that will be used to design, apply and assess the learning outcomes of the climate change game.

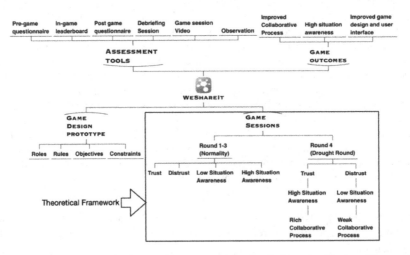

Fig. 3. Theoretical and Methodological Framework for the design of a Climate Change Game for Trans-boundary water resources management that utilizes disasters as an "opportunity for change." The rectangle is a visual representation of the theoretical framework within the context of game sessions. It is a representation of how the three theories (Gaming, trust and situation awareness) are conceptualized and used to design game sessions to improve the Collaborative Process. For the theoretical framework, we adjusted the Schul et al. [39] and Lowry et al. [40] theory of trust and distrust to a water resources management context and added situation awareness and the YUTPA model of trust [41–43].

Apart from assessing the changes in trust and distrust we also intend to assess the effect of climate-induced disasters on situation awareness. When climate change-induced disasters replace normality, there is disruption of perceptions of a safe and predictable system and situation awareness increases. Recent studies show that increased situation awareness may reduce disaster losses by half [44]. Normality encourages 'business as usual' thinking. Therefore, if "business as usual" is poor collaboration, it is difficult to change from non-collaboration to collaboration, while normality exists. Especially when past non- non-collaborative actions have not led to adverse outcomes or the consequences are not immediate, and the connections are not clear. Thus, positive or non-significant results reinforce trusting beliefs that the system is safe and predictable and there is little need for investigating the system further.

On the other hand, climate change induced disasters disrupt normality, and the previous trusting beliefs regarding the safety and predictability of the system are brought to question. Lowry et al. [40] carried out a research that established that with low levels of normality, the distrust of the system increased, which led to high awareness levels. With the distrusting beliefs, individuals are compelled to investigate the system, and they discover that it is not safe nor predictable. What we were not confident of is what happens after they come to this discovery. Before Lowry et al. researchers regarded distrust as a negative attribute, which led to no prior empirical assessments on the contribution of distrust to situation awareness and collaboration [40]. Surprisingly, early research in the 1950s until 1970s highlighted the positive aspects of distrust [45]. Then there was a wave of research mainly focusing on the positive aspects of trust [45, 46] and a few studies on the contribution of dissent [47, 48], without efficiently addressing distrust. Therefore, the contribution of distrust to collaborative actions is also a new research focus has begun to be re-assessed.

We made four adjustments to the Schul et al. [39] and Lowry et al. [40] theory. First, we included climate change-induced disasters as the factor that disrupts normality to increase system distrust and enhance situation awareness. The initial model did not include climate-change induced disasters. Second, we extended the theory from individuals to teams. While playing the WeShareIt game, some people play in teams. We assumed that team rationality is a total of the individuals in that team [39]. Third, we incorporated the assumption that increases in trust/distrust within the various WeShareIt teams will significantly affect collaboration, which will then affect the quality of the decisions made. Fourth, in the game design and assessment, there is a distinction between distrust of the system and distrust of other individuals (i.e., other players in the game). Consequently, we grouped parameters to measure distrust of the system under situation awareness and distrust of individuals and teams under trust and distrust.

Subsequently, we developed research instruments to assess increases in trust, situation awareness, and collaborative actions. The research instruments were inbuilt in the game itself, and external assessment tools. The external assessment tools consist of pre-game, in-game & post-game questionnaires, video recordings, observations and a debriefing session. Research measurements were developed to measure situation awareness, trust, and collaborative process. To assess situation awareness, we adopted the ten-question Situation Awareness Rating Technique (SART) [49] approach. The players were requested to subjectively rate their level of awareness based on a 7-point

Likert scale, before the start of the game and at the end of the game. We incorporated the situation awareness assessment questions in the pregame and postgame online questionnaires.

Furthermore, we assessed trust by some frameworks that were incorporated in the pregame, in-game (leaderboard) and postgame questionnaires. We developed a 16 question (in Swahili) rating scale, using the YUTPA conceptual framework [50] and its four dimensions (time, place, action, relation), for the leaderboard. Additionally, we used two techniques to assess trust, the first to assess the personality and the second; for self-assessment of one's level of trust at the beginning of the game and the end of the game. The personality inventory in the pregame questionnaire was developed using questions from the North-western University personality project website[2]. This website uses the Synthetic Aperture Personality Assessment (SAPA) method to assess the data and classifies personalities in the Big Five categories[3]. In addition to the personality test, the participants assessed their level of trust at the start and end of the game using 18 questions filtered from the IPIP Scale measuring constructs for trust[4]. We designed a research approach to assess collaborative actions using the in-game data, observation reports, debriefing notes and the recorded videotapes. Detailed descriptions and assessments of the various components of the theoretical framework are not within the scope of this paper. Therefore, each theory will be assessed separately, and discussed in detail, in subsequent papers.

4   Nile WeShareIt Climate Change Game

Before designing the WeShareIt climate change game, we assessed whether there are existing games that match the WeShareIt game specifications. In the assessment, we came across over fifty sophisticated climate change games [51]. Conversely, the focus of these games was mainly on the climate change negotiations at the global scale (for example, WORLD CLIMATE [52]) and decision support to reduce green gas emissions (for example, PLANET GREEN GAME, 2007 [53]). There are a few that focused on disaster risk reduction (for example, BEFORE THE STORM [54]/EARLY WARNING, EARLY ACTION, 2009 [55]). Alternatively, there are more recent climate change games that focus on water management and skills development (for example, AQUA-PLANNING [56] and FLOODED [57]).

From our assessment, we could not find a single game that met all the game specifications that we had defined for the WeShareIt Game. As a consequence, we developed WeShareIt as a new game aimed at focusing on the interaction between climate change adaptation, disaster risk reduction & management, water management, benefit sharing (energy, food, and nature), trust-building, situation awareness, and collaboration.

---

[2] http://personality-project.org.

[3] Openness, Conscientiousness, Extroversion, Agreeableness, and Neuroticism.

[4] http://ipip.ori.org/newNEOKey.htm#Trust.

WeShareIt is a hybrid board game designed to explore whether disaster diplomacy can foster water cooperation through joint planning, production, and trade in energy, food, and nature, within the Nile Basin. The game consists of five select boards. The goal of WeShareIt is for policymakers to get as many "happy faces" as possible. There are also regional collaboration strategies that need to be met by each player or a team of players. We designed the game with multiple continuing rounds, each consisting of a pay-out session (A) and a water allocation session (B). In the session, A, food, wood fuel (nature) and hydro-electric energy are harvested, bought and sold, in the trade round. After the trade, players invest in public services or buy solar panels (to reduce their energy need). In session B, the players may adjust their water allocation strategies to make their citizens happy and meet their regional collaboration strategies.

5   Game Application and Findings

Game design, testing and a series of iterations took place between October 2014 and October 2015. On 22 October 2015, WeShareIt was played by ten policymakers from the Kenyan Ministry of Water and Irrigation in Maji House (Ministry Headquarters), Nairobi, Kenya [36]. The players played three regular rounds and one drought round. In the drought round, their resources (food, energy, and nature) are halved. Since the players had not developed a joint action plan to buffer the river basin from future disasters, they were not prepared for the fourth round. None of the countries could meet their citizens' needs in the fourth round (see Fig. 4).

The findings discussed in this paper are general findings that seek to investigate the contribution of gaming to pre-disaster capacity development. The three contextual factors (trust, situation awareness and collaboration), identified during the scenario construction stage emerged during the game sessions as critical determinants of the outcomes. First, the riparian states could not **trust** other countries to be their sole providers or suppliers for their basic needs (food and energy). Second, the players barely made water allocation changes because these changes required trust and a robust collaborative process. Figures 4.1 and 4.2 indicate a correlation between trust and collaboration. When there was distrust, there was barely any collaboration between the players. Trust led to increased collaboration. Third, there was a false sense of security. This false perception led to low situation awareness. As a consequence, all countries were pre-occupied with local investments to be self-sufficient (national strategy to produce locally, all food and energy needs, without undermining the environment), and did not address trans-boundary strategies (cooperate and produce food and energy only according to one's comparative advantage). As a result, they were ill-prepared for the drought round.

From the players' statements in Fig. 4, we identified a shift in their mental models on managing uncertainties. One of the players representing Ethiopia made the first two statements (1 and 2) during the first three rounds. Later, he made the last statement, during the debriefing session. An assessment of the statements indicates that at first instance, the player was not ready to collaborate and was more focused on taking care of national interests. In the first three rounds, players did not incorporate uncertainties in their planning. Consequently, the players remained within their national social

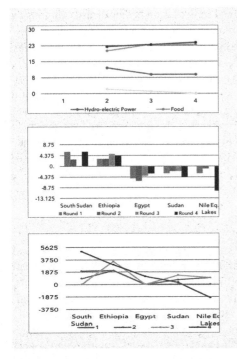

1. TRUST & DISTRUST
Fig. 4.1 | Water Allocation Changes in 3 rounds

"Even though I have a high energy productivity factor and I have the capacity to provide energy for the entire basin, I cannot convert all my food parcels into energy. How can I trust other countries to produce food for my citizens. That is not politically feasible. In addition, how assured am I that other countries will buy my energy, at competitive prices, once I have made the conversions."

2. COLLABORATIVE PROCESS
Fig. 4.2 | Citizens' Happiness Scores in 4 rounds

" I am well aware of the regional collaborative strategies but I did not implement them in any round. My first priority is to ensure that I have enough food and energy for my citizens. After that is achieved, then I may consider other countries."

3. SITUATION AWARENESS
Fig. 4.3 | Investments made by the players in 4 rounds

"As I was representing Ethiopia I thought my country had everything, because I always had surplus. So everything was okay, until the time when the rain failed and there was drought, I had no food. That is when I realized that we need to cooperate. I need these other countries. Cooperation is very important amongst us in our countries and even when we are working together in an institution."

Fig. 4. On the left side is quantitative data illustrated by three (3) graphs to explain three significant findings of the initial game sessions. On the right side are excerpts of players' perceptions that were expressed during the game and at the debriefing stage that illustrate that the main factors that challenges were distrust, weak collaboration, and low situation awareness. Figure 4.1: Minimal changes to the original allocations despite the allocations producing adverse outcomes for three of the five players in subsequent rounds. These minimal changes were attributed to lack of trust in other countries to produce basic needs (energy and food) on behalf of other countries. Figure 4.2: Minimal collaborative actions between countries despite having three (3) countries having three (3) successive negative scores from the previous rounds. There was much focus on seeking internal solutions to the problems and not joint planning and decision-making. Figure 4.3: Low situation awareness characterized by long-term planning without taking into account deep uncertainties and disasters. Figures 4.2 and 4.3 have a similar trend, leading us to conclude that there was a correlation between where the countries were investing their resources and the game outcomes. All the countries invested in strategies aimed at making their citizens happy and took little account of the overall basin needs. When faced with climate change, the water resources diminished significantly reducing the hydro-electric energy and food supplies, and none of the countries could meet their citizens' needs, despite the comprehensive planning that had taken place before-hand.

networks (riparian state) and maintained the established roles and identities without questioning the game rules. However, after the drought, the players stopped playing and sought advice and the opinion of other players on how to address uncertainties. In the discussions, new roles and identities began to emerge. For example, Ethiopia and South Sudan understood their roles as respectively energy and food providers. The last statement (Fig. 4.3) corroborates players increase in situation awareness. Players realized the value of cooperation because it prepared them to address future uncertainties, including disasters.

Moreover, there was more collaboration in round four than all the previous rounds. Figure 4.2 indicates a steep decline in adverse outcomes for Egypt for round 4 and a subsequent decrease in positive outcomes for Ethiopia, which was occasioned by the increased trust and situation awareness after the drought round. Ethiopia decided to forego some of its national priorities and ensure that it produces and sells sufficient energy to other riparian states, leading to a positive change for Egypt. The drought round increased situation awareness and raised the levels of trust to facilitate collaboration. Additionally, the sudden awareness that the system is unsafe and unknown led to distrust of the system and initiated a collaborative process, to address their challenges.

Despite weak collaboration in the first three rounds, the players ranked the collaborative process in the game highly (see Fig. 5). By their responses, we identified areas in the collaborative process in which they have sufficient capacity and the areas in which the players are in need of further support. We concluded that future work should give more priority to the capacity development of policymakers to (i) focus on collective interests, (ii) successfully negotiate and (iii) manage conflicts.

Furthermore, the participants were requested to rate their overall satisfaction with the game: 40% were extremely satisfied, 50% were very satisfied, and 10% were satisfied. No player was dissatisfied with the game session. Based on the positive outcome, we concluded that we could use WeShareIt game as a pre-disaster capacity development tool and gaming as a useful tool in preparing policymakers to utilize disasters as an opportunity for change.

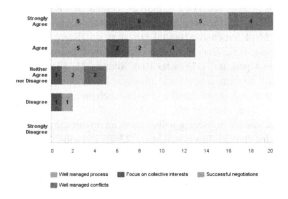

Fig. 5. The responses we received from the ten (10) players to Question 6 of the post-game questionnaire. The question is: "what is your analysis of cooperation in the game?"

Based on the player's recommendations, future work may entail decision support on complex interactions between the social, physical and built environments to minimize future adverse outcomes. We plan to do this through the use of already established frameworks like the Cynefin Domains of Knowledge model [58] Moreover; we plan to improve on the current game and customize it for a smaller catchment in the Nile basin, known as the river Nzoia catchment. Additionally, we plan to play it with key policymakers, in the river Nzoia catchment.

6 Concluding Remarks

In this paper, we discuss the emerging concept of disaster diplomacy with specific reference to gaming. Thus, background information is provided to contextualize the opportunities that may face the Nile Basin by 2050 when we use climate change disasters as an opportunity for change. Also, three barriers emerge to the efficient utilization of climate change disasters as an opportunity for change: low trust, low situation awareness, and weak collaboration. Consequently, we developed a theoretical framework aimed at addressing the three barriers. After that, based on the already developed framework, a game known as WeShareIt was designed and applied in Nairobi, Kenya. Based on the initial game findings, it is evident that climate change induced disasters may provide an opportunity for change if the Nile Basin policymakers overcome the three. In particular, shared learning through a well-designed and applied climate change game can help policymakers overcome these barriers. Future work will entail more detailed assessments of game findings and provision of specific policy analysis support to the policymakers.

References

1. UNISDR (United Nations International Strategy for Disaster Reduction), Living with risk. A global review of disaster reduction initiatives. United Nations, Geneva (2004)
2. Baragona, S.: 2017 Most Expensive Year for US Natural Disasters. Economy (2018)
3. Zhang, B.: Top 5 Most Expensive Natural Disasters in History (2013)
4. Mochizuki, J., Chang, S.E.: Disasters as an opportunity for change: Tsunami recovery and energy transition in Japan. Int. J. Disaster Risk Reduct. 21, 331–339 (2017)
5. Birkmann, J., et al.: Extreme events and disasters: a window of opportunity for change? Analysis of organizational, institutional and political changes, formal and informal responses after mega-disasters. Nat. Hazards 55(3), 637–655 (2010)
6. Archer, D., Boonyabancha, S.: Seeing a disaster as an opportunity – harnessing the energy of disaster survivors for change. Environ. Urban. 23(2), 351–364 (2011)
7. Kelman, I.: Beyond disaster, beyond diplomacy. In: Natural Disasters and Development in a Globalizing World, pp. 110–123 (2003)
8. Kelman, I.: Disaster diplomacy: can tragedy help build bridges among countries, p. 6. Fall, UCAR Quarterly (2007)
9. Kelman, I.: Disaster diplomacy: how disasters affect peace and conflict. Routledge, Abingdon (2011)
10. Kelman, I.: Hurricane Katrina disaster diplomacy. Disasters 31(3), 288–309 (2007)
11. Enserink, B., Onencan, A.: Nile Basin Scenario Construction (2017)
12. Onencan, A., et al.: Coupling nile basin 2050 scenarios with the IPCC 2100 projections for climate-induced risk reduction. In: Humanitarian Technology Science, Systems and Global Impact, HumTech2016, Boston, USA (2016)

13. Kelman, I.: Acting on disaster diplomacy. J. Int. Aff. **59**(2), 215 (2006)
14. Quarantelli, E., Lagadec, P., Boin, A.: A Heuristic Approach to Future Disasters and Crises: New, Old, and In-Between Types (2017)
15. Kelman, I.: Reflections on disaster diplomacy for climate change and migration. In: Sudmeier-Rieux, K., Fernández, M., Penna, I.M., Jaboyedoff, M., Gaillard, J.C. (eds.) Identifying Emerging Issues in Disaster Risk Reduction, Migration, Climate Change and Sustainable Development, pp. 197–210. Springer, Cham (2017). https://doi.org/10.1007/978-3-319-33880-4_12
16. Onencan, A.M., Enserink, B.: THE NILE BASIN BY 2050: strategic foresight on the nile basin water governance, p. 28 (2014)
17. Saritas, O., Nugroho, Y.: Mapping issues and envisaging futures: an evolutionary scenario approach. Technol. Forecast. Soc. Change **79**(3), 509–529 (2012)
18. Onencan, A.: TU Delft serious game elevates Nzoia (2017)
19. Mileti, D.S.: A Reassessment of Natural Hazards in the United States. Joseph Henry Press, Washington, D.C (1999)
20. Eakin, H., et al.: Opinion: urban resilience efforts must consider social and political forces. Proc. Nat. Acad. Sci. **114**(2), 186–189 (2017)
21. Waugh, W.L., Streib, G.: Collaboration and leadership for effective emergency management. Publ. Adm. Rev. **66**(s1), 131–140 (2006)
22. Zhou, W., et al.: Generating textual storyline to improve situation awareness in disaster management. In: 2014 IEEE 15th International Conference on Information Reuse and Integration (IRI). IEEE (2014)
23. Paton, D.: Preparing for natural hazards: the role of community trust. Disaster Prev. Manag.: Int. J. **16**(3), 370–379 (2007)
24. Sattler, K.L., et al.: Gaming: a unique way to teach active shooter preparedness and response in healthcare. Prehospital Disaster Med. **32**(S1), S214 (2017)
25. Lawrence, J., Haasnoot, M.: What it took to catalyze uptake of dynamic adaptive pathways planning to address climate change uncertainty. Environ. Sci. Policy **68**, 47–57 (2017)
26. Graafland, M., Bemelman, W.A., Schijven, M.P.: Game-based training improves the surgeon's situational awareness in the operation room a randomized controlled trial. Surgi. Endosc. **31**, 4093–4101 (2017)
27. Ong, D.C., Zaki, J., Gruber, J.: Increased cooperative behavior across remitted bipolar I disorder and major depression: insights utilizing a behavioral economic trust game. J. Abnorm. Psychol. **126**(1), 1 (2017)
28. Sanchez, E.: Competition and Collaboration for Game-Based Learning: A Case Study. In: Wouters, P., van Oostendorp, H. (eds.) Instructional Techniques to Facilitate Learning and Motivation of Serious Games. AGL, pp. 161–184. Springer, Cham (2017). https://doi.org/10.1007/978-3-319-39298-1_9
29. Blanson Henkemans, O.A., et al.: Learning with Charlie: a robot buddy for children with diabetes. In: Proceedings of the Companion of the 2017 ACM/IEEE International Conference on Human-Robot Interaction. ACM (2017)
30. Meera, P., McLain, M.L., Bijlani, K., Jayakrishnan, R., Rao, B.R.: Serious game on flood risk management. In: Shetty, N.R., Prasad, N.H., Nalini, N. (eds.) Emerging Research in Computing, Information, Communication and Applications, pp. 197–206. Springer, New Delhi (2016). https://doi.org/10.1007/978-81-322-2553-9_19
31. Mayer, R.C., Davis, J.H., Schoorman, F.D.: An integrative model of organizational trust. Acad. Manag. Rev. **20**(3), 709–734 (1995)
32. Endsley, M.R.: Toward a theory of situation awareness in dynamic systems. Hum. Factors: J. Hum. Factors Ergon. Soc. **37**(1), 32–64 (1995)

33. Klabbers, J.H.: The Magic Circle: Principles of Gaming & Simulation. Sense Publishers, Rotterdam (2009)
34. Spada, H., et al.: A new method to assess the quality of collaborative process in CSCL. In: Proceedings of the 2005 Conference on Computer Support for Collaborative Learning: Learning 2005: The Next 10 Years! International Society of the Learning Sciences (2005)
35. Nile Basin Initiative (NBI): State of the River Nile Basin Report, Nile Basin Initiative, Entebbe, Uganda (2012)
36. Onencan, A., et al.: WeShareIt Game: strategic foresight for climate-change induced disaster risk reduction. In: Humanitarian Technology: Science, Systems and Global Impact 2016, HumTech2016. Procedia Engineering, Boston (2016)
37. Onencan, A., et al.: Weshareit: a Nexus approach to nile basin water resources management. In: Decision Making Under Deep Uncertainty (2015)
38. Nile Basin Initiative (NBI): Press statement issued by Hon. Mutaz Musa Abdalla Salim Chairperson of the Nile Council of Ministers and Minister of Water Resources and Electricity of the Sudan at the close of the 4th Nile Basin Development Forum, in Building Sustainable Trans-boundary Cooperation in a Complex River Basin: Challenges, Lessons and Prospects (Theme), N.B. Initiative (ed.), Nairobi, Kenya, p. 4 (2014)
39. Schul, Y., Mayo, R., Burnstein, E.: The value of distrust. J. Exp. Soc. Psychol. 44(5), 1293–1302 (2008)
40. Lowry, P.B., et al.: Is trust always better than distrust? The potential value of distrust in newer virtual teams engaged in short-term decision-making. Group Decis. Negot. 24(4), 723–752 (2015)
41. McKnight, D.H., Choudhury, V.: Distrust and trust in B2C e-commerce: do they differ? In: Proceedings of the 8th International Conference on Electronic Commerce: The New e-commerce: Innovations for Conquering Current Barriers, Obstacles and Limitations to Conducting Successful Business on the Internet. ACM (2006)
42. Dimoka, A.: What does the brain tell us about trust and distrust? Evidence from a functional neuroimaging study. MIS Q. 34, 373–396 (2010)
43. McKnight, D.H., Cummings, L.L., Chervany, N.L.: Initial trust formation in new organizational relationships. Acad. Manag. Rev. 23(3), 473–490 (1998)
44. Girons Lopez, M., Di Baldassarre, G., Seibert, J.: Impact of social preparedness on flood early warning systems. Water Resour. Res. 53(1), 522–534 (2017)
45. Guo, S.-L., Lumineau, F., Lewicki, R.J.: Revisiting the foundations of organizational distrust. Found. Trends® Manag. 1(1), 1–88 (2017)
46. Lewicki, R.J., McAllister, D.J., Bies, R.J.: Trust and distrust: new relationships and realities. Acad. Manag. Rev. 23(3), 438–458 (1998)
47. Dooley, R.S., Fryxell, G.E.: Attaining decision quality and commitment from dissent: the moderating effects of loyalty and competence in strategic decision-making teams. Acad. Manag. J. 42(4), 389–402 (1999)
48. Schulz-Hardt, S., et al.: Group decision making in hidden profile situations: dissent as a facilitator for decision quality. J. Pers. Soc. Psychol. 91(6), 1080 (2006)
49. Taylor, R.: Situational Awareness Rating Technique (SART): The development of a tool for aircrew systems design. AGARD, Situational Awareness in Aerospace Operations, 17 p (1990). (SEE N 90-28972 23-53)
50. Nevejan, C.: Witnessed presence and the YUTPA framework. PsychNology J. 7(1), 59–76 (2009)
51. Reckien, D., Eisenack, K.: Climate change gaming on board and screen. Simul. Gaming 3 (2), 44 (2013)
52. Massachusetts Institute of Technology/Climate Interactive, World Climate (2006)
53. Starbuck Company and Global Green, Planet Green Game, USA (2007)

54. Red Cross/Red Crescent Climate Centre, Before The Storm, The Hague, Netherlands (n.d.)
55. PetLab, Early Warning, Early Action. New York, NY (2009)
56. Floersheim-Weilbach, Aqua-Planing, Germany (n.d.)
57. Mannsverk, S.J.: Flooded-A Location-Based Game for Promoting Citizens' Flood Preparedness. Institutt for datateknikk og informasjonsvitenskap (2013)
58. Snowden, D.J., Boone, M.E.: A leader's framework for decision making. Harvard Bus. Rev. **85**(11), 68 (2007)

Maritime Spatial Planning – A Board Game for Stakeholder Involvement

Xander Keijser[1(✉)], Malena Ripken[2], Harald Warmelink[3],
Lodewijk Abspoel[4], Rhona Fairgrieve[5], and Igor Mayer[3]

[1] Rijkswaterstaat, Zuiderwagenplein 2, 8224 AD, Lelystad, P.O. Box 2232,
3500 GE Utrecht, The Netherlands
xander.keijser@rws.nl
[2] COAST - Centre for Environment and Sustainability Research, Carl von
Ossietzky University of Oldenburg, P.O. Box 2503, 26111 Oldenburg, Germany
[3] NHTV Breda University of Applied Sciences, Monseigneur Hopmansstraat 1,
4817 JT Breda, The Netherlands
[4] Ministry of Infrastructure and Water Management, Rijnstraat 8,
2515XP The Hague, P.O. Box 20901, 2500 EX The Hague, The Netherlands
[5] Scottish Coastal Forum, Area 1-A South,
Victoria Quay, Edinburgh EH6 6QQ, UK

Abstract. The Maritime Spatial Planning (MSP) Challenge game: Short Sea Shipping (SSS) Edition is a table-top strategy board game, designed for policy-makers and stakeholders involved in MSP, short-sea shipping and the Blue Economy. It is a 'serious game', allowing the development of a better understanding of the issues involved in MSP through creative and imaginative role playing, taking into account the relevant professional and personal experience of the players. The authors present and discuss the use of the MSP Challenge board game to test how, and to what extent, the concept can help stakeholders understand Maritime Spatial Planning.

Keywords: Maritime Spatial Planning · Stakeholder involvement
Serious gaming · Board game · Short sea shipping · Blue Growth

1 Introduction

European countries have relied on access to seas and oceans for their economic and social development for many centuries [1]. As a result, these areas have experienced increased pressures, both in terms of space and uses made of the marine environment. Many different activities take place at sea; ranging from shipping, fisheries, oil and gas extraction, to offshore wind energy and military activities. As increased use is made of offshore marine resources, the requirement becomes greater for countries to work more effectively together if those resources are to be utilised sustainably. Simultaneously, new and evolving policies focus on tools to integrate different marine demands in space and resources [2].

Uncoordinated planning and management of marine space can result in underperformance of the (blue) economy and/or the overexploitation of resources (e.g. marine

© Springer International Publishing AG, part of Springer Nature 2018
H. K. Lukosch et al. (Eds.): ISAGA 2017, LNCS 10825, pp. 58–66, 2018.
https://doi.org/10.1007/978-3-319-91902-7_6

ecosystem goods and services) [3]. Marine or Maritime Spatial Planning (MSP) is defined as "a process of public authorities of analyzing and allocating the spatial and temporal distribution of human activities in marine areas to achieve ecological, economic and social objective" [4]. Further, MSP is described as "optimizing sea use and ensuring the integrity of the ecosystem at the same time" [5]. MSP has been developed in response to these current challenges and is still a rather new governmental approach in most parts of Europe [6].

MSP has been introduced in different countries [7] and can be considered a much needed approach to manage and organize the use of the sea and oceans. Stakeholder participation and involvement is an important factor to the success of MSP [8]; and has furthermore been identified as being key to MSP [9]. Stakeholder involvement and cross-border cooperation provide opportunities to deepen mutual understanding about MSP issues, explore and integrate ideas and generate new options and solutions [8]. However, according to Pomeroy and Douvere (2008), stakeholder participation alone is not enough. Stakeholders need to be (and feel) empowered to enable their full engagement [8].

Collaborative tools, such as serious gaming/simulation gaming (SG), can be used to facilitate stakeholder engagement and, in turn, to gather evidence about the human-level processes involved. This improves the available body of literature and, thereby, increases trust in scientific evidence [10]. According to Morf et al. (2013), there is a need of personal experience and interactive practice in MSP, as planning can hardly be taught and learned individually or by books [11].

As a result, the MSP Challenge: Short Sea Shipping (SSS) Edition board game has been developed. It is designed to let stakeholders experience some of the dynamic and complex interactions in ecosystem-based MSP in relation to short sea shipping and Blue Growth and to start 'thinking and talking' about the interrelations among different sea uses and objectives.

This paper discusses 'How and to what extent the MSP Challenge: Short Sea Shipping board game can help stakeholders understand MSP?' First, we describe the main design characteristics of the MSP Challenge SSS board game. We continue the discussion to consider 'To what extent can MSP professionals broaden and improve their understanding of MSP following gameplay?' Finally, we address the question of 'To what extent do individual and professional backgrounds and perspectives influence participants' general understanding of MSP as a result of gameplay?'

2   MSP Challenge Board Games

The MSP Challenge: Short Sea Shipping (SSS) edition was developed for a high level meeting on short sea shipping in Amsterdam on 15 February 2016, held as part of the NL Presidency of the EU Council [12]. It is an adaptation into board game form of the electronic simulation game 'Maritime Spatial Planning Challenge 2050' [10, 13]. Following the success of the Short Sea Shipping edition, other versions of the MSP Challenge board game have been developed [13–15] for different groups of stakeholders concentrating on different aspects of, and contexts for, maritime spatial planning. In this paper we do not make a significant distinction between these games. More information about the different versions and design decisions can be found on www. mspchallenge.info [13].

The MSP Challenge SSS is a 'table top strategy board game' designed for policy-makers and stakeholders with an interest in the field of MSP [12, 13]. The game is designed to run for between one to three hours, depending on the setting, involving twelve to thirty players.

The goal is to let players experience some of the dynamic and complex interactions between Short Sea Shipping and Maritime Spatial Planning (MSP). The main challenge for the players is to achieve Blue Growth (BG) and Good Environmental Status (GES) in their national and shared marine waters through the spatial allocation of economic functions and ecological features and the development of short sea shipping [12, 14, 15].

The game is played in the fictional sea basin called the 'Rica Sea' (see Fig. 1), which gives players a level playing field. The Rica Sea is shared by three countries: Bayland, Peninsuland and Island. These countries have their own maritime heritage and ideas about the future development of the Rica Sea. The map shows various parameters, such as cities/ports and water depths; important information for maritime spatial planners [12, 14, 15].

Fig. 1. Impression of the MSP Challenge board game in use with tokens to illustrate different marine activities in the Rica Sea.

In each country, players assume the roles of Maritime Spatial Planners, Nature Conservationists or a representative of a marine-related industry, such as Shipping, Fisheries, (Renewable) Energy or Tourism & Recreation. The players receive some background information about the Rica Sea and policy objectives per country. Furthermore, players will receive 'opportunity maps' at some point during the game-play. These maps give the '*best available scientific evidence*' which hint at opportunities and threats for achieving a blue economy [12, 14, 15].

At the start of the game, the game board is set up by the facilitators and shows a few 'opportunity areas' such as ports, cultural sites, wrecks, bird areas, etc. However, most of the sea area is still undeveloped; it is up to the players to further develop the 'Rica Sea' taking into account the countries' national policy objectives and wider international objectives, like achieving BG and GES. This is done by placing various tokens and threads on the game board [12, 14, 15].

These tokens and threads, symbolize all kinds of human activities (e.g. energy, fisheries), ecological functions (e.g. bird and habitat areas) and shipping (e.g. cargo, ferries). There are 25–40 different tokens and 5–10 different coloured threads. The number of different tokens and threads, and combination in which they are placed on the board, is up to the players. During the game, the players may gradually find out that they get into each other's way and this should players start 'thinking and talking' about the interrelations among the different objectives [12, 14, 15].

The game is facilitated by a moderator and a Game Overall Director (G.O.D.). The G.O.D., a policy expert, has the authority to give additional information, decide or intervene in all matters that are unclear or not provided for in the game. At the start of the game, the moderator briefly explains the rules and objectives of the game. At chosen intervals, the moderator pauses the game in order to facilitate a discussion on some key observations. The G.O.D. plays an important role in the game, giving or asking feedback and explanation from the real MSP world. After the game, the moderator explains key concepts and practices of MSP processes and an evaluation takes place with the players on successes and apparent inconsistencies in developing a Blue Economy for the 'Rica Sea' [12, 14, 15].

3 Method

Our empirical research strategy has thus far been mostly quantitative in nature, using questionnaires to obtain information on participants' level of MSP understanding and its possible influential factors after each session. The questionnaires were intentionally brief (2 pages) as the gameplay is already demanding. The questionnaire consisted of background questions (demographics, sector of employment, pre-existing MSP involvement, perspective on sustainability) and statements (scale: 1 = strongly disagree; 5 = strongly agree) on game play experience (general perceived usability and playability of the game), and MSP appreciation and understanding. We included one open question for comments and feedback, and we noted our general observations as facilitators and observers of the sessions.

In this paper we analyze data from the following gameplay sessions:

- Session in Millport (3 h), Scotland on 15 October 2016 - 9 respondents (all but one female; all working in the UK, with one originating from Ecuador)
- Session at Baltic MSP Forum in Riga (1 h), Latvia on 24 November 2016 - 13 respondents (7 female; 5 male; originating from and working in several different European countries)
- Session at North Sea Days in Scheveningen (1 h), the Netherlands on 6 October 2016 - 22 respondents (14 male; 8 female; all but one originating from the Netherlands, all but two working in the Netherlands)
- Session with two game boards at Atlantic Strategy Stakeholder Conference in Dublin (1 h), Ireland on 26 September 2016 - 32 respondents (16 male; 15 female; mostly originating from and working in Ireland and the UK).

Of the 76 respondents in total, 36 (47%) were male and 38 (50%) were female. Most respondents (50%) worked in the non-profit sector (e.g. science and academia,

NGOs), followed by those who worked in the public sector (36.5%; e.g. government, public administration, public policy advice). A final 12.2% worked in the private sector (e.g. fishing, shipping, tourism, energy). Given the limited set of data, all further statistical analyses are non-parametric (Figs. 2 and 3).

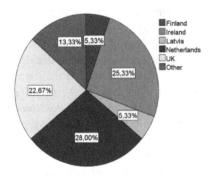

Fig. 2. Distribution of countries of employment.

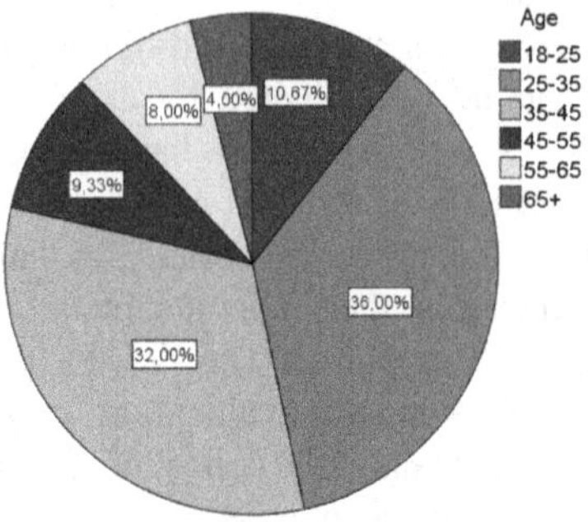

Fig. 3. Distribution of age of participants.

We conducted various descriptive, reliability and correlation analyses to answer our research questions. We were able to calculate and work with two components: a component representing five statements on overall game experience assessment (usability, playability, enjoyment) and a component representing four statements on overall MSP understanding. These and other ordinal and scale variables were not normally distributed. Thus we were mindful to conduct only non-parametric analyses.

4   Results

Table 1 shows that, in general, respondents scored positively on our measures of MSP understanding.

Table 1. Obtaining a general understanding of MSP – key descriptives

Measure	Mean ± SD	Min–Max	Median	Mode
'I know better what MSP is.' (N = 75)	3.73 ± 1.03	1–5	4	4
'I can better imagine the different viewpoints on MSP.' (N = 73)	3.96 ± 0.95	1–5	4	4
'I gained more insight into what the important factors in MSP are and how they (can) influence each other.' (N = 74)	3.77 ± 0.87	1–5	4	4
'I gained insights on how different planning scales (local, regional, national, international. etc.) can influence decisions made.' (N = 74)	3.53 ± 1.06	1–5	4	4
General understanding of MSP (N = 72; Cronbach's Alpha: .835)	3.76 ± 0.80	1.75–5.00	4.00	N/A

The overall component, derived from all four statements, indicates a positive overall response, though not highly positive. Additionally, roughly one-fifth of the respondents provided insightful remarks pertaining to their understanding of MSP. Seven respondents remarked critical aspects and common challenges of MSP, thereby indicating that they better understand MSP itself. For example:

- 'Really interesting and innovative way [for] getting people to think about the different interests and viewpoints of the various stakeholders.'
- 'The game shows clearly how governance and communication links work in reality. Everyone undermines the planners and mind[s] their own interest.'
- 'Nice to see how you experience that you first go for your own interests, then national, and only then international in this game. Actually isn't good, but this is how it worked. Also: everyone wants to plan as much as possible.'

Another eight respondents provided remarks that signaled a lack of understanding of MSP characteristics and issues, mostly because they attributed their experience to flaws in game design and facilitation rather than the collective play and MSP itself. For example:

- 'In terms of set up players tend to [remain] in the space in front of them, and not move around the table.
- 'Personally would have benefited from more information about tokens e.g. requirements for building of wind power, transport options for oil + gas, etc.'
- 'Clearer game rules and objectives, and consequences of actions would make the game clearer and more fun … The chaos would then get less, I think (without consequences nobody feels responsible).'

4.1   Factors Influencing MSP Understanding

Gameplay Experience
Table 2 shows that overall respondents assessed the gameplay experience positively. Kendall's tau and Spearman's rho tests revealed significant, though rather limited, positive correlations between the gameplay experience assessment component and MSP understanding (respectively .227, $p = .012$ and .304, $p = .011$).

Table 2. General gameplay experience assessment – key descriptives.

Measure	Mean ± SD	Min–Max	Median	Mode
'I think it is easy to learn how to play the game.' ($N = 74$)	3.86 ± 0.80	1–5	4	4
'I think the information provided in the game is clear.' ($N = 75$)	3.56 ± 0.81	1–5	4	4
'I feel creative while playing the game.' ($N = 75$)	4.00 ± 0.85	2–5	4	4
'I think the game is fun.' ($N = 75$)	4.48 ± 0.58	3–5	5	5
'I enjoy playing the game.' ($N = 73$)	4.40 ± 0.66	3–5	4	5
Gameplay experience assessment ($N = 72$; Cronbach's Alpha: .691)	4.06 ± 0.50	2.80–5.00	4.20	N/A

Kruskal-Wallis tests revealed statistically significant differences between the four gameplay sessions on both gameplay experience assessment ($p = .024$) and MSP understanding ($p = .000$). Further Kruskal-Wallis tests also revealed significant differences between the different countries of origin ($p = .000$) and employment ($p = .028$) on MSP understanding. The distributions on gameplay experience assessment and MSP understanding for each are shown in the boxplots below (Figs. 4 and 5).

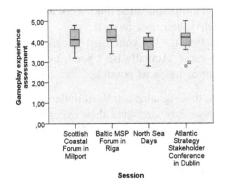

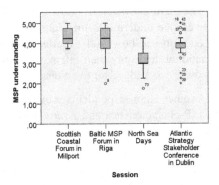

Fig. 4. Distribution of gameplay experience assessment per session.

Fig. 5. Distribution of MSP understanding per session.

Employment Sector

Another Kruskal-Wallis test revealed statistically significant differences ($p = .008$) between sectors of employment on the distribution of MSP understanding. The distributions on MSP understanding for each category are shown in the table below (Fig. 6).

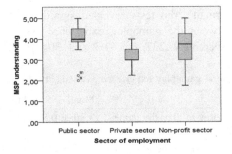

Fig. 6. Distribution of MSP understanding per sector of employment

Sustainability Perspective

Table 3 shows how we measured two different perspectives on sustainability - 'soft' vs. 'hard' – with a significant though rather limited negative correlation between the two (Spearman's rho: $-.334$, $p = .005$; Kendall's tau: $-.294$, $p = .005$).

Table 3. Sustainability perspectives – key descriptives.

Statement	Mean ± SD	Min–Max	Median	Mode
'Depletions in natural resources and decline of biodiversity can be compensated for through economic growth and improvements in technology.' ('soft' sustainability; $N = 71$)	2.55 ± 1.32	1–5	2	1
'Human activity and economic development should not be allowed to undermine natural systems and processes that are vital to the existence of humans.' ('hard' sustainability; $N = 71$)	4.42 ± 0.77	2–5	5	5

Twenty-one respondents (29.6%) at least slightly agreed with the 'soft' sustainability statement. Kruskal-Wallis, Spearman's rho and Kendall's tau tests revealed only a significant correlation between 'soft' sustainability perspective and MSP understanding (respectively $p = .010$; .353, $p = .003$; .289, $p = .002$).

5 Discussion and Conclusion

From our data analyses we conclude that, in general, MSP stakeholders from any sector and background can enjoy and appreciate the experience of a 'serious game' on Maritime Spatial Planning (MSP). Whether they understand MSP better afterwards depends not only on key session characteristics (such as quality of facilitation, number of participants, timing, scenarios and the gameplay itself), but also on key characteristics of the participant's own professional background, notably their perspective on sustainability and sector of employment. Participants from public and non-profit sectors and those with a 'soft' sustainability perspective seem to be more open towards MSP. Cultural differences in organization and communication might have an influence on the game play and its effect on MSP understanding, but our data is inconclusive in this respect.

Although our data shows a positive relationship between participation and understanding of MSP, we cannot conclude that gaming is more effective than other, more conventional means such as presentations or publications. Further studies could be conducted in a quasi-experimental manner to determine this. Other future research could also focus on the role of gaming in the MSP process itself; to what extent does gaming influence actual MSP processes and outcomes?

Acknowledgement. The research leading to these results acknowledges the contribution of the NorthSEE, BalticLINes and SIMCelt projects, which receive funding from the European Union's Interreg VB Programmes North Sea Region (NSR), Baltic Sea Region (BSR) and the European Maritime and Fisheries Fund (EMFF).

References

1. Douvere, F., Ehler, C.N.: New perspectives on sea use management: initial findings from European experience with marine spatial planning. J. Environ. Manag. **90**, 77–88 (2009). https://doi.org/10.1016/j.jenvman.2008.07.004
2. Kannen, A.: Challenges for marine spatial planning in the context of multiple sea uses, policy arenas and actors based on experiences from the German North Sea. Reg. Environ. Change **14**, 2139–2150 (2014). https://doi.org/10.1007/s10113-012-0349-7
3. Halpern, B.S., Walbridge, S., Selkoe, K.A., Kappel, C.V., Micheli, F., D'Agrosa, C.: A global map of human impact on marine ecosystems. Science **319**, 948–952 (2008)
4. Ehler, C., Douvere, F.: Marine spatial planning: a step-by-step approach toward ecosystem-based management. Intergovernmental Oceanographic Commission and Man and the Biosphere Programme. IOC Manual and Guides no. 53, iCa M Dossier no. 6. UNESCO, Paris (2009)
5. Gee, K., Kannen A., Heinrichs, B.: BaltSeaPlan vision 2030 for Baltic sea space, Hamburg (2011). www.baltseaplan.eu/index.php/BaltSeaPlan-Vision-2030;494/1. Accessed 05 Jan 2017
6. Kidd, S., Shaw, D.: The social and political realities of marine spatial planning: some land-based reflections. ICES J. Mar. Sci. **71**(7), 1535–1541 (2014)
7. UNESCO: Marine spatial planning initiative, UNESCO, Paris, France (2013). http://www.unesco-ioc-marinesp.be/msp_around_the_world
8. Pomeroy, R., Douvere, F.: The engagement of stakeholders in the marine spatial planning process. Mar. Policy **32**, 816–822 (2008). https://doi.org/10.1016/j.marpol.2008.03.017
9. Fletcher, S., McKinley, E., Buchan, K.C., Smith, N., McHugh, K.: Effective practice in marine spatial planning: a participatory evaluation of experience in Southern England. Mar. Policy **39**, 341–348 (2013). https://doi.org/10.1016/j.marpol.2012.09.003
10. Mayer, I., Zhou, Q., Keijser, X., Abspoel, L.: Gaming the future of the ocean: the marine spatial planning challenge 2050. In: Ma, M., Oliveira, M.F., Baalsrud Hauge, J. (eds.) SGDA 2014. LNCS, vol. 8778, pp. 150–162. Springer, Cham (2014). https://doi.org/10.1007/978-3-319-11623-5_13
11. Morf, A., Perus, J., Steingrímsson, S.A., Ekenger, M., Evans, S., Mayer, I., Zhou, Q.: Results of the 2nd Nordic Workshop on Marine Spatial Planning and an update for 2014: Use and Management of Nordic Marine Areas: Today and Tomorrow, Nordic Working Papers, Reykjavik, Iceland (2013)
12. Maritime Spatial Planning Challenge Short Sea Shipping Edition Handbook (2016)
13. www.mspchallenge.info
14. Maritime Spatial Planning Challenge Scottish Marine Region Edition Player's Handbook (2016)
15. Maritime Spatial Planning Challenge Blue Development Edition Handbook (2017)

Challenges in the Transition Towards a Sustainable City: The Case of GO2Zero

Geertje Bekebrede[1]([⊠]), Ellen van Bueren[2], Ivo Wenzler[2], and Linda van Veen[1]

[1] Faculty of Technology Policy and Management,
Delft University of Technology, Delft, The Netherlands
G.bekebrede@tudelft.nl
[2] Faculty of Architecture, Delft University of Technology,
Delft, The Netherlands

Abstract. Cities face a challenging task in reducing CO_2 emissions. Multiple technical solutions on district level as well as household level are available; multiple stakeholders with different values and possibilities to intervene are involved; and their actions highly influence the performance. To get a better understanding of these complexities and to contribute to a community-based transition process towards a CO_2 city, a simulation game was developed. This game, GO2Zero, represents an abstract district that is challenged to reduce the CO_2 emission to zero. Multiple stakeholders take actions, observe the challenges, and deal with these challenges with the final objective a sustainable district. This paper illustrates the first sessions with this game and show that different strategies of stakeholders lead to different challenges, ways to solve these, and a variety of outcomes.

Keywords: CO_2 emissions · Simulation game · Sustainability
Table top game

1 Introduction

The depletion of fossil fuel sources for our energy systems requires new ways and new sources to fulfil our energy demand. More importantly these sources have a large influence on the CO_2 emission. Other sources than fossil fuel ones (wind, sun, biomass) and related technologies (wind turbines, solar cells, biomass combustion) are available and implemented. At this moment, this is done insufficiently. A large transition towards more sustainable energy systems is necessary. This requires not only the use of renewable sources but requires a more holistic approach that addresses cost savings, energy efficiency and institutional innovation as well.

The current transition process is scattered. Although the urgency for this transition is well known, stakeholders act alone and their actions and implementations are limited to what they individually can do. Is it possible to coordinate a collaborative transition process, how would the roles of stakeholders change, and what does this mean for the sustainability?

© Springer International Publishing AG, part of Springer Nature 2018
H. K. Lukosch et al. (Eds.): ISAGA 2017, LNCS 10825, pp. 67–74, 2018.
https://doi.org/10.1007/978-3-319-91902-7_7

To test and explore different strategies, it was decided to develop a simulation game about the transition process with the aim of reducing CO_2 emissions on a district level. Simulation gaming is considered as an approach to freely experiment with different strategies and experience and reflect on the consequences of one's actions [1]. Furthermore, a simulation game can be considered as a complex system in itself, that makes it possible to represent a real world complex system [2, 3]. In the game, multiple stakeholders on a district level can work together, experience, and learn how a transition process can be organized, who needs to take the lead and how to achieve collaboration and alignment among stakeholders. This game is intended for European city stakeholders. Before this game could go life it had been tested with students from Tilburg University.

This paper presents the results of these student sessions. The main questions are: does this game provide enough freedom to experiment with different strategies, does it result in a variety of outcomes, is it a game nice to play?

We will first introduce the challenges in the transition towards a sustainable city. In Sect. 3, we will describe the game GO2Zero, which is developed by Delft University of Technology in cooperation with DNV GL. Section 4 describes the research approach, and the results of the sessions are described in Sect. 5. We end with the conclusions that the game provides the possibility to experience challenges in the transition processes towards sustainable cities and could be a starting point for a collaborative design of this process.

2 Transition Towards Sustainable Energy Cities

Cities can be considered as complex socio-technical systems [4]. Due to the characteristics of these complex systems, planning and steering the system towards a new system state is difficult and maybe even impossible. Looking at energy transition processes on a district level, we observe a network of a variety of stakeholders, formally and informally dependent on each other, and many technical and managerial possibilities, which are highly connected and interacting. That means the system can show emergent behavior, which could be unexpected and undesirable.

Main actors on a district level are the municipality, inhabitants of the district, the social housing corporation, businesses, but also the energy network operator and energy companies. These stakeholders operate on different levels and make decisions based on different values. Whereas a citizen mainly focusses on its direct living environment, a network operator or energy company reaches a larger geographical level. Although, in general, the actors would agree that sustainability is important, the ways in which this can be achieved varies from high-level top-down interventions to small-scale bottom-up initiatives.

In addition, the variety of technical solutions and the relationships between them are large. A number of possibilities are available, from reducing energy consumption by insulation, double glazing, and energy saving appliances, to producing energy on a household scale (e.g. heat pumps, photovoltaic (PV) panels) and a district scale (e.g. PV farms, wind farms, and using rest heat from industry), or changing energy sources from using gas towards using heat. The problem with these measures is that they could negatively influence each other. If households insulate their houses and install heat pumps, the demand for heat from the network will decline and investing in a heat network will not be efficient. Placing multiple PV panels on roofs might require changing the capacity of the electricity network.

Finally, the technical system and the stakeholder network interact. Owners decide about placing PV panels, which require an action from network operators to adapt the networks; subsidies from a municipality steer the selection of measures causing different performances of the system. These interactions lead to emergent behavior on the level of the district and consequently on the national and international scale.

Challenges

Getting a city towards a state of zero CO_2 emission faces some challenges.

- Stakeholders must invest first, while the return of investment is uncertain. PV panels will not be optimally used when they were closed from the network with insufficient capacity.
- The transition is a kind of chicken and egg story; on the one hand, the electricity network must be ready and on the other hand stakeholders need to invest in sustainable measures. It is not clear where to start.
- If everybody is deciding on their own, coordination problems will occur. Who needs to take this initiative to coordinate this process?
- Many stakeholders look at municipalities to organize this process. A municipality can follow a more top-down approach in which the local government in leading (by rules and regulations, incentives etc.) or follow a more bottom-up approach where the individual stakeholders take the lead and take actions based on their priorities and expectations.

3 The Game GO2Zero

GO2Zero is a multiplayer tabletop game, developed as part of the EU project Cityzen. The development followed the game design philosophy of Harteveld [5] and the design approach of Duke and Geurts [1]. The main objective of the game is to get a better understanding of the challenges of the transition process towards zero emissions in cities and to provide an experiential space to explore different transition strategies. In the development, we started with a thorough system analysis, including interviews with different stakeholders in Europe to understand the main variables, relations and challenges. In the design of the game, we set some clear boundaries to make the game more playable and more focused. Therefore, the transportation sector was left outside the scope, just as the commercial businesses in a district.

The game GO2Zero simulates a transition process towards sustainable energy. Multiple players, divided over different roles need to take actions to reduce energy consumption, increase sustainable production and make the district CO2 free. A board, with 12 houses with their families and gas and electricity networks, represents the district (See Fig. 2). All households have four piles of fiches representing the energy consumption (heat and electricity), the energy production, and the CO2 emissions. The potential local production areas also have a place on the map.

The participants play the families, municipality, grid operator, technology contractors, housing corporation and the local energy company. Half of the families rent a house from the housing corporation and the other half are house owners. All households have a grey energy contract with a national energy company (played by the facilitator) to start with. The grid operator is responsible for ensuring sufficient capacity on the grid. The needed capacity will change due to actions of the families and the housing corporation, but also by newly installed production capacity of the local energy company. The participants are placed at different tables in the room, with a placemat containing information about their personal situation, available contracts, and assets. They are allowed to move around and communicate with each other.

The challenge in the game is to reduce the CO_2 emissions in the district back to ZERO! Additionally, participants should achieve energy consumption reduction by 50%, and produce all energy locally. The transition process is not determined yet, so the participants need to think about strategies to reduce energy demand, and produce green energy locally. Cooperation and coordination is necessary, but they must consider their personal values as well as their financial possibilities and consumption pattern.

Fig. 1. Discussion with grid operators (picture used with permission)

Fig. 2. Representation of the district. The piles represent CO_2 emission, energy use and consumption per household

A gaming session of GO2zero starts with a briefing about the background of the energy problem and an introduction to the game. The game starts with a strategy phase where participants have time to read the information and develop a strategy. The game takes place in several rounds consisting of three steps: (1) payments, (2) negotiation, and (3) consumption. In the first step, households receive their salary and they have to pay their rent, energy bills, grid costs and municipality taxes. During the second step, all stakeholders can buy technology assets, negotiate about costs, make appointments, change contracts, and organize community meetings (See Fig. 1). In the third step, the city map is adapted to the new situation. A complete gaming session has four rounds. After the rounds, the final score is registered and all participants have to count their money and get an overview of their individual situation.

Then a debriefing starts, during which participants share and discuss their results, followed by sharing of emotions surfaced during the game, and reflect on the overall outcomes of the game. Further, they discuss what has happened, which challenges they faced and how this could be done differently. Finally, together they look forward to what this could mean for the transition process in the real cities.

4 Participants and Research Set-up

The game was play-tested with the municipality of Amsterdam (The Netherlands) and Dubrovnik (Croatia). From these sessions, the design of the game and materials have been improved, like the game flow and amount of possible measures. In this paper, we focus on the realism and utility of the final design with student sessions.

4.1 Participants

The game was played with first year students following a public policy making course at Tilburg University. At the end of the course, they played GO2Zero, to experience the policy making and decision-making concepts discussed in the lectures in a simulated real-life situation. In total 46 Dutch students played the game. The average age was 19.6 years (sd. 2.4), more women than men played the game, respectively 64% and 36%. They were randomly divided in three groups consisting of 15, 15 and 16 students. This was an optimal number of players for the game.

4.2 Research Set up

As this is one of the first sessions of the final game, we were especially interested in the game play, the possibilities within the game, and experiences of players. To collect data about these points, we used the following methods:

- Game results; each round results of the situation in the game were collected.
- Game observations: each group had one general game leader and one or two teachers to observe the game play and listen to the discussion between participants.
- Postgame questionnaire which focused on the game experiences and changing perspectives about the transition process. All participants received a link to an online survey.

5 Results

The results are divided in game outcomes to observe the varieties of strategies and game experiences to present the game play according to participants.

5.1 Game Outcomes

All groups started from the same position, which means that the houses have a low energy label (G or H), which is an indicator of the sustainability of the house, and they use non-sustainable energy sources for their consumption. We observed different strategies and results between the three teams. Table 1 shows the outcomes on the three main indicators. In general, none of the groups reached the final objective on any of performance indicators. This was hardly possible, as the game has been designed for four rounds of playing and due to time limitations, we played two rounds.

Table 1. Results of the different groups on the three main key performance indicators.

	Target	Team 1	Team 2	Team 3
CO2 reduction	100%	46.7%	45.5%	33.4%
Reduction energy consumption	50%	27.0%	33.6%	14.8%
% local produced	100%	29.5%	6.7%	3.0% (52%)[a]

[a]Group 3 build a couple of local production assets, which had not been connected to the network at the end of the session. Otherwise, the local production would have been 52%.

Team one clearly focused on reducing CO_2 emissions by changing the grey energy contracts to a contract with energy generated by nuclear power. This had a large impact on CO_2 emissions. Secondly, the households focused on energy reduction and local production via PV panels. They did this without any communication with the grid operator. Consequently, the network had insufficient capacity to deal with the new production. In the second round, the grid operator invested in increasing the grid capacity and the households applied energy reduction measures. This lead to an overly dimensioned network and a waste of resources.

The second group focused most on the reduction of energy. Together with some sustainable energy contracts, they were about halfway the CO_2 reduction targets and reached the highest reduction in energy use. With this group, the grid operator was also not part of the discussion about how to execute the transition. They had the idea that they could only react on the actions of others and need to follow the dynamics.

The third group had a strong grid operator, who took the leading position. To survive as a company, they had the strategy to focus on district production instead of household production. They actively discussed with the local energy company about investments in the grid and new production assets. In this session, the households had less influence and needed to pay higher grid costs. In the results, this is not yet visible, as the installed power was not connected to the grid at the end of the game. If it had been connected, the energy from local production would have been 52%, which would have been substantially higher than in other groups, especially taking into account that their energy consumption was higher.

During the debriefing, it became clear that it was not so easy to align the strategies among the stakeholders. Although they share the same ambition, when it comes to discussing investments problems occur, which lead to a deadlock. The discussion about implementing a heat network was a good example; everybody had agreed that this was a good solution, but nobody wanted to invest. Finally, the heat network was not implemented. A second general observation was that stakeholders focused on the well-known measures as PV panels, insulation and double-glazing. They did not research other opportunities.

5.2 Game Experience

In the postgame survey, we asked for players' experiences while playing this game. The number of responses of the postgame questionnaire was 24 (51%). Table 2 presents averages of answers to the statements (on a 5-point Likert scale). The participants agree that the game was relevant (M = 3.9, SD = 0.5) and they put themselves into their role (M = 3.9, SD = 0.6). Further, they slightly agree on the clarity of aim, the level of detail, and the realism of dynamics. In the debriefing, we observed that the students were surprised that in reality stakeholders often do not communicate well and believed that you could take decisions only with complete information. Further, they slightly agree that they enjoyed playing the game and they would like to play again. From the reactions in the open questions, we conclude that a better introduction of the different roles is needed as students lack knowledge about different roles. In addition, they asked for more time, so they would have the opportunity to finish the game. Both points influenced their experiences.

Table 2. Statistics about game play experiences

Statement	Average (n = 24)	St. deviation
The aim of GO2Zero was clear	3.5	1.0
The aim of GO2Zero was relevant	3.9	0.5
I really put myself into my role	3.9	0.6
Given the aim of the simulation, the performance indicators were sufficiently detailed	3.5	1.2
Given the aim of the simulation, the dynamics were sufficiently realistic	3.5	1.3
I enjoyed taking part in GO2Zero	3.6	1.1
I would like to play GO2Zero again	3.5	1.1

6   Discussion and Conclusions

The goal of the GO2Zero game is to provide more insights in the challenges of a transition process towards sustainable cities. Our observations, coupled with the results of the sessions, show that the game provides room for testing a variety of strategies and related outcomes. Further observations showed that a good alignment between different stakeholders is necessary to stimulate the transition process and to optimally use limited resources. Especially the role or involvement of a grid operator seemed to be critical in this transition. A second observation was that well known and easy to apply measures had been taken, like new appliances and PV panels. Other less known measures as heat pumps were not implemented.

The post survey shows that participants liked to play the game and would like to play the game again. The experience could become better if the roles had been explained better and if there was enough time to finish the game. The participants agreed that this game gave more insights in challenges of the transition process.

Based on the results, we conclude that GO2Zero represents a complex system in a playable way and gives room for discussion. More respondents are needed to measure the changing opinion about the transition process by playing this game.

Acknowledgement. The game development and sessions played have been part of the EU FP7 supported project 'City-zen, new urban energy'. The game has been developed in collaboration with DNVGL.

References

1. Duke, R.D., Geurts, J.L.A.: Policy Games for Strategic Management: Pathways into the Unknown. Dutch University Press, Amsterdam (2004)
2. Bekebrede, G.: Experience Complexity: A gaming approach for understanding infrastructure systems. Gildeprint Drukkerijen, Enschede (2010)
3. Frank, A.: Establishing games, gaming and policy exercises as tools for urban and regional planning - Are we there yet? In: Duke, R.D., Kriz, W.C. (eds.) Back to the Future of Gaming, pp. 80–92. W. Bertelsmann Verlag, Bielefeld (2014)
4. Holland, J.H.: Hidden Order How Adaptation Builds Complexity. Addison-Wesley, Reading (1995)
5. Harteveld, C.: Triadic Game Design: Balancing Reality Meaning and Play. Springer, London (2011). https://doi.org/10.1007/978-1-84996-157-8

Preferred Team Roles and Communication Patterns in Teamwork – Is There a Formula for Effectiveness? – Case Study Analysis

Anna Palyga$^{(\boxtimes)}$ (iD)

Kozminski University, Warsaw, Poland
apalyga@kozminski.edu.pl

Abstract. Preferred team role composition is said to influence team work effectiveness and communication patterns within teams. It is often recommended to balance team members in terms of socio-emotional and task-oriented preferred roles. However results obtained during this study indicate that there might not be such a possibility in the managerial environment. Hereby we present case studies of two extremely unbalanced teams in terms of socio-emotional and task-oriented role preference and its relationship with communication patterns in teamwork effectiveness. As suggested by literature, neither of these extremities is fully beneficial in terms of game play results. However it seems that a team consisting of only task-oriented participants performed better than purely socio-emotional oriented team. The first part of this article summarizes theoretical background and outlines the method used in this study. In the second part we present case studies of chosen unbalanced teams with in-depth analysis of their communication patterns.

Keywords: Team communication patterns · Preferred team roles
Serious games · Effectiveness

1 Introduction

Team work, team communication and effectiveness are a commonly combined and extensively researched areas in context of Business Simulation Games (BSG). Findings related to these topics come from many fields (i.e.: management, psychology, computer science, sociology, education, marketing, game-theory, etc.), and thus, BSG as a research domain, tend to be highly interdisciplinary. As a result an interdisciplinary approach is also highly recommended by scholars and practitioners of the field, especially for research methods employing serious games [1].

The majority of authors agree on the importance of the role of communication in experiential learning and serious game-based learning courses [2–7]. In fact, this consensus is reached, across all the fields related, stating communication to be central to any team actions. However, authors generally disagree on the way learning effectives is reached and measured.

This study derives from process-oriented research method for teamwork effectiveness assessment in BSG that was elaborated to take into account the dynamics of

© Springer International Publishing AG, part of Springer Nature 2018
H. K. Lukosch et al. (Eds.): ISAGA 2017, LNCS 10825, pp. 75–89, 2018.
https://doi.org/10.1007/978-3-319-91902-7_8

the game processes and encompass qualitative and quantitative measures [8]. The aforementioned method was employed to examine a group of master level business students taking part in a business simulation games course, and will be briefly introduced for the purposes of this paper. The aim of this study however, is to elaborate in greater detail on chosen inter-dependencies and processes captured by the above mentioned method.

1.1 Communication and Effectiveness in Teams in Business Simulation Games

Communication in group processes research derives from the psychological domain of group dynamics. In order to define a 'group' or a 'team' there is usually a list of their descriptive characteristics created. It is worth noting that Levi [9] particularly stresses the importance of interpersonal interactions among the group members, stating the communication to be the main and most important group process. Nevertheless, their definitions also underline direct interactions and performance, together with complementary skills of the members as teams' core qualities [10]. Thus, communicative behaviours were one of the core components of the case study analyses in this research. In addition, Barnlund's Transactional Model of Communication was used at the conceptual stage of the original study [11].

Existing studies of team work, lack sound empirical evidence around serious games effectiveness. This fact is attributed to the diversity of measures for effectiveness and communication assessment, plurality of data collection methods, and overall suboptimal study designs [12]. Several researchers point out to the necessity of further exploration of this matter, as serious games are discussed in the literature to be powerful learning tools [13–16].

It is also important to mention that the general logic and methodological approach of original study for communication effectiveness in teamwork was derived from studies in group development models, where two criteria were considered for group development models construction and analysis: (1) process- and (2) outcome-oriented [17].

1.2 Belbin's Self Perception Inventory – Team Roles and the Balance Between Socio-emotional and Task Role Preferences

Belbin defines preferred team roles as "a tendency to behave, contribute and interrelate with others in a particular way", pointing out that they are to be understood as a limited set of beneficial behaviors that bring meaningful input into the teams actions and can be divided into a few interconnected groups [18]. Each role is characterized in Appendix 1.

The questionnaire itself is being widely used in managerial practice. The main reason for that might be the fact that it addresses a literature gap regarding practice of working teams, especially in the field of balanced teams composition [19]. In this study the questionnaire was used to determine the balance of socio-emotional and task – oriented roles in researched teams.

There is ample research literature regarding relationship between team work effectiveness and Belbin team roles balance that confirms its existence [20] and lack of it [21].

Polish validation of this questionnaire, which was used for the purpose of this study is described as a valuable tool. However, its authors underline that this method should be approached as experimental, as it lacks an in-depth research of accuracy of its scales [22].

To determine whether the team is balanced or not, Fisher, Hunter and Macrosson method was used. Each members result was classified according to two categories: (a) socio-emotional or (b) task-oriented [23].

2 Method

The method of the original study was described in great detail in the authors former article, [8]. For the purpose of this paper the method will be briefly outlined to provide a point of reference.

The aim of the original research was to scrutinize team work effectiveness in context of team communicative behaviors. In this study the main focus will regard the preferred team role balance/imbalance results and combining them with communication behaviours obtained.

2.1 Socio-emotional and Task-Oriented Role Balance

First, the preferred team roles of the team members were diagnosed by Belbin's Self-Perception Inventory [24]. The results of each member were classified according to two categories: (a) socio-emotional or (b) task-oriented – using Fisher, Hunter and Macrosson method [23]. Next, the ratio of both categories was assessed as balanced or not by the rule of thumb as suggested by the authors. See Table 1 below for Belbin's role categorization.

Table 1. Preferred group role categories. Own elaboration.

Socio-emotional oriented	Task-oriented
Chairman (coordinator)	Shaper
Company worker (implementer)	Plant
Resource investigator	Monitor-evaluator
Team worker	Completer-finisher

As a result, the "profiles" of teams were obtained, indicating balance or imbalance of preferred roles.

2.2 Team Work Effectiveness Measures for Communication Behaviours and Engagement in Teamwork

Financial Game Results. Financial results were expressed by stock price of the company (in Euro) point to teamwork effectiveness by outcome-oriented measure. Financial results are used to rank the researched teams. The final ranking of the companies (teams) was prepared and the teams were divided in two categories: "winning" or "losing", including first and second degree winning and losing teams.

Communicative Behaviours. Communicative behaviours were measured through video analysis of team members' behaviours during gameplay. Communicative behaviours relate to teamwork effectiveness as process-oriented measures. The analysis was run by trained behavioural judges who categorized observed behaviours. There were three categories of behaviours defined – see Fig. 1 below:

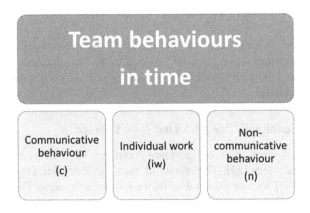

Fig. 1. Communicative behaviours of examined teams.

Communicative Behaviour (Code: c). Such behaviour: (1) contains an intention directed to a partner of interaction and (2) the behaviour is not an operation on an object serving other purpose but communication [25].

Individual Work (Code: iw). Operations on objects, when a person does not communicate directly with other team members and is busy with individual activity. For example: reading course materials, making necessary calculations with computer.

Non-communicative Behaviour (Code: n). Opposing the definition of communicative behaviour. This included all behaviours containing no intention towards the partner of interaction and serving other purposes than communicating with another team member.

Active Engagement in Team Activities. The level of active engagement was assessed by trained behavioral judges based on a video recording of game play situation. The experts were assessing the observed engagement on a 5-level Likert scale, where: 1 = "no active engagement in team activities, the team is not working" and 5 = "all team members actively engaged in team activities, full engagement".

2.3   Subjects

The research was conducted at the authors' university, during Business Simulation Games courses (employing "TOPSiM" managerial game). The subjects were the last year, part-time business students of master-level studies, aged from 21 to 42 (mean age = 27). Four student classes were researched in total, one of which was removed from the analysis of this study due to missing data. The students had previously finished their courses in finance, accounting, strategic management, marketing.

2.4   Research and Data Analysis Procedure

Research Procedure. The students gathered in their classroom were informed by the teacher about the opportunity to take part in a research study regarding group processes. The research situation was separated from the standard course situation, by introducing a researcher.

Next, the professor would leave the classroom. The researcher described the research procedure, and provided Belbin Self Perception Inventory for the subjects. After the questionnaire was filled, the teacher was invited back to the classroom and started the class by instructing participants to form 4–6 person teams [26].

All teams worked in the open space of the classroom, where two video cameras were registering their behaviors.

Data Analysis Procedure. After registering team members behavior in the classroom, the video material was processed for the use of behavioral judges: from each decisive round (90 min each) first 15 and last 15 min sections were selected for analysis. The experts were given assessment sheets, instructions regarding behavioral categories, and received training.

To provide the highest internal consistency of assessment, the experts were asked to work in pairs – discussing to agree on a certain behavior categorization if in doubt.

The research material was categorized by judges according to the instructions given: communicative behaviors and active engagement in team work were noted and categorized every 30 s of the video, for every person from each team. Dominant behaviors were categorized and noted down.

3   Results

3.1   Financial Results of Teams

For the financial results of each group and its teams see tables in Appendix 2. Financial results were used in character of grouping variable to rank researched teams.

3.2   Socio-emotional and Task–Oriented Balance in Teams

Table 2 below summarizes socio-emotional and task – oriented balance in teams, that was created based on Belbin Self-Perception Inventory questionnaire results. The table contains additional information on final rankings of teams derived from their financial results. In addition, the number of roles that emerged in teams were noted.

Table 2. Socio-emotional and task – oriented balance in teams with ranked game results

	Ranking order	Team no	Game result	Socio-emotional/task - oriented proportions [%]	Number of present roles
Group 1	1	4	Winning 1	20/80	6 of 8
	2	1	Winning 2	20/80	6 of 8
	3	3	Losing 2	25/75	4 of 8
	4	2	Losing 1	25/75	5 of 8
Group 2	1	3	Winning 1	40/60	7 of 8
	2	4	Winning 2	60/40	8 of 8
	3	1	Losing 2	20/80	7 of 8
	4	2	Losing 1	**100/0**	6 of 8
Group 3	1	1	Winning 1	20/80	7 of 8
	2	2	Winning 2	**0/100**	4 of 8
	3	4	Losing 2	50/50	8 of 8
	4	3	Losing 1	20/80	7 of 8

This overview of researched teams shows that eight out of twelve teams were imbalanced towards task-oriented roles, while only one team held the opposite. There is one nominally balanced team, however, in cases of teams number one and two, in group three, there is a ratio pointing towards balance, as these two teams were composed of odd number of members (5 people). Thus, this could be interpreted as a presence of three balanced teams out of twelve researched teams.

It is also worth noting that each group forms its own micro-world. Group one is most homogenous in terms of team role imbalance – all of its teams have more task-oriented preferences than socio-emotional ones. Ratios for winning teams are 20:80 and for losing 25:75.

Group two is not homogenous, with winning teams tendency towards balanced ratios (40:60 and 60:40), while losing teams with a bias towards extreme values: losing team number one with 100:0 and losing team number two with ratio 20:80.

Group number three is also not homogenous. Winning team 1 and losing team 1 exhibited the same ratios of socio-emotional and task-oriented role preferences, which is 20:80. The only nominally balanced team with ratio 50:50 was a second degree winner. Second degree losing teams lacked team members with socio-emotional preferences.

Additionally, there was a summary of the number of different roles appearing in each team. Number of present roles varies from 4 to 8 (out of 8), and only two teams displayed a complete set of eight team roles. One of them was a second degree winner (team number 2 in group 2), and the other was ranked as second degree losing team (team number 4 in group 3).

Teams marked in bold (team number 2 in group 3, and team number 2 in group 2) were chosen for deeper analysis of their communicative results as extremely unbalanced team roles of all teams that were researched.

3.3 Communicative Behaviours and Active Engagement Results of Two Extremely Unbalanced Cases

Two teams were chosen for further in-depth investigation of their communicative patterns based on their extreme team role imbalance. Summary charts were created for team number two in group two and team number two in group three (see Figs. 2 and 3).

First Degree Losing Team. The team number 2 in group 2 (see Fig. 2) finished the game as a first degree losing team (Losing 1). There were no preferences for task-oriented roles diagnosed in this team. General communicative behaviours in time (per round) seemed consistently focused on communication and individual work: with communication varying from 56% to 45% and individual work varying from 42% to 49% throughout all decisive rounds. Non-communicative behaviours were consistently marginal throughout the whole gameplay varying form 1.54% to 6.33% with 6.33% being the highest ratio of non-communicative behaviours displayed, which appeared in round 3.

In closer analysis of communicative behaviours observations for the beginning and the end of each decisive round the bar graphs showed that this particular team's members communicated with one another more frequently in second halves of their decisive rounds.

Even though there were numerous communication behaviours displayed, the team started off from rank position number 3 after the first round. They managed to shift to second rank after round 2, and after that the team gradually dropped their position to the bottom of the ranking.

It is also worth noting that the team started the game off with extremely engaged attitude of all its members (scoring 4.94 points out of 5 in behavioural judges assessment), which lasted to the end of round 2. After that round the displayed engagement dropped to be assessed 3.07 points and in next two rounds it gradually shifted to the value of 3.93. This particular breaking point of engagement occurred simultaneously with a drop in the ranking position.

Second Degree Winning Team. The team number 2 in group 3 (see Fig. 3) finished their game as a second degree winner (Winning 2). There were no preferences for socio-emotional-oriented roles diagnosed in this team. General communicative behaviours in time (per round) seemed to gradually increase, with two 7–8% drops in round one and three. The team started off with 46.86% communicative behaviours ratio and finished with the ratio of 70.83% communicative behaviours, consequently increasing communication throughout their gameplay. Their individual work per round varied from 45.61% to 20.42%. Non-communicative behaviours of this team held the level below 1% for 3 out of five decisive rounds. However in round 1 and round 3 they increased to 7.53% and 8.76% respectively.

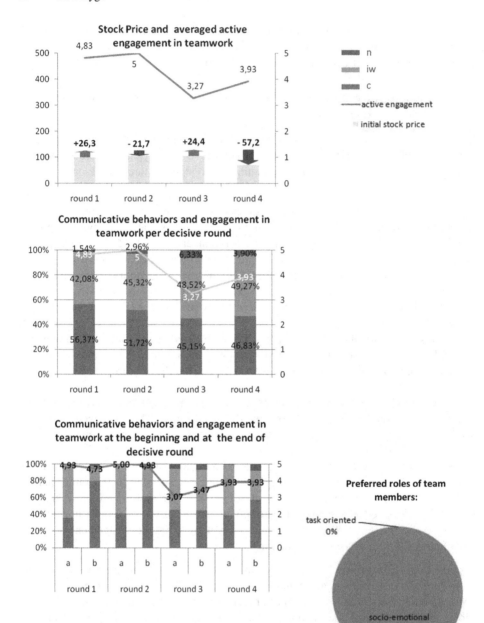

Fig. 2. Chart of the first degree losing team (Team no 1 in Group 2)

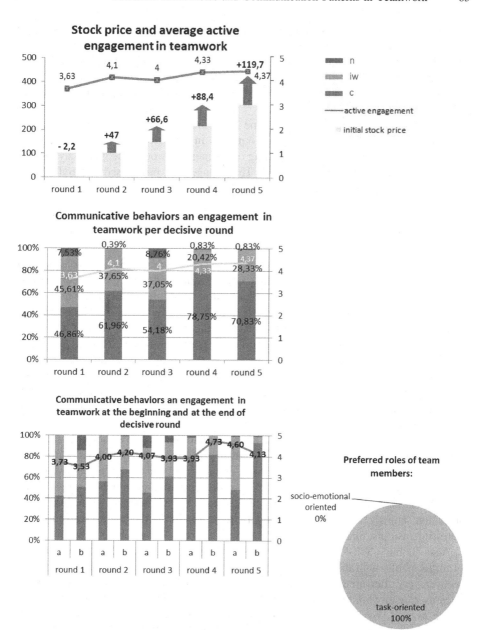

Fig. 3. Chart of the second degree winning team (Team no 2 in Group 3)

In closer analysis of communicative behaviours observations for the beginning and the end of each decisive round the bar graphs show that this particular team members communicated with one another more frequently in the second halves of their decisive rounds, reaching their most extreme difference in last - fifth - round shifting from 48.33% to 93.33%.

The team started the game off ranked second in round 1 and shifted to rank 1 for rounds 2,3, and 4. In the fifth round – simultaneously to the communication behaviours biggest shift - the team lost their leading financial position and finished the game ranked as second.

This particular team started the game with moderately engaged attitude of its members (scoring 3.53 averaged points out of 5 in behavioural judges assessment). However, their engagement was increasing consequently through the gameplay (to end the game scoring 4.37 averaged points). The engagement progressed in parallel with financial progress of this team.

4 Discussion

Communication processes can be viewed as transactions, where two conditions need to be fulfilled: (1) each person is simultaneously a sender and a recipient of verbal and non-verbal messages, and (2) all parties involved in the communication are influenced and influence one another [11].This approach illustrates how team communication is a dynamic process that undergoes constant changes, therefore, this study focused on both: results and processes taking place during the gameplay. Thus, methods employed for the purpose of data collection and analysis of this study were combined in accordance to both, process- and outcome-oriented approaches of measuring effectiveness. This was performed in order to bring a wider and more detailed picture to the research situation. Nevertheless, these tools also comprise certain limitations that had to be taken into consideration.

Some of them were already addressed by Palyga and Wardaszko in their original study on process-oriented research method for teamwork effectiveness assessment in Business Simulation Games [8]. To name the foremost, it was stated that there is no possibility for results generalization, as the scale of original study was not large enough. Secondly, the research method forged for the purpose of this study is still untested and needs further calibration. Thirdly, although the results of application of the method brings some very interesting insights, there is no causal reasoning allowed to be run here.

Also, Belbin's Self-Perception Inventory (SPI) is widely criticized as a tool that does not conform fully with all psychometric requirements of a psychological test [27, 28]. It is, however, very often used by researchers and practitioners for its coverage of very relevant concerns in teamwork theory and practice. SPIs relationship with teamwork is not conclusive as well, however some researchers claim this fact to be a reason for further exploration of this tool's properties and applications [29, 30]. Nonetheless, Polish validation of this questionnaire which was used for the purpose of this study is claimed by its authors as worth attention and offering some valuable properties.

Another important issue to be addressed, concerns the procedural decisions regarding this study. Firstly, the students participating in the research situation were allowed to create their teams by themselves. Such decision was made in order to obtain a natural team composition, allowing better communication from the start [31–36]. It is also worth addressing that the cameras used to record the teams could influence teams behaviors by distracting participants attention. Nonetheless, a direct observation by behavioral judges could intensify such phenomenon even more. In order to mitigate such influence, the participants were informed about (1) cameras presence prior to research beginning and (2) possibility of withdrawal from participation in research at every moment of the recording. All questions and requirements about anonymity, confidentiality and procedures of recording were answered. On the side of behavioral judges there was instruction given to note behavioral indicators of interest in cameras presence (like direct gazing, pointing and looking at the devices). The judges reported few indications of interest in recording devices, but the amount was considered insignificant.

Results obtained in the three researched student groups might serve as an example of how each group forms different internal culture and how each team develops its own "personality" over time [6]. Results obtained by two teams chosen for case study analysis emerged as extremely unbalanced in terms of socio-emotional and task-oriented role preference. Imbalance in favor of task-oriented roles was observed in all researched groups (majority of the teams) which could constitute a premise about managerial population possessing such characteristic. However the sample size does not allow such reasoning and permits to interpret this observation only as a suggestion for further exploration.

Two extremely imbalanced teams came to the attention of the close observation and analysis of this study. Obtained results suggest that neither of extremities in preferred roles (either 100% task-orientation, nor 100% socio-emotional-orientation) is fully beneficial in terms of team effectiveness. It is suggested in the reference literature that excessive focus on only one role type might restrain the other and lead to a regression of group development [37]. However, in the light of this research, it seems that the team consisting of only task-oriented participants performed more effectively than purely socio-emotionally oriented team. This study does not attempt to answer the question why such situation occurred, yet its results might serve as a premise to explore this matter further.

Appendix 1. Belbin Team Role Typology

Type	Symbol	Typical feature	Positive qualities	Allowable weaknesses
Company worker	CW	Conservative, predictable, dutiful	Organising ability, Practical common sense, Hardworking, Self discipline	Lack of flexibility, unresponsiveness to unproven ideas
Chairman	CH	Calm, self controlled, self confident	A capacity for treating and welcoming all potential contributors on their merit; and without prejudice. A strong sense of objectives	No more than ordinary in terms of intellect or creative ability

(*continued*)

(*continued*)

Type	Symbol	Typical feature	Positive qualities	Allowable weaknesses
Shaper	SH	Highly strung, dynamic, outgoing	Drive and a readiness to challenge inertia, ineffectiveness, complacency or self deception	Proneness to provocation, irritation and impatience
Plant	PL	Individualistic, serious minded, unorthodox	Genius, imagination, intellect and knowledge	Up in the clouds, inclined to disregard practical details or protocol
Resource investigator	RI	Extroverted, enthusiastic, curious, communicative	A capacity for contacting people and exploring anything new. An ability to respond to a challenge	Liable to lose interest once the initial fascination has passed
Monitor evaluator	ME	Sober, unemotional, prudent	Judgement, discretion, hard headedness	Lacks the inspiration or the ability to motivate others
Team worker	TW	Socially orientated, rather mild, sensitive	An ability to respond to people and to situations, and to promote team spirit	Indecisiveness at moments of crisis
Completer finisher	CF	Painstaking, orderly, conscientious, anxious	A capacity for follow through. Perfectionism	A tendency to worry about the small things. A reluctance to "let go"

Source: Belbin (2004)

Appendix 2 – Game Results

	Share price in EUR					Final rank
Group 1	Round 0	Round 1	Round 2	Round 3	Round 4	
Team 1	100	106,6	136,2	189,2	255,5	Winning 2
Team 2	100	120,1	78,8	145,6	158,7	Losing 1
Team 3	100	173,5	128,5	182,8	235,8	Losing 2
Team 4	100	104,7	171,4	214,3	275,3	Winning 1

	Share price in EUR					Final rank
Group 2	Round 0	Round 1	Round 2	Round 3	Round 4	
Team 1	100	141,3	156	122,9	137,8	Losing 2
Team 2	100	126,3	104,6	129	71,8	Losing 1
Team 3	100	159,9	101,8	162,6	194,6	Winning 1
Team 4	100	115,4	80,3	136,1	186,7	Winning 2

	Share price in EUR						Final rank
Group 3	Round 0	Round 1	Round 2	Round 3	Round 4	Round 5	
Team 1	100	78,4	142,9	189,7	299,1	519	Winning 1
Team 2	100	97,8	144,8	211,4	299,8	419,5	Winning 2
Team 3	100	112	99,4	168	125,7	0	Losing 1
Team 4	100	76,6	135,5	125,6	168,6	134,2	Losing 2

References

1. Duke, R., Geurts, J.: Policy Games for Strategic Management. Dutch University Press Amsterdam (2004)
2. Kriz, W.C.: Lernziel Systemkompetenz. Planspiele als Trainingsmethode. Vandenhoeck & Ruprecht, Göttingen (2000)
3. Kriz, W.C.: Creating effective interactive learning environments through gaming simulation design. J. Simul. Gaming **34**(4), 495–511 (2003)
4. Kayes, D.C., Kayes, A., Kolb, D.A.: Experiential learning in teams. Simul. Gaming **36**(3), 330–354 (2005)
5. Kriz, W.C., Hense, J.: Theory-oriented evaluation for the design of and research in gaming and simulation. J. Simul. Gaming **37**(2), 268–283 (2006)
6. Hergeth H.: Team behavior and team success: results from a board game simulation. Dev. Bus. Simul. Exp. Learn. **34** (2007). http://www.absel.org
7. Kriz, W.C., Nöbauer, B.: Teamkompetenz: Konzepte – Trainingsmethoden – Praxis, 4th edn. Vandenhoeck & Ruprecht, Göttingen (2008)
8. Palyga, A., Wardaszko, M.: Process-oriented research method for teamwork effectiveness assessment in business simulation games. Dev. Bus. Simul. Exp. **1**, 233–239 (2016)
9. Levi, D.: Group Dynamics for Teams. 5th edn. California Polytechnic State University, Sage Publications Inc., San Luis Obispo (2016)
10. Bitkowska, A.: Zarządzanie Procesami Biznesowymi W Przedsiębiorstwie. Vizja Press & IT, Warszawa (2009)
11. Barnlund, D.C.: A transactional model of communication. In: Akin, J., Goldberg, A., Myers, G., Stewart, J. (eds.) Language Behaviour: A book of Readings in Communication Mauton and Co./N.V. Publishers, The Hague, pp. 45–63 (1970)
12. All, A., Nuñez Castellar, E.P., Van Looy, J.: Measuring effectiveness in digital game-based learning: a methodological review. Int. J. Serious Games **1**(2), 3–21 (2014)
13. Annetta, L.A., Minogue, J., Holmes, S.Y., Cheng, M.-T.: Investigating the impact of video games on high school students' engagement and learning about genetics. Comput. Educ. **53**, 74–85 (2009)
14. Wrzesien, M., Raya, M.A.: Learning in serious virtual worlds: evaluation of learning effectiveness and appeal to students in the E-Junior project. Comput. Educ. **55**, 178–187 (2010)
15. Hainey, T., Connolly, T., Stansfield, M., Boyle, L.: The use of computer games in education: a review of literature. In: Patric, F. (ed.) Handbook of Research on Improving Learning and Motivation Through Educational Games: Multidisciplinary Approaches, pp. 29–50. Waterford Institute of Technology, Ireland (2011)
16. Girard, C., Ecalle, J., Magnan, A.: Serious games as new educational tools : how effective are they ? A meta-analysis of recent studies. J. Comput. Assist. Learn. **29** 207–219 (2013). https://doi.org/10.1111/j.1365-2729.2012.00489.x
17. Chidambaram, L., Bostrom, R.P.: Group Development (I): a review and synthesis of development models. Group Decis. Negot. **187**, 159–187 (1996)
18. Belbin, M.: Team Roles at Work. Butterworth-Heinemann, Burlington (1993)
19. Partington, D., Harris, H.: Team role balance and team performance: an empirical study. J. Manag. Dev. **18**(8), 694–706 (2014)
20. Hirschfeld, R.R., Jordan, M.H., Feild, H.S., Giles, W.F., Armenakis, A.A.: Becoming team players: team members' mastery of teamwork knowledge as a predictor of team task proficiency and observed teamwork effectiveness. J. Appl. Psychol. **91**(2), 467–474 (2006)

21. Smith, M., Polglase, G., Parry, C.: Construction of student groups using Belbin: supporting group work in environmental management. J. Geogr. High. Educ. **36**(4), 585–601 (2012)
22. Witkowski, S.A., Ilski, S.: Walidacja Kwestionariusza Ról Zespołowych: Przegląd Psychologiczny, **43**(1), 47–64 (2000)
23. Fisher, S.G., Hunter, T.A., Macrosson, W.D.K.: The structure of Belbin's team roles. J. Occup. Organ. Psychol. **71**(3), 283–288 (1998)
24. Belbin, M.: Management Teams: Why They Succeed or Fail, 2nd edn. Butterworth-Heinemann, Oxford (2004)
25. Goldin-Meadow, S., Mylander, C.: Gestural communication in deaf children: the effects and noneffects of parental input on early language development. Monogr. Soc. Res. Child Dev. **49**, 3–4 (1984)
26. Wolfe, J., Chacko, T.L.: Team-size effects on business game performance and decision making behaviours. Decis. Sci. **14**, 121–133 (1983)
27. Furnham, A., Steele, H., Pendleton, D.: A psychometric assessment of the Belbin team-role self-perception inventory. J. Occup. Organ. Psychol. **66**(3), 245–257 (1993)
28. Aritzeta, A., Swailes, S., Senior, B.: Belbin's team role model: development, validity and applications for team building. J. Manag. Stud. **44**(1), 96–118 (2007)
29. Senior, B.: Team roles and team performance: is there 'really' a link? J. Occup. Organ. Psychol. **70**(3), 241–258 (1997)
30. Chong, E.: Role balance and team development: a study of team role characteristics underlying high and low performing teams. J. Behav. Appl. Manag. **8**(3), 202 (2007)
31. Faria, A.J., Wellington, W.: The effect of time pressure, team formation and planning on simulation/game performance. In: Crookall, D., Arai, K. (eds.) Simulation and Gaming Across Disciplines and Cultures. Sage Publications (1994)
32. Wolfe, J., McCoy, R.: Should business game players choose their teammates: a study with pedagogical implications. Dev. Bus. Simul. Exp. Learn. **35**, 315–328 (2008). http://www.absel.org
33. Wolfe, J., McCoy, R.: Those who do and those that don't: a study of engaged and disengaged business game players. Dev. Bus. Simul. Exp. Learn. **38**, 383–389 (2011). http://www.absel.org
34. Thavikulwat, P., Chang, J.: Pick your group size: a better procedure to resolve the free-rider problem in a business simulation. Dev. Bus. Simul. Exp. Learn. **37**, 14–22 (2010). http://www.absel.org
35. Thavikulwat, P., Chang, J.: Two free-rider-accepting methods of organizing groups for a business game. Dev. Bus. Simul. Exp. Learn. **39**(2012), 26–34 (2012)
36. Thavikulwat, P., Chang, J.: Hybrid methods of organizing groups for a business game. Dev. Bus. Simul. Exp. Learn. **42**, 91–101 (2015)
37. Bales, R.: A set of categories for the analysis of small group interaction. Am. Sociol. Rev. **15**(2), 257–263 (1950)

Games and Simulations

Facilitating 21st Century Skills and Increasing Active Learning Environment of Students by Games and Simulations

Songsri Soranastaporn[1(✉)], Nophawan Yamchuti[2],
and Urairat Yamchuti[2]

[1] Mahidol University, Nakhon Pathom Province, Thailand
songsri.sor@mahidol.ac.th
[2] Thonburi University, Bangkok, Thailand
{Nophawan-y,urairat-y}@thonburi-u.ac.th

Abstract. This paper presents teachers training to design, develop, and apply educational games and simulations in their class. The development of training teachers to design, develop, and apply educational games and simulations in their class in the era of 21st century and educational reform during 2006–2016 are discussed. Pedagogical knowledge and application as well as techniques of design, development, and application of educational games are offered. Benefit of games and simulations from teachers' products is revealed. The development and application of educational games and simulations may be one of efficient tools in the 21st Century where teachers need to integrate language, culture, innovation and information technology for their teaching.

1 Introduction

In the era of 21st century, globally, many young learners have difficulties in using their high order thinking skills, collaborating with others, or creating new ideas or products. These learners need to be trained in such skills, so they can survive and live happily. This calls for educational reform, and learning and teaching methods and techniques need to be change in accordance with the complexity of society, economics, and technology. A new approach such as active learning is introduced by educators to increase quality of learners. In this approach, one technique to enhance active learning is to employ games and simulations.

21st Century Skills
Students need to be prepared very well for living in the era of 21st century. Students must be equipped with three core skills, including learning and innovation skills, information, media and technology skills, and life and career skills in order to succeed in their work, life, and citizenship [1]. See Fig. 1. These skills need to be integrated across a curriculum and instructions through standards such as ASEAN University Network-Quality Assurance (AUN-QA) and assessments such as the Common European Framework of Reference for Languages (CEF or CEFR).

© Springer International Publishing AG, part of Springer Nature 2018
H. K. Lukosch et al. (Eds.): ISAGA 2017, LNCS 10825, pp. 93–102, 2018.
https://doi.org/10.1007/978-3-319-91902-7_9

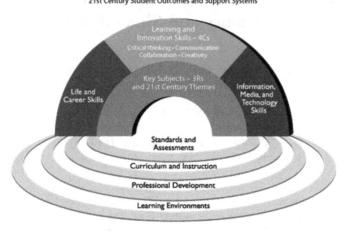

© 2007 Partnership for 21st Century Learning (P21)
www.P21.org/Framework

However, mostly, the current curriculums are not designed to produce students for embedding such 21st century skills in tomorrow's world [2]. This is because Internet and computer technology are under constant development. Charles Fadel, from Global Lead, Education Cisco Systems, Inc [3] stated that "The Internet is changing the way we work, live, play, and learn" (p. 21). All students must be trained to use high order thinking skills such as critical thinking and problem solving skills as well as life and career skills. At the same time, students must be equipped with innovation and creativity skills, information, media and technology skills [3]. See Table 1.

Table 1. What's new about 21st century skills?

New understanding of coverage	New areas of emphasis
Critical thinking and problem solving skills for EVERYONE	Innovation and creativity skills
Life and career skills for EVERYONE	Information, media and technology skills

Presently, learning and innovation skills include 7C and 3R. See Table 2.

What approach and teaching techniques should we use to build up those various skills for our students? How will we train them? We chose active learning and games and simulations.

Active Learning

Whenever experiences stimulate *mental activities that lead to meaningful learning,* this is *active learning* [5]."Active learning involves providing opportunities for students to

Table 2. 7C and 3R in learning and innovation skills

7C	3 R
• Critical Thinking & Problem Solving	• Reflectiveness
• Communication	• Resilience
• Collaboration	• Risk Taking
• Creativity & Innovation	
• Curiosity & Inquiry	
• Cultural Understanding	
• Care for our self, others, and the planet	

Source: [4] http://www.banb7.sa.edu.au/docs/capabilities_
dispositions.pdf

meaningfully talk and listen, write, read, and reflect on the content, ideas, issues, and concerns of an academic subject" [6] (p. 6). Active learning characterizes as follows: Students are involved in more than listening. Less emphasis is placed on transmitting information and more on extending students' skills and ideas. Students are involved in higher-order thinking (analysis, synthesis, and evaluation). Students are engaged in activities (e.g., reading, discussion, and writing). Greater emphasis is placed on students' exploration of their own attitudes, values, and prior experiences [7].

Techniques of applying active learning to class included active listening, active writing, visual-based active learning, brainstorming, collaborative learning, peer teaching, problem-based learning, case studies, class discussions, questioning sessions, role playing, drama, and simulations [8].

Games and Simulations

Kapp and O'Driscoll [9] *state that games and simulations are very useful for learning.* Students collaborate, share their vision, work together to achieve a common goal, have fun and excitement, and put high levels of energy when they play games *and simulations* with their friends. Computer games especially online games enhance the cognitive advantages of learning because of repetition. Students as players play games again and again when games are over and over for getting a higher score, to beat a colleague, or to reach the next higher level. This motivates players to play more and more. Games also provide a goal and an immediate feedback for players, so they have direction and learn while they play games. In *simulations, students have chances to act as in a real situation, so their* cognitive elements are transferable.

Classically, simulation games include 6 elements [10]. *Roles*: What roles are involved in situations? What is the status? How are persons in each role affected by the problem situation? *Goals*: What are the goals of individuals and groups in the situation? Goals in simulation games which involve conflict or problem solving should not be the same for every group. *Alternatives*: What alternatives do individuals or groups have in trying to achieve their goals? Do they make decisions and use high order thinking skills? *"Chance" element:* Do students as players can anticipate in some situations and cannot in others? *Focus on interaction*: Do students have interaction within or between their groups while they are playing games in order to achieve the goals? There is no need to have "winner" or "loser" in simulation games when games are ended. Finally, *debriefing*: Do students talk about and examine what happen during the games including feeling, actions, and reactions? Do students demonstrate creativity and innovation of products or learning after playing games?

To conclude, educational games and simulations or simulation games need to be designed and developed based on both global and local environment. Students actively learn through games and simulations, and teachers should design their simulation games which include roles, goals, alternatives, "chance" element, focus on interaction, and debriefing elements.

2 How We Train Our Students

In this section, we shared our experiences of training our student teachers to design and develop their games and simulations.

2.1 Course and Purposes

The 93001: Language, Culture, Innovation and Information Technology in Education course is offered for student teachers. The main purposes of the course are to train students: (1) to use both native and target languages academically and efficiently, (2) to apply teaching theories, technology, culture to create new tools and new teaching materials. We, then, discussed what strategies we should use. We decided to use games and simulations as a tool and product for this course. The reasons are the following. Kids like to play games, pupils have chances to simulate what they will do in their real life, culture can be integrated while playing games and simulations, teacher-students can design and create their games suit to their pupils and contexts in a limited of time. Moreover, teacher-students use 4 language skills because they are trained and assigned to design, develop and implement their games and simulations systematically and scientifically by using research methodology, explain and demonstrate their games and simulations in teacher-students' class before implementing in their own class. Write up their games and simulations as a paper and present in a conference.

2.2 Target Group

The target group is teacher-students who study a teacher certificate program during 2006–2015 at *Thonburi University*, Thailand. There are about 110–120 teacher-students in each year and 30 are put into classes based on their level of teaching, viz., kindergarten, primary, secondary, and vocational. Most of them are young teachers, but a few are old. All have graduate bachelor degrees, and most are subject matter experts in their fields. However, none have a professional teacher license. In this paper, this group is called students; whereas, pupils is used for a group of students who are taught by these teacher-students. I refer to the first author, and we refer to all three authors.

2.3   Training

We use active learning approach to train our students to design, develop, and apply educational games and simulations in their class. This is because our students have chances to use their high order thinking skills, involve in creating and using their products, and get their feedback from us and their peers after they finish playing their games and simulations.

2.3.1 Pre-training

We plan to integrate games and simulations (G & S) development into the course: *Language, Culture, Innovation, and Information Technology in Education* (2-2-5), so one hour is allocated for this activity in each week. Then in the next semester, students bring their games and simulations to experiment in their class, write their paper, and present their experiments in the ThaiSim national conference. We plan to introduce examples, the concept, process of game and simulation development, and debriefing little by little. Students have chances to think, create, design, develop, use, and evaluate their games and simulations. We play as a helper and supporter.

2.3.2 Training

The process of this training activity is shown in Fig. 1.

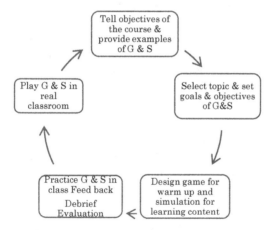

Fig. 1. A process of training game and simulation development for teachers

Introduction of objectives of the course and provide examples of G & S

I describe the objectives of the course and the major activity which students will have to do. Students need to learn language, culture, innovation, and information technology in education. These four elements must be integrated into their own games and simulations. They will design and develop their own games and simulations. By doing these, they use information technology (IT) techniques and skills to search, read, and evaluate what information they find from the Internet. They have to summarize information and have conversation within their group. Then they write information in their own words and present to class. While searching and reading information, students learn culture of Thai or other countries. Microsoft Word, PowerPoint, Google drive and form, Facebook, LINE, Skype, and SPSS are introduced via learning by doing, so students embed necessary IT skills. By the end of the course, I hope students will produce their own games and simulations which are considered as innovation for their teaching.

I divide students into 4 groups according to the level of teaching: kindergarten, primary, secondary, and vocational and ask two students to work together to create their game and simulation as a core activity of this course. One example of games and simulations of each level is introduced for students, and they play for the purpose of learning and experience, before they develop their own games and simulations.

Selection of Topic and Contents

Students know well their learning and teaching situation, so I ask them to discuss with their partners to choose the topic from their courses and prepare their contents according to the topic they choose to develop their games and simulations. The criteria are set for choosing their topic: the topic is difficult to understand or complicated, it acts as a background for the next one, and students will use it in their real life. Students search for and study theories of learning, games, and simulations. Then they select one or two theories which are relevant to the topic they choose and suitable for teaching technique they will use.

Setting up Goals and Objectives of Learning

A direction is very crucial; as a result, I ask students to set up goals and objectives of learning for this topic. Goals of games are broader; while, objectives for the contents are more specific. My students and I discuss goals and objectives of learning in order to make clear and have mutual understanding. Then they note down these goals and objectives of learning. I remind them that when they design their games and simulations, they have to look at their goals and objectives of learning so they will not get lost.

Design Educational Games and Simulations

Six elements of designing educational games and simulations [10] are explicitly explained, and students need to apply these elements in their games and simulations.

Roles: Each pair of students identifies a learning situation: level, age, numbers, and characteristics of students, subject taught, times and duration of teaching, and equipment. Games and simulations must be designed appropriate to their students' group. Games are encouraged to use as an input of a lesson; while, simulations are employed for students to act, react, and interact as in a real situation. For example, in a class of graphic design, students do matching tools of Adobe Photoshop before doing simulations with their graphic team to design name cards and sale in Facebook. Each group has to try hard to attract their customers. Members of each group function differently such as a manger, 3 graphic designers, a marketing and sale person, and a secretary.

Goals: Students set up the goals and objectives of their games and simulations. Goals are broader; while, objectives are narrower. Goals are focus on learning from playing games, and objectives are emphasized on content knowledge. For examples, goals of this game are: (1) to enhance team work and co-operation and (2) to encourage students to use high order thinking skills. Objectives of this game: After students finish playing this game, they will be able to: (1) indicate the names of functions of the industry tools correctly and (2) select appropriate tools for using in each situation.

Alternatives: Students have to create their own games, so they have chances to make decisions and use high order thinking skills. At the same time, they have to design their games which encourage their pupils to think and make decisions while playing the games too.

"Chance" Element: Students design games and simulations and apply them in class within 6 months and all are manual games, so as players, they can anticipate what will happen in some situations and what will not happen in other situations.

Focus on Interaction: Small games which serve as input of the lesson have less interaction than simulations. After students' attention is attracted to focus on their lesson, they do the simulation. Students should design this simulation to provide for students to have interaction within and between groups. Though no need to have "winner" or "loser" in simulation games when games are ended, most students design their game for competition.

Debriefing: All groups need to *debrief* after they finish their games and simulations. Students prepare four to five open-ended questions to ask their pupils. The examples of questions are:-

(a) How do you feel after playing games and simulations?
(b) What did you learn from playing games and simulations?
(c) What should be done to improve playing games and simulations?
(d) Can you use what you learnt from playing games and simulations to your real life or daily life and study? How? Please explain.

At this point, all students compile their devices for using in as well as write their manual of their games and simulations.

Trial out
Students have to trial out 2 times at least. I ask my students to test their games and simulations in my class. Their friends pretend to be pupils. Two students check devices as stated on the manual and examine the objectives, a process of running simulations in their own classes, and debriefing of games and simulations. Two students act as observers and one serves to a time keeper. After each group finished its games and simulations, both my students and I provide comments and suggestions. Students take comments and suggestions to improve their games and simulations. They play their games and simulations one more time before applying games and simulations in their own class rooms.

Apply
Students run their games and simulations in their own classes. Pictures and video are taken during the games with two purposes: to review and improve and to be evidences.

Evaluation

Students report their results of running games and simulations in their real classrooms. How is the climate of their class? Do their pupils like and willing to learn more? What did their pupils say about playing games and simulations? To increase reliability of games and simulations, two students of each pair run their games and simulations in their respective schools to see that (1) pupils like games and simulations and (2) the mean scores before and after playing games and simulations of each group increase or not.

2.3.3 Post-training

Students improve their games and simulations, and they prepare to present and run their games and simulations in conferences. The purposes of this activity are to have experts evaluate these games and encourage students to share and experience an activity at the national level.

3   Reflection of Actual Practice

Training games and simulations for teacher-students enhance their 21st Century Skills and active learning as follows.

21st Century Skills

Designing and developing games and simulations provide opportunities for students to use high order of thinking which are *critical thinking and problem solving*. Students have to analyze their pupils and learning environment before setting the goals and objectives of games, simulations, and learning. Then they have to select the most suitable topic, design, develop, test, and apply in their classroom which students must complete this process in limited time. Students need to study existing games and simulations before starting to think of developing their own games and simulations, so they have to search, read, compare, and make their games and simulations different from the previous ones so they *inquire* new information and knowledge. Thus, students are asked to create new games and simulations which are considered as their *creativity and innovation*. Students work in pairs, in a small group, and in the whole class while they design and develop their games and simulations. They have to *communicate and collaborate* with their partners and friends.

All students and pupils are Thai, so *cultural understanding* is not a problem or concern. About 2–3 pairs teach Thai dance or Thai language, so they integrate Thai culture into their games. Those students who teach kindergarten have to carefully design their games and simulations to avoid any accidents from running or competing.

Students practice their games and simulations in class and do debrief at the end of games and simulations, and have chances to *reflect* their feeling, knowledge, and experiences. Two students brought one game and simulation which created by two of them to experiment in each of their class. Each pairs of students mostly teach in different schools. Thus, students have to be flexible and adjust more or less, so their games and simulations are suitable for running in the two real classes. Students are required to present their games and simulations in a conference which there are 4–5 senior teachers act as evaluators to evaluate their games and simulations. Most students are young and have never had experience to make any presentation. They have to *take risk*, but they did, courageously, by practicing before presenting their games and simulations in the conference.

Active Learning

Training students to design, develop, and employ games and simulations in classrooms can be considerate as embedded *active learning* to this group. The process of training game and simulation development for teachers (Fig. 1) facilitates active learning. Students have to talk and discuss the learning situation of their class, and then analyze the situation before synthesis their situation and knowledge of their subject contents with games and simulations. The ultimate goal of this activity is to produce games and simulations which are new and suitable for their pupils. This idea and process is congruent with Rusbult [5] which students create games and simulations leading to meaningful learning. The process also co-responds to Meyers and Jones [6] because it provides students to have meaningfully conversation and communications of four skills. Students reflect their learning and experience with their peer while they practice and with their pupils while they run their games and simulations in the debrief session. To conclude, games and simulations create active learning as Bonnell and Eison [7] stated because students use their high order thinking skills, they engage in games and simulations, and they explore their attitudes and experiences after playing games.

Consequence

After integration games and simulations into one course: *Language, Culture, Innovation, and Information Technology in Education* 3 credits (2-2-5) for 6 years, the program developed a new course *Simulations and Games for Learning* 2 credits (2-0-4) for the teacher certificate program.

4 Limitation

Time is limited, so only one topic or lesson is used for developing a game and a simulation to experiment in only 1–3 hours according to the level of pupils. This contrasts with the learning idea which is an accumulating process little by little. We as teachers encourage them to continue design and develop their games and simulations for their class because the results from their experiments reveal that pupils are alert and active. They have fun and learn while playing games and simulations.

Levels of students: There were 4 levels of students in this program: kindergarten, primary, secondary, and vocational level. Moreover, there is one more group which works under informal education section in this program. They were mixed with different levels for the first six years because students were put into class according to 'first come, first serve' basis. Then students were put into each level of their teaching in the last two years. The reasons are that the purpose, design, process, motivation, and care and management of each level are quite different. When they work in groups, either pairs, small groups, or the whole class, they feel they have more mutual understanding because they have the same background.

Games and Simulations Design: In the early period of training, all students designed only manual games and worked in groups of 4–5 members. From our observation, only 2 students worked; while, the other two sat and watched. Thus, we decided to make the group smaller by pairing them. We encouraged students who taught or had knowledge and skills in computer or information technology to apply their knowledge and skills to develop their computer games. This is still embryo because limited of time, knowledge, and experience, so mostly, students used PowerPoint to present or run their games and simulations.

5   Conclusion

In the 21st Century where teachers need to integrate language, culture, innovation and information technology for their teaching, one of efficient tools may be development and application of educational games and simulations. The learning situation should be analyzed first, and the element of games and simulations need to be considered and included in the process of games and simulations design and development.

References

1. Partnership for 21st Century Learning: P21, Framework for 21st Century Learning. Framework for 21st Century Learning 2-page PDF (2007)
2. The North Central Regional Educational Laboratory and the Metiri Group (NCREL): enGauge 21st Century Skills: Literacy in the Digital Age (2003). http://pict.sdsu.edu/engauge21st.pdf
3. Fadel, C.: 21st Century Skills: How can you prepare students for the new Global Economy. CISCO (2008). http://www.oecd.org/site/educeri21st/40756908.pdf
4. Capability & Disposition (2017). http://www.banb7.sa.edu.au/docs/capabilities_dispositions.pdf
5. Rusbult, C.: 1. Active-Learning Theories (constructivism,…) 2. Teaching Strategies for Effective Instruction (2007). http://www.asa3.org/ASA/education/teach/active.htm
6. Meyers, C., Jones, T.B.: Promoting active learning: strategies for the college classroom. Jossey-Bass, San Francisco (1993)
7. Bonnell, C.C., Eison, J.A.: Active learning: creating excellent in the classroom. ASHE-ERIC Higher Education Report No. 1. School of Education and Human Development, The George Washington University, Washington, D.C. (1991)
8. Florida State University, Instruction at FSU: A Guide to Teaching & Learning Practices, Chapter 8: Using Active Learning in Classroom (2012). https://distance.fsu.edu/instructors/instruction-fsu-guide-teaching-learning-practices
9. Kapp, M.K., O'Driscoll, T.: Learning in 3D: Adding a New Dimension to Enterprise Learning and Collaboration. Wiley, San Francisco (2010)
10. Roger, M.V., Goodloe, H.A.: Simulation games as method. Educ. Leadersh. **30**, 729–732. (1973). http://www.ascd.org/ASCD/pdf/journals/ed_lead/el_197305_rogers.pdf

User Satisfaction with Organizational Learning Time-Efficiency in *Topaasia Cards*

Otso Hannula[1] and J. Tuomas Harviainen[2(✉)]

[1] Aalto University, Espoo, Finland
[2] Hanken School of Economics, Helsinki, Finland
jiituomas@gmail.com

Abstract. This paper discusses the ways in which design games are used as scaffolds for knowledge creation. Using players' reports on time-efficiency in deployments of Topaasia Cards, it demonstrates that play appears to foster creative dialogue and meaningful interaction that lead to user experiences of positive organizational knowledge creation.

Keywords: Design games · Knowledge creation · Organizational learning
User experience research

1 Introduction

This paper discusses design games as a method for knowledge creation necessary for developing practices and organizational processes by providing a space for playful creativity. Although playfulness and creativity have been linked in organizational life [13] and many solutions to foster playful activities in organizational contexts have been created (e.g. [8, 15]), the use of service design games for organizational learning remains an understudied area.

In this paper we begin this inquiry by discussing design games, an existing tradition of applying games in organizations, and describe how they foster playfulness and creativity for organizational learning. We propose that design games increase creative thinking in discussions about current working practices and thereby contribute to knowledge creation.

To achieve this end, we use a case example to examine two research questions:

RQ1: How do design games foster creative discussion for organizational learning?
RQ2: How are such tools perceived by their players?

To answer these questions, we first introduce service design games as organizational learning tools.

© Springer International Publishing AG, part of Springer Nature 2018
H. K. Lukosch et al. (Eds.): ISAGA 2017, LNCS 10825, pp. 103–109, 2018.
https://doi.org/10.1007/978-3-319-91902-7_10

2 Design Games as Creative Interventions

Design games are a method of participatory design which uses game rules and material to serve different interests in the design process. They are a loose group of structured, often somewhat shallow forms of play, conducted for service innovation, improvement, or knowledge creation [9]. No exact definition of design games exists, and as a phenomenon they tend to be defined more by their context than with any specific game properties [5]. Yet they have been documented as being highly efficient for the purposes of facilitating collaboration, because they enable the sharing of experiences [2, 16]. A design game may just as well be a card game, a role play, a physical exercise, or something digital. This flexibility, together with their shallow structures, together enables designers to easily tailor the games for various organizations' and stakeholders' needs [9].

According to the seminal Play framework of Vaajakallio [15], the use of design games can best be understood through three perspectives. For the designer, the game is a tool for gathering input from a number of participants in an organized manner. For the player, it is a mind-set that allows associative and representational thinking across space and time. Finally, for the designer of a particular design game, the game forms a structure for creating materials and roles for the participants [15, 16].

The Play framework implies that for the designer the playfulness and creativity in design games exist in service to the design process. Design games organize dialogue and collect contributions from multiple participants, and promote exploration at the expense of negotiation or compromise [2]. This means that as a whole, design games' potential as an organizational learning intervention has been left underexplored. Especially design games applied in service design have been used to interrupt routines and focus on building new understanding [10].

Design games work on principles of expansive learning (as per [3]) and the development of practices through shared discourses [6]. According to expansive learning, the development of practices takes place when the members of a community identify contradictions in their collective activity and respond to the contradictions by reorganizing their activity [4]. Mainemelis and Ronson [13] have studied the role of playfulness in fostering creativity in organizations, and identified five creativity-relevant cognitive processes supported by play: *problem framing, divergent thinking, mental transformations, practice with alternative solutions,* and *evaluative ability.* Design games aim to support all of these, by fostering discourses and thinking patterns that enable creativity, exploration, problem-forming, while giving each player a level field to propose ideas and evaluate those proposed by others [15]. Our case example *Topaasia Cards* focuses on precisely this kind of discussion support.

3 Case Topaasia Card

Our case example, *Topaasia Cards*, is designed and sold by Finnish company Gälli-washere. *Topaasia* is a family of organizational learning games which combine a dialogue for developing practices (as per [7]) and simple game rules which structure the discussion on shared topics and provide some competitiveness to the interaction.

Topaasia Cards can be played without a facilitator and the game is intended to be played multiple times over a period of time for continuous reflection. Different decks, such as "Sales" or "Projects", are available.

In *Topaasia Cards* (Fig. 1), players choose a topic of discussion for each round, and play a card from their hands. Each card has a suit which corresponds to a theme of development within the game, as well as a keyword which refers to a specific item of development. The selected cards are shuffled to hide which player chose which card, and the group decides which card is the most important one. That card is then moved aside together with the chosen topic marker. Out of those, at the end, the most pressing issue is selected for further development. One game usually takes from 30 to 45 min of play, and is able to optimally accommodate four to eight players.

Fig. 1. A *Topaasia Cards* deck, rulebook, package and hourglass timer. (Gälliwashere)

In order to facilitate a dialogue on developing practices, the game uses cards act as shared points of reference. The text on the card acts as a trigger for the player to consider each card's potential significance, and each player's best cards are further discussed once the cards have been played. The downside of this is that some key topics may not come up for discussion because that particular card was not played during the game. To manage this risk, best results are acquired from multiple rounds played either simultaneous or by the same group over time.

A key feature of *Topaasia Cards* at the time of this research the goal of getting the most points by playing cards that will be picked the best by the group. Because of this competition, the game might be perceived as more engaging than design games without competitive elements or clear winners (e.g., [8]).

4 Data

Our data set comes directly from the producing company, Gälliwashere. After each session, the players could choose to use the feedback system, *Kiteyttäjä*, to provide a summary of their play and provide data for the game designers. Different versions of the feedback system have included questions related to development suggestions, usefulness, etc., but we have focused our analysis to the five questions present in all submitted feedback, presented in Table 2.

At the time of writing this paper, *Topaasia Cards* been played over 300 times in over 100 companies. Exact numbers are not available because of the voluntary nature of the feedback system. A total of 53 answers were received from play sessions with an older version of *Kiteyttäjä* (January 1, 2015 to May 12, 2016) and 54 with a newer one (May 13, 2016 to August 19, 2016) (Table 1).

Table 1. Feedback questions of *Topaasia Cards* (translated by Harviainen)

How useful was the session, compared to the time you used (1 = No benefit compared to time; 3 = Equally useful compared to time [as other methods]; 5 = Produced significantly more value compared to time.)
How well was the play session organized on a scale of 1–5, with 5 being the best?
Do you have suggestions on how the session could have been improved?
What functioned well in the session?
Other feedback?

5 Results

Gälliwashere gathered evaluations for each game session with the instructions that the answers should be determined by group consensus after the play session. The average time-effectiveness evaluation was 3.74 (n = 53) for the older version and 3.78 (n = 54) for the new version. Neither data set contained any ratings of 1 (the lowest), and only one rating of 2 each. A total of 28 answers rated the sessions with an evaluation of 3, denoting that the session in question was perceived to be as time-effective for organizational learning as other methods. 66 gave a rating of 4, for somewhat more time-effective, and 10 gave a rating of 5, meaning extremely useful. The last 25 ratings were all 4 or above, which suggests that the iterative design may be improving its performance rate (see Table 2).

Table 2. Summaries of user group feedback on time-efficiency

	Useless 1	2	As useful 3	4	More useful 5
Old *Kiteyttäjä*	0	1	17	30	5
New *Kiteyttäjä*	0	1	11	36	5
TOTAL	0	2	28	66	10

Although the available data does not allow for deep analysis, we can see that the consistent majority (71%) of Gälliwashere clients perceived that the play was more useful for organizational learning than other methods they had tried. Given how difficult it is to convince corporate clients to see cost-effective benefits in play, we find this significant, especially since many clients have continued using the game after the initial workshops in which it was introduced. So while part of "work", the play still also seems to preserve a voluntary aspect to it as well (see e.g., [11]), especially given the high approval ratings. It appears that a combination of playful engagement, competition, and constant reflection is able to lead to organizational learning – or at least the experience that organizational learning is taking place.

It must be noted, however, that *Topaasia* play seems to be quite backcasting-oriented. This is not necessarily a bad thing: the identification of existing challenges, risks and potentials through the examination of present data is a key advantage of organizational gaming. *Topaasia Cards* thus provides important insight on the current state of the organizations within which it is played.

While user satisfaction is no gauge for organizational learning, we believe that its correlations with existing findings on knowledge creation point to there being actual benefits in this sort of play. We next turn to those correlations.

6 Discussion and Conclusions

According to Tsoukas [14], organizational knowledge creation takes place in dialogues, but all dialogues are not equally useful for that purpose. Dialogue has to be productive and therefore requires a type of commitment and engagement in which participants relate to each other and make it obvious that they want to work together. The participants have to separate themselves from the organization's existing practices in order to reflect on them, while still remaining aware of existing practices to create relevant knowledge. However, should participants try and protect their own interests by engaging in calculated participation at the expense of productive dialogue, knowledge creation and transfer fail.

We believe that *Topaasia Cards* excels at fostering productive dialogue. As each proposition in the card games is group arbitrated, the desire to win is re-appropriated for the purpose of knowledge creation. The reflective work required for both learning and assessment of competitive learning games is thus embedded in their play. Thereby, the game scaffolds the creation of new organizational knowledge, and also enables its players to pinpoint information needs of which they, or even the organization as a whole, may not have been aware before.

Service design games tend to be very efficient in facilitating knowledge creation, as they encourage creative discussions, shared reflection and task-completion oriented thinking in a playful mode [7]. The *Topaasia* games take this further. Through their competitive-reflective mode, they on the one hand enable participants to fuse those three information needs into a single whole, making task completion, context, and information creation one integrated process. They also increase time-on-task, a factor noted as a key facet of game-based learning (e.g., [12]). At the same time, they enable fluent switching between a goal-oriented and a reflective mind-state and a playful-speculative-competitive mind state (as per [1]) when players navigate optimal play choices based on their existing organizational knowledge. *Topaasia Cards* exemplifies the way in which those co-exist in a learning game. Whereas organizational play tends to be focused on just efficiency, and is thus often constrained [17], design games can create a safe space for innovative exploration - and make that exploration highly enjoyable.

The expansive learning potential of these kinds of games is in providing methods for interrupting the routines of organizations by allowing players to "bring in" their existing practices and contradictions and setting up a space in which the players feel at liberty to engage in playful examination of the existing practices and modelling new solutions.

Ethical Statement and Funding. The authors have no connection to Gälliwashere excluding this particular research project.

Parts of this research were supported by grant 10-5514 from Liikesivistysrahasto.

References

1. Apter, M.J.: A structural phenomenology of play. In: Kerr, J.H., Apter, M.J. (eds.) Adult Play: A Reversal Theory Approach, pp. 13–29. Swets & Zeitlinger, Amsterdam (1991)
2. Brandt, E., Messeter, J., Binder, T.: Formatting design dialogues – games and participation. CoDesign **4**, 51–64 (2008)
3. Engeström, Y.: Learning by Expanding: An Activity-theoretical Approach to Developmental Research. Orienta-Konsultit, Helsinki (1987)
4. Engestrom, Y.: Innovative learning in work teams: analyzing cycles of knowledge creation in practice. In: Engeström, Y., Miettinen, R., Punamäki, R.-L. (eds.) Perspectives on Activity Theory, pp. 377–404. Cambridge University Press, Cambridge (1999)
5. Eriksen, M.A., Brandt, E., Mattelmäki, T., Vaajakallio, K.: Taking design games seriously: re-connecting situated power relations of people and materials. In: Proceedings of the 13th Participatory Design Conference, pp. 101–110. ACM, Windhoek (2014)
6. Gherardi, S.: Organizational learning: the sociology of practice. In: Easterby-Smith, M., Lyles, M.A. (eds.) The Blackwell Handbook of Organizational Learning and Knowledge Management, pp. 43–65. Wiley, Hoboken (2011)
7. Hannula, O., Harviainen, J.T.: Efficiently inefficient: service design games as innovation tools. In: Morelli, N., de Götzen, A., Grani, F. (eds.) Service Design Geographies, pp. 241–252. Linköping University Electronic Press, Linköping (2016)
8. Hannula, O., Irrmann, O.: Played into collaborating: design games as scaffolding for service co-design project planning. Simul. Gaming **47**, 599–627 (2016)
9. Harviainen, J.T., Vaajakallio, K., Sproedt, H.: Service design games as innovation tools, knowledge creators, and simulation/games. Simul. Gaming **47**, 559–565 (2016)
10. Kaario, P., Vaajakallio, K., Lehtinen, V., Kantola, V., Kuikkaniemi, K.: Someone else's shoes-using role-playing games in user-centered service design. In: ServDes 2009 (2009)
11. Klapztein, S., Cipolla, C.: From game design to service design: a framework to gamify services. Simul. Gaming **47**, 566–598 (2016)
12. Landers, R.N., Landers, A.K.: An empirical test of the theory of gamified learning: the effect of leaderboards on time-on-task and academic performance. Simul. Gaming **45**, 769–785 (2014)

13. Mainemelis, C., Ronson, S.: Ideas are born in fields of play: towards a theory of play and creativity in organizational settings. Res. Organ. Behav. **27**, 81–131 (2006)
14. Tsoukas, H.: A dialogical approach to the creation of new knowledge in organizations. Organ. Sci. **20**, 941–957 (2009)
15. Vaajakallio, K.: Design Games as a Tool, a Mindset and a Structure. Aalto University, Helsinki (2012)
16. Vaajakallio, K., Mattelmäki, T.: Design games in codesign: as a tool, a mindset and a structure. CoDesign **10**, 63–77 (2014)
17. Vesa, M., Hamari, J., Harviainen, J.T., Warmelink, H.: Computer games and organization studies. Organ. Stud. **38**, 273–284 (2017)

The Design and Evaluation of a Multi-player Milk Supply Chain Management Game

Mizuho Sato[1]($\boxtimes$), Manami Tsunoda[2], Hitomi Imamura[2],
Hajime Mizuyama[2], and Masaru Nakano[1]

[1] Graduate School of System Design and Management, Keio University,
4-1-1 Hiyoshi, Kohoku-ku, Yokohama, Kanagawa 223-8526, Japan
mizuho.sato@sdm.keio.ac.jp
[2] Department of Industrial and Systems Engineering,
Aoyama Gakuin University, 5-10-1 Fuchinobe, Chuo-ku, Sagamihara-shi,
Kanagawa 252-5258, Japan

Abstract. There are various brands of milk with different "best use before" dates in supermarkets. Each milk package must be sold by this corresponding selling time limit, which is set as two-thirds of the time of its best used before date from production under the so-called one-third rule. If the milk remains unsold when the selling time expires, milk waste occurs. This paper gives a detailed design of a milk supply chain game that simulates the situation and carries out the game experiments. In addition, a questionnaire is completed before and after the experiments to help evaluate the educational effect of the game in increasing awareness of food waste.

Keywords: Milk industry · Dairy farm · Supermarket · Supply chain
Waste

1 Introduction

Many milk-based drinks are currently available in the marketplace and the nutritional benefit that milk provides, such as calcium, is well known. As most Japanese people are said to be deficient in this [1], the recommendation is that they drink milk regularly. However, there is a decreasing trend in its consumption and a large amount of raw milk is reportedly wasted every year. For example, in 2006, as much as 1,000 tons of raw milk was wasted, with an economic value of approximately 76 million yen [2]. The production volume of raw milk decreases in summer and increases in winter because the body condition of a cow is weakened by the summer heat and recovers in winter [3]. In contrast, the demand for milk from consumers increases in summer and decreases in winter.

For milk with a certain "best used by" date, the period corresponding to two-thirds of the best used by date from production is set as the selling duration and a supermarket has to sell the milk within this period under the so-called one-third rule. There are various brands of milk packages with different best used by dates being sold in supermarkets. If some remain unsold when the selling duration is over, the milk is wasted. Thus, at the International Simulation and Gaming Association (ISAGA)

© Springer International Publishing AG, part of Springer Nature 2018
H. K. Lukosch et al. (Eds.): ISAGA 2017, LNCS 10825, pp. 110–118, 2018.
https://doi.org/10.1007/978-3-319-91902-7_11

conference in 2016, we proposed a milk supply chain game that simulates this situation [4]; in this paper, we elaborate on the design of the milk supply chain game including an auction model and consumer agents. Several other papers are available as references for our study, which designs and evaluates a milk supply chain management game. For example, in one study, a pedagogical game mimicking negotiations in a supply chain was proposed [5]; and in another, the role of gaming simulation in policy research was discussed [6]. Our study was conducted based on this literature, namely, our game experiments were conducted with university students focusing on milk waste under two cases: with and without the one-third rule. In addition, a questionnaire survey was conducted both before and after the game experiments to evaluate the educational effects of the game in increasing food waste awareness and, thereby, ultimately decreasing waste.

2 Methodology

2.1 Game Scenario

The game scenario is shown in Fig. 1. The major stakeholders in a milk supply chain include dairy farmers, milk manufacturers, supermarkets, and consumers. Players are assigned to the roles of three milk manufacturers and three supermarkets, and the transactions between the two roles are modeled as an auction. Dairy farmer roles are modeled by a computer agent, which automatically receives orders for purchasing raw milk from manufacturers. Customer behavior is modeled by a logit model. Therefore, the total number of human players is six.

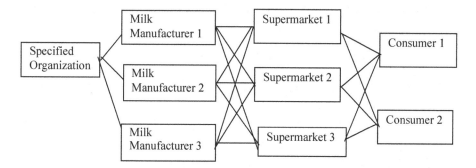

Fig. 1. Game scenario

Once every two days, an auction is conducted between milk manufacturers and supermarkets. The game was played for 13 days fictionally from October 1 to October 13 and the auction was done five times in this game. Each milk manufacturer tries to sell as much milk as possible to as many supermarkets as possible as at high a price as possible, and each supermarket tries to buy milk from as many milk manufacturers as possible as at low a price as possible. The milk manufacturer players make a production plan so that milk waste does not occur, and the supermarket players need to consider customer behavior. The milk size available is only 1L.

2.2 Player Actions

2.2.1 Milk Manufacturers

Each of the milk manufacturer players can check the total sales account, total waste of milk, amount of raw milk, production plan, total stock of milk, and the result of the last auction at any time.

9 am: Delivery plan

(1) The player creates a delivery plan for milk based on the previous day's auction result.
(2) If the volume of milk sold can be met by the total stock, there is no work for the player here.
(3) If the volume of milk sold exceeds the total stock, the player has to decide how much milk to move to each of the supermarkets 1 to 3.

1 pm: Production plan and the raw milk order (only Tuesday and Friday)

(1) On Tuesday: the amount of milk production will be decided for Friday, next Monday, and next Tuesday.
(2) On Friday: the amount of milk production will be decided for next Wednesday and Thursday.
(3) According to the production plan, raw milk is ordered.
    The raw milk ordered on Tuesday is delivered on Thursday, and this milk can be used as of Friday. The raw milk ordered on Friday is delivered on Tuesday, and this milk can be used as of Wednesday (Table 1).

3 pm: Auction time

(1) It is possible to bring to the auction the milk stocked in the warehouse and available by 5 pm of the auction day.
(2) The player offers the volume and selling price of the milk produced every day.

5 pm: Reconsideration of the production plan

The production plan drafted on Tuesday and Friday can be modified the day before (the last decision).

9 pm: Check the sales

Today's sales and the amounts unsold raw milk and milk waste are counted.

To achieve the most points, it is important that the manufacturer player makes good decisions. The points of this player are calculated as follows:

Table 1. Time schedule of the flow of raw milk

Order	Received	Day used
October 1 (Tues)	October 3 (Thu)	October 4 (Fri)
October 4 (Fri)	October 8 (Tue)	October 9 (Weds)

<Plus points>

- The volume of the sales * sale price

<Minus points>

- The purchased amount of raw milk * 10
- The amount of milk that could not be sold * 30% of the price decided by the auction.

2.2.2   Supermarkets

Each of the supermarket players can check the total sales account, total milk waste, stock of milk, and the result of the last auction any time.

9 am: Shelf stacking

The player decides how much milk of each brand with a best sell before date should be moved from the warehouse to the shelf as well as the selling price.

1 pm: Shelf stacking

The player confirms the sales of the milk that were moved to the shelf at 9 am and decides the further amount of the milk to be moved from the warehouse to the shelf and the selling price.

3 pm: Auction time

The player decides on and offers for a purchase amount and a price of the milk produced by the milk manufacturers 1 to 3 on each production date.

5 pm: Shelf stacking and discount

(1) The player moves some milk to the shelf as done at 9 am and 1 pm.
(2) The player may discount the price of milk that has been stacked on the shelf.

9 pm: Confirmation of sales

Today's sales and the amount of the milk wasted are counted.
To gain the most points, it is important for the supermarket player to make good decisions. The points of the supermarket player are calculated as follows:

<Plus points>

- The sales price * (1-discount rate) * the amount of milk sold

<Minus points>

- The amount of milk that cannot be sold * 10
- The purchased amount of milk * the purchase price from the manufacturer.

2.3   Auction Model

The transaction between the manufacturers and the supermarkets is modeled as a double-sided auction. The auction is conducted separately for the milk produced on each day by each milk manufacturer. The manufacturer bids the minimum price and the maximum amount and each supermarket bids the maximum price and the maximum amount for the milk. Then, the bids are aggregated into the supply and demand curves, and who buys how much of the milk at what price is determined by the intersection point between the curves.

2.4 Logit Model

A logit choice model represents the consumers' preference in which the total utility is determined by the sum of the partial utilities on the price, the discount rate, and the best use before date. The parameter values of the model are estimated through the choice based conjoint analysis. Eighteen university students answered a questionnaire with 20 choice questions created for the analysis and the parameter values were estimated for each respondent. The respondents can be clustered into three groups by applying cluster analysis to the data. Accordingly, three types of consumer agents were created.

In the game, a consumer agent appears following an exponential distribution, and she/he chooses which milk to buy from those on the shelf or decides not to buy any according to the logit choice model with the parameter values corresponding to her/his group. Further, the supermarket he/she goes to is determined by the probability proportional to the mean utility gained in each supermarket by a consumer of the group on the day before.

3 Results

3.1 Milk Manufacture

(1) The difference in milk waste between the cases with and without the one-third rule was analyzed. When the rule was used in the game, the packaged milk waste increased. This is because when the rule was not imposed, the milk manufacturers could sell the milk for 12 days, however, when the rule was imposed in the game, they could sell the milk only for four days. Of note, the number of selling days was significantly fewer.

(2) The data on milk waste on Wednesday, October 2 are shown in Figs. 2, 3, 4 and 5. If the one-third rule is used, the selling time limit of this milk is Sunday, October 6. Since the auction is conducted once every two days, it is only possible to sell this milk on Thursday, October 3. On the other hand, in the case without the rule, this milk can be sold four times during the game period. Thus, when the rule was used, in every round (from 1 to 4) more milk waste was caused for the milk manufacturer. When the one-third rule is used, therefore, a price decision can be made only once, and hence, it is critically important.

(3) However, the difference in the amount of raw milk waste between the cases with and without the one-third rule was not large. This is because the players can review the production plan every day.

3.2 Supermarket

Milk waste occurred between two and four times more when the one-third rule was used during this game. However, when the rule was not used, there was no milk waste

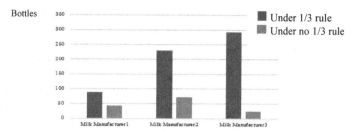

Fig. 2. The waste of milk at the first trial (October 2)

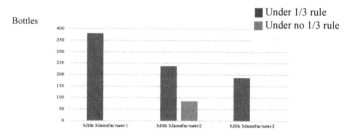

Fig. 3. The waste of milk at the second trial (October 2)

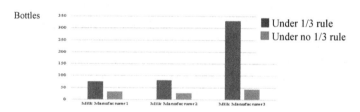

Fig. 4. The waste of milk at the third trial (October 2)

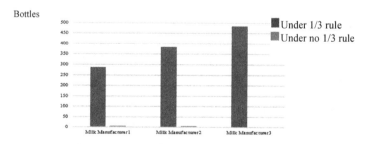

Fig. 5. The waste of milk at the fourth trial (October 2)

or very little. When the rule was imposed, it was clear that the quantity of wasted milk was large. When the rule was used, the sales period was four to seven days. However, when it was not used, the sales period was 11 days. Thus, the sales period without the rule was longer than with the rule. Therefore, when the one-third rule was imposed, the players could not sell a large amount of stock without wasting milk.

The volume of milk purchased, the volume of milk sold, unsold milk, and waste in the fourth trial is shown in Tables 2, 3 and 4. When the one-third rule is not used, the players can sell a large amount of milk and decrease the amount of wasted milk. Because of this situation, the supermarket players can choose milk with the best sell by date he/she wants to buy from the manufacturer. The supermarket can sell the milk for a longer time and the decision-making period is also longer. Thus, the players are able to consider the consumer's demand as well. When playing without the one-third rule, the supermarket players are able to sell more milk efficiently with less waste than in the alternative case.

Table 2. Milk manufacturer 1 (milk purchased, sales volume, unsold milk, and waste)

	With one-third rule	Without one-third rule
Volume of milk purchased	1986	1360
Sales volume	1046	1238
Unsold milk	863	122
Milk waste	77	0

Table 3. Milk manufacturer 2 (milk purchased, sales volume, unsold milk, and waste)

	With one-third rule	Without one-third rule
Volume of milk purchased	2280	1380
Sales volume	1292	1330
Unsold milk	400	50
Milk waste	588	0

Table 4. Milk manufacturer 3 (milk purchased, sales volume, unsold milk, and waste)

	With one-third rule	Without one-third rule
Volume of milk purchased	2279	1604
Sales volume	1149	1489
Unsold milk	538	115
Milk waste	592	0

3.3   Change in Customer Behavior

Before and after the game, we conducted a survey questionnaire on consciousness regarding food waste. Before the game, we asked the game players, for example, "Do you know the one-third rule?" Only 20% of the players knew the rule (this meant that the majority, 80% did not). Therefore, it was important for these players to learn about the rule. In the survey after the game, we asked, "Have you ever heard news about food waste in Japan?" Of the players, 70% had heard such news, however, only 25%

indicated a consciousness of food waste. In addition, we asked, if "the best use before date of the food has passed, do you still eat the food?" About 60% of the players indicated that they would not eat such food. Although there were many players who knew about the problem of food waste, they did not know the details around the problem.

After the game, we asked, "Do you think about the problem of food waste?" In this survey, 53% of the players who answered stated that we all should think about the problem. However, in the survey before the game, only 30% of the players answered this way. Thus, there was a 23% increase in consciousness regarding food waste after the game. Furthermore, before the game, the ratio of players who checked the refrigerator before going shopping was less than 50%; however, after the game, this increased to 87%. More than 90% of the players answered that they will pay more attention to food waste from now.

4   Study Limitations and Future Considerations

In terms of study limitations, research indicates that a student's ability to apply knowledge is important in solving an internal pricing problem in a supply chain and that such knowledge could affect the results. In addition, the findings should be reconfirmed by using new data to assess the reliability of the results [7]. Thus, it is also important for us to confirm the results with other data and carefully evaluate the effectiveness of the game for the reduction of food waste.

Future study considerations are as follows:

(1) This game tests only 13 days, so we need to lengthen the period and check for milk waste.
(2) Here, the difference in milk waste between the cases with and without the one-third rule was analyzed. Thus, we should try another system, for example, a half rule.
(3) As the players here were university students, we should try to use this game with milk manufacture workers, supermarket workers, and others.
(4) In a supermarket, there are many brands of milk with different sell before dates are being supplied. Therefore, we should incorporate more items into the game.
(5) It remains to be answered whether our game is effective as an educational tool that can actually decrease food waste.

5   Summary

We gathered the following insights from our study results:

(1) By analyzing the questionnaire before and after the experiments, the effectiveness of the game was clarified.
(2) We found that it was possible to subdivide consumers according to their buying behaviors regarding milk, as revealed in the consumer questionnaire.

(3) We were able to effectively compare milk waste between the cases with and without the one-third rule in this game. More waste was created when the players were under the rule. Thus, we saw the importance of reconsidering the impact of the one-third rule.

(4) We were able to develop a serious game that can be used effectively to enhance consumer consciousness around decreasing food waste.

References

1. Ministry of Health, Labour and Welfare: National Health and Nutrition Survey, Japan (2016)
2. Keizai, N.: Hokuren's first raw milk disposal, news (2006). Accessed 18 Mar 2006
3. Japan Dairy Industry Association Information. http://www.nyukyou.jp/detail/farming/farming01.html
4. Sato, M., Mizuyama, H., Nakano, M.: Milk supply chain management game for waste reduction. In: Naweed, A., Wardaszko, M., Leigh, E., Meijer, S. (eds.) ISAGA 2016, SimTecT 2016. LNCS, vol. 10711, pp. 302–314. Springer, Cham (2018). https://doi.org/10.1007/978-3-319-78795-4_21
5. Gumus, M., Love, C.E.: Supply chain sourcing game: a negotiation exercise. Decis. Sci. J. Innov. Educ. **11**, 3–12 (2013)
6. De Caluwé, L., Geurts, J., Kleinlugtenbelt, W.J.: Gaming research in policy and organization: an assessment from the netherlands. Simul. Gaming **43**(5), 600–628 (2012)
7. Fuglseth, M.A., Grønhaug, K., Jörnsten, K.: Students' ability to apply their knowledge in a gaming exercise: an exploratory study. Scand. J. Educ. Res. 1–21 (2016). https://doi.org/10.1080/00313831.2016.1212255

What is the Game? Study of Subjective Perceptions

Elena Likhacheva[✉]

Department of General Ecology, Faculty of Biology, M.V. Lomonosov Moscow
State University, Leninskie Gory, 1, Build. 12, 119234 Moscow, Russia
likhacheva@mail.bio.msu.ru

Abstract. The use of simulation games in education requires coherence in their understanding as methods of instruction. Variety of definitions of the game concept has been put forth; but is still difficult to give an unambiguous and universally accepted one. To identify how a simulation game is understood by its participants the study of subjective perceptions of game was undertaken. Results obtained showed that, primarily, the game is described by all participants as an active form of learning-by-doing (regardless of gaming experience). Participants' subjective perceptions of game reality are mostly influenced by experience of participation in simulation games. The perception of game also depends on the cultural context.

Keywords: Simulation games · Subjective perceptions · Learning-by-doing

1 Introduction

The use of simulation games in education requires coherence in their understanding as methods of instruction. For example, variety of definitions of the game concept has been put forth; but is still difficult to give an unambiguous and universally accepted one. It is natural that people with diverse backgrounds have different subjective opinions. To identify how a simulation game is understood by its participants the study of subjective perceptions of a game was undertaken. We wanted to detect similarities and substantial differences, depending on game experience, gender and cultural context (here as represented by language – English or Russian).

2 The Study

To conduct this investigation, we developed a questionnaire [1]. For the purpose of obtaining spontaneous answers of participants the questionnaire contained the open type questions as they provide an opportunity to give answers in free form and are not restricted by rigid statements. The survey involved 125 attendees of the several Russian and International conferences, seminars, schools on interactive methods (including participants of ISAGA Summer School-2005 and several ISAGA conferences). The participants differed in gaming experience, gender and cultural contexts (Table 1).

© Springer International Publishing AG, part of Springer Nature 2018
H. K. Lukosch et al. (Eds.): ISAGA 2017, LNCS 10825, pp. 119–125, 2018.
https://doi.org/10.1007/978-3-319-91902-7_12

Table 1. Distribution of participants by their game experience, gender and cultural context (N = 125)

Game experience		Gender			Cultural context (language)	
Absence	Presence	Men	Women	Did not specify	Russian speaking	English speaking
54	71	40	77	8	89	36

Game experience was determined by the participant's answer to the first question: "What is your experience of playing/facilitation games?" 54 persons out of 125 participants (43.2%) had no experience or had an insignificant one (participation in 1–2 games); 71 persons (56.8%) had an experience of participation in simulation games, facilitation and their designing.

89 persons (71.2%) were Russian-speaking people (including the CIS countries), out of them 54 persons had no or an insignificant experience, 35 persons had such experience (rarely in designing); 36 (28.8%) – English-speaking participants (all had a game experience).

117 participants specified their gender: 40 men, 77 women. Due to the small number of the participants who did not specify gender, the comparative analysis between this group and two other groups (men and women) was not carried out.

The age was specified by 52 participants (covers the range from 22 to 68 years). Due to the small amount of participants who indicated their age the comparative analysis of different age groups was not carried out.

As long as there were no English-speaking participants without game experience, to exclude an influence of game experience on final results the comparison only between the following groups was executed:

1. The Russian-speaking participants with (N = 35) and without (N = 54) experience;
2. Russian-speaking (N = 35) and English-speaking (N = 36) participants having an experience of participation, facilitation and designing of simulation games;
3. Men (N = 40) and women (N = 77).

Analysis was performed using the content-analysis technique [2]. Procedure of content-analysis included the text splitting into meaningful units and calculation of frequency and number of the text units. A certain category was given to each statement (if possible) or unit. The attribution of a text unit to a certain category sometimes caused difficulties, since being included by different participants into various contexts the unit got a slightly different meaning. In other words, the strict categorization of the data was impossible without loss of the semantic nuances given to the same concept (phenomenon, object, etc.) by different participants. Thus, the meaning of the same statement sometimes was set to several categories, for example: "For me the game is an interesting pastime and an opportunity to be not myself, but another person", received categories: (1) game is interesting; (2) it is related with rest, pastime, etc.

After the calculation of the allocated specific categories they were grouped into more general blocks, for example: self-cognition; sphere of personality; cognitive sphere, etc. Then calculation of their occurrence for each of the groups of participants and comparison were carried out. Statistical significance of differences between groups of participants was checked by the $\chi2$–Pearson criterion ($p < 0.01$) [3] (MATLAB R2007b package).

3   Results Obtained and Discussion

Participation in simulation games allowed participants without game experience or with insignificant game experience to learn new things about games, to reconsider their views on learning. It changed their perception (including perception of games). Game is described by them as an active form of education. Training, learning is mentioned as the goal and meaning of simulation games. Thereby the participants without an experience of participation in games or with insignificant one perceive simulation game, first of all, as a form of learning.

Experienced participants consider the game as a synthesis of knowledge and experience, they connect simulation games with efficiency and productivity, and they consider personal experience of participation in the games and receiving practice as important. They define game as a set of several features (list of its characteristics): "Model of life, a type of human activity, the source of energy, knowledge and feelings". These participants distinguish simulation games from methods of conventional education by:

- Subject-subject approach to learning (the learner is active in the process of instruction);
- Higher motivation of participants;
- More effective use of the available resources;
- Orientation of methods of conventional education towards the transfer of knowledge.

The goal and meaning of simulation games for participants with game experience are cognition, including development of thinking (in particular, environmental and logical thinking). Personal experience of participation, practice, and orientation to the problem-based learning were mentioned as variants of meaning of simulation games.

Thus, the participants with experience of participation in games (especially, their design and facilitation), perceive simulation games more broadly than inexperienced participants (more answers). The game is perceived by them as an effective way to learn something new through complicity and activity, experimenting, practice. This special way of learning through personal experience gives the chance and an impulse for the development of cognitive and motivational spheres of the personality. We propose that in a process of accumulation of game experience the perception of differences between simulation games and methods of conventional education shifts, first, from the narrower to broader (more categories) and, secondly, from external, unstable interest in games towards internally driven cognitive interest and motivational involvement.

In order to identify an influence of a cultural context on the participants' subjective perceptions of game reality we carried out the comparative analysis of the answers of

English-speaking and Russian-speaking participants, who had an experience of designing, facilitation and participation in simulation games.

Russian-speaking participants more often experienced difficulties while formulating the specific answers to the questions "What did the game experience change for you? What new have you learned about yourself?"; they answered that they didn't learn anything new about themselves and about the games more frequently. While answering the question about the differences between simulation games and conventional education these participants experienced difficulties more often than English-speaking participants, as the specific differences between the games and traditional methods of learning were not revealed (answers are terse and short): "Yes, it differs". Russian-speaking participants associate games with a form of cognition, transfer of knowledge, opportunity for an application of knowledge to practice (an emphasis on cognitive aspect of simulation games is made). The development of thinking, in particular, of environmental thinking was mentioned as the goal of the simulation games. These participants more often mentioned the development of cognitive abilities (a cognitive component of the games), visual presentation and interest as advantages of simulation games.

It is interesting that Russian-speaking participants with game experience significantly more often did not give answers to the question "What did the game experience change for you? What new have you learned about yourself?" than Russian inexperienced participants. May be this result could be connected with cultural context: generally English-speaking participants, all with experience in games, gave answers to this question in contrast to experienced Russian-speaking participants. We propose that traditions of life in Russian-speaking countries imply closeness and intimity concerning information about oneself.

English-speaking participants specified that games had an impact on their thinking and allowed them to learn new about themselves and about the sphere of the personality in games. Apparently, as a result, these participants mention development of the personality and learning as the goals and meanings of simulation games. For many participants with experience game is specially modeled reality, "a magic door to the special world": "... educational games: they are as attractive initiation to the world of special reality which cannot be transferred in other ways" (the English-speaking teacher, the designer, the researcher of simulation games; experience of studying, use, teaching and game-design – more than 19 years). Games involve the person in learning and change: "For the personality it gives an opportunity to be oneself because I'm active and alive!".

Thus, Russian-speaking participants perceive the game through the development of the cognitive sphere of the participant's personality. English-speaking participants perceive it more as learning through feeling of immersiveness, active involvement and an opportunity for personal development. Representation of game reality in a world of English-speaking participants has a clear emotional accent: unlike methods of conventional education, game for them is the tool allowing to express emotions freely in the game environment.

In order to identify an influence of a gender on subjective perceptions of participants we carried out the comparative analysis of the answers of men and women. Significant differences were revealed in the answers to a question "What are the goal and the meaning of the simulation games?" Men significantly more often than women answered that modeling of a situation and transfer of its results to the real life is the goal of game.

In order to identify the factors which have the strongest impact on the subjective perceptions of the game reality we summarized the amount of differences for each group of participants in Table 2. In the 1st column of the Table questions are shown; in 2nd column the number of participants is shown; in the 3rd column the number of the categories revealed by means of the content-analysis is shown. The numbers in the 4th, 5th, 6th columns show the amount of categories with significant differences between groups of participants.

The greatest number of differences – 38 – was revealed in the groups differing by game experience (column 5). Thus, the experience of participation in simulation games mostly influences subjective perceptions of the game reality. Participants without game experience perceive games as a form of learning. For experienced participants the game is not only an effective way of learning, but is also a way to acquire/develop motivational sphere of personality.

In a group of the participants differing by a cultural context and with game experience 14 differences (column 6) were revealed. The smallest number of differences – 1 – was revealed in a group of the participants differing by gender (column 4). Thus, an influence of a cultural context (Russian-speaking and English-speaking) on subjective perceptions is much less important than gaming experience. The gender actually does not influence the subjective perceptions of game reality.

We also compared and identified questions that provided significant differences in answers. From Table 2, in a group "Presence/absence of game experience in a group of Russian-speaking participants" (column 5), the greatest number of differences (9) was revealed in the answers to the question "Do you have any experience of the use of interactive and game learning methods? What results have you got from their application?" Experienced participants use these methods of education and can describe results of their work in more detailed answers in contrast to inexperienced participants.

In a group "Presence/Absence of game experience in cultural contexts" (column 6), the greatest number of differences (4) was revealed in the answers to the questions "What did the game experience change for you? What new have you learned about yourself?" and "What are the goal and the meaning of the simulation games?"

In general, the greatest number of differences (10) was revealed in answers to a question "What are the goal and the meaning of the simulation games?" We propose that every participant (despite game experience, gender and cultural context) has his/her own understanding of things that happen in games and of the goals, aims, and meanings that simulation game has. Thus, the debriefing becomes the key value for promoting the holistic understanding of game and of the meanings that it has; and it also provides new meanings for everyone.

An analysis of the answers to the questions "Did your opinion about the subject of the game change after the game …?" and "What disadvantages does the interactive simulation method of learning have?" did not reveal significant differences (0).

Table 2. Summary of Statistically Significant Differences in the Answers of Different Groups of Participants ($p < 0.01$)

1	2	3	4	5	6	7
Questions	N participants	N categories discovered	Gender	Presence/absence of game experience in a group of Russian-speaking participants	Presence/absence of game experience in cultural contexts	Total (sum)
What did the game experience change for you? What new have you learned about yourself?	124	38	0	4	4	8
Did your opinion about the subject of the game change after the game (the specific subject of specific game)?	33	7	0	0	–	0
Do you have any experience of the use of interactive and game learning methods? What results have you got from their application?	85	17	0	9	–	9
What is the game for you (simulation, educational, role, etc.)?	106	32	0	4	1	5
Does the simulation game differ from the conventional education? How? Please, define.	103	25	0	4	1	5
What are the goal and meaning of the simulation games?	124	35	1	5	4	10
What advantages an interactive simulation method of education has?	121	50	0	6	3	9
What disadvantages an interactive simulation method of education has?	121	26	0	0	0	0
What personal qualities the facilitator must possess?	104	52	0	6	1	7
Total	–	282	1	38	14	53

4   Conclusions

We carried out the comparative analysis of the subjective perceptions of participants differing by a game experience, a gender and a cultural context. Results obtained showed that, primarily, the game is described by all participants as an active form of learning (regardless of gaming experience). Participants' subjective perceptions of game reality are mostly influenced by experience of participation in simulation games. The accumulation of gaming experience makes the perception of differences between conventional forms of education and simulation games broader, and shifts from pragmatic motives (cognition), simple curiosity and excitement of gaming to the motivational component of educational games.

There are fewer differences in answers between participants belonging to two cultural groups than between two groups differing by a game experience. It is interesting that subjective perceptions of game reality of English-speaking participants are more emotional (in contrast to Russian-speaking participants): unlike conventional forms of education, game allows participants to freely express their emotions in communication. The gender actually does not influence subjective perceptions of the reality of game.

All participants perceive game as the space which unites the processes of acquiring of new knowledge and of its application – learning-by-doing. The perception of game depends on experience of gaming and on the cultural context. These specifics should be considered in facilitation of games, especially during briefing and debriefing of particular game.

Simulation games on sustainable cities are used not only with academic and scientific purposes but also as a tool of managers' education, with participants of diverse origin and background. Therefore, it is important for facilitators to know that participants may represent games differently, to understand how these perceptions can be documented and adapt the process of game.

References

1. Zaikova, A.V.: Study of School Teachers' Representations and Personal Attitudes towards Interactive Methods of Education (Issledovanie predstavlenii i lichnostnogo otnosheniya uchitelei obshcheobrazovatel'noi shkoly k interaktivnym metodam obucheniya). CD-ROM "From Environmental Knowledge to the Picture of the World. XXV years of the Laboratory of Ecology and Protection of Nature of the Department of Higher Plants of M.V. Lomonosov Moscow State University" ("Ot ekologicheskikh znanii k kartine mira. XXV let laboratorii ekologii i okhrany prirody kafedry vysshikh rastenii MGU im. M.V. Lomonosova"). ANO, Ekopolispress, Moscow (2005)
2. Bogomolova, N.N., Stefanenko, T.G.: Content-Analysis: Special Workshop on Social Psychology (Kontent-analiz: Spetspraktikum po sotsial'noi psikhologii). MGU, Moscow (1992)
3. Nasledov, A.D.: Math Methods of Psychological Study. The Analysis and Interpretation of Data. Tutorial (Matematicheskie metody psikhologicheskogo issledovaniya. Analiz i interpretatsiya dannykh. Uchebnoe posobie), 3rd edn., Rech', SPb (2007)

Games as Research Instrument

Assessing the Residential Energy Rebound Effect by Means of a Serious Game

Oscar Garay Garcia[1], C. Els van Daalen[1(✉)], Emile Chappin[1],
Bas van Nuland[2], Iman Mohammed[1], and Bert Enserink[1]

[1] Faculty of Technology, Policy and Management, Policy Analysis Section,
Delft University of Technology, Jaffalaan 5, 2628BX Delft, The Netherlands
c.vandaalen@tudelft.nl
[2] The Barn Games, Delft, The Netherlands

Abstract. Residential energy efficiency improvements often have a smaller effect than expected. Although there is agreement on the existence of this effect, called the rebound effect, there is no agreement on the size of the effect. The objective of this study was to investigate the potential of using serious games to assess this effect. We used a game in which participants play home owners who manage their households in terms of energy consumption. Results of experiments with 50 players showed signs of the rebound effect when players with a low efficiency house reduced their energy consumption more than players with a high efficiency house. In addition, some issues related to previous studies were addressed, such as the possibility to perform an ex-ante assessment and to conduct the study in a controlled environment. Calculations of the size of the rebound effect depended on the approach used to determine the expected effect and showed differences between appliances.

Keywords: Rebound effect · Energy savings · NRG game
Game as a research instrument

1 Introduction

Improvements in household energy efficiency often do not lead to the energy savings which are expected. If energy efficiency is improved by 10%, one would also expect energy consumption to be decreased by 10%. However, due to the rebound effect, energy consumption is not reduced by that same percentage. Although there are different definitions in the literature, the following definition is explanatory and clear: "The rebound effect is the extent of the energy saving produced by an efficiency investment that is taken back by consumers in the form of higher consumption" [1, p. 2].

Figure 1 illustrates how the rebound effect works in household energy consumption [2]. First, technical improvements produce a more comfortable indoor environment and reduce the energy use. Second, this energy use reduction increases the disposable income which, together with a more comfortable indoor environment, produces an increment of the household lifestyle. Finally, a better lifestyle with more disposable income produces extra energy consumption (either in the same energy service

© Springer International Publishing AG, part of Springer Nature 2018
H. K. Lukosch et al. (Eds.): ISAGA 2017, LNCS 10825, pp. 129–138, 2018.
https://doi.org/10.1007/978-3-319-91902-7_13

producing a direct rebound effect, or in other energy services producing an indirect rebound effect). The latter partially offsets the initial energy reduction. This process of offsetting initial energy savings is called the rebound effect.

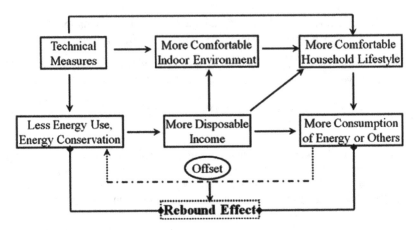

Fig. 1. Formation process of the rebound effect. (Source: [2].)

The rebound effect has been widely studied and analyzed (see [3–6], among others). Although the scientific community agrees that the rebound effect is true and can be measured, the size of the rebound effect is unclear since different scholars have calculated and measured different magnitudes of the effect [3–5].

Four main methodologies have been used in previous studies to measure the rebound effect: econometric studies of historical data, quasi-experimental analysis, direct surveys, and benchmarking techniques. One of the reasons why the extent of the rebound effect is unclear is that previous attempts to measure the rebound effect have some methodological issues [6–8]. Econometric and quasi-experimental studies provide ex-post information. In such studies it is difficult to isolate the rebound effect from other effects. Direct surveys suffer from biases as they do not rely on independently observed behavior. Benchmarking depends on data collected in other studies which suggests that there is not an exact fit between the studies and the objective to estimate rebound effects mainly due to socio-economic differences between the groups under study.

Serious games have a number of advantages compared to the studies above, in that in a game: variables can be controlled, an ex-ante analysis can be done, and a control group can be added. However, there are not only advantages to using a serious game. Since we are working with a representation of the real world, the applicability to the actual context is always an issue. Additionally, developing and using serious games is time-intensive which in practice limits the realism of the games used and the representativeness of the studies using serious games.

In this study, a serious game will serve as a laboratory environment to assess the rebound effect. This research aims to address the methodological problems identified in previous research and investigate the potential of using a serious game to assess the rebound effect.

The remainder of this paper is organized as follows. In Sect. 2 the game which is used to assess the rebound effect and the experimental setup are explained. Section 3 provides the results of the assessment and Sect. 4 concludes the paper.

2 Using the NRG Game to Assess the Rebound Effect

2.1 The NRG Game

The serious game which is used to assess the rebound effect in this study is called the NRG game. The NRG game was originally developed to test the influence of different interventions, such as information, feedback, discounts and subsidies, on energy conservation in households. The NRG game simulates the basic decisions households make regarding energy consumption.

The players' objective in the game is to manage their household in terms of energy consumption. Players must pay gas and electricity bills, can buy new appliances, produce energy using solar panels or wind turbines, sell appliances to get some money back, increase thermal or electric efficiency by investing in thermal insulation or smart meters, and so forth.

The main screen of the game is shown in Fig. 2, which shows the house a player has. Players can navigate through their house, and during the course of the game money becomes available to spend in order to simulate the income people would receive in real life.

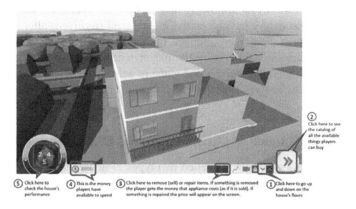

Fig. 2. Screenshot of the main screen of the NRG game.

The players can see a catalogue containing all available appliances that can be acquired (Fig. 3(a)) and they see the extent to which appliances are luxury and eco-friendly (Fig. 3(b)). The higher the luxury level of an item, the more expensive it is and the more comfort it adds. The higher the eco-friendly level of the item, the more expensive it is and the less energy it consumes. All (types of) energy consuming appliances in households are covered in the game with realistic relative performance and costs.

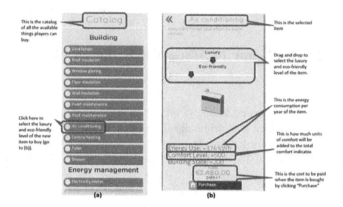

Fig. 3. Screenshot of part of the item catalogue in the NRG game.

After each round, players can monitor their performance in the game: their energy consumption, their energy production (if they decided to produce energy), their total comfort level, the condition of all the appliances and furniture they have in their houses, the total money they spend on electricity and gas, and the annual income they receive.

After players make any decision in the game, the choice they have made is stored. Specifically, the game stores the following information: the appliance, the comfort and eco-friendly level selected by the player, the money paid (received) after the purchase (sale), the money left in the player's budget, the total energy and gas consumption in the house after the decision, the money the player will have to pay at the end of the round for energy bills, and the round of the game in which the decision was made. This information is used to analyze the players' behavior and way of thinking regarding energy consumption.

2.2   Using the NRG Game to Assess the Rebound Effect

For the purpose of this study, we modelled two types of houses in the game. The only difference between these two houses is the energy efficiency level. One is called a "low efficiency house" and the other one a "high efficiency house". Players are randomly assigned to one of these houses. We observed and analyzed whether these two different but comparable groups of people behaved differently in the game. The "high efficiency" house represents a house with improved energy efficiency and the "low efficiency house" represents a house in which energy efficiency has not been improved.

Players were asked to follow three steps to complete the experiments. First, they were asked to answer a pre-game questionnaire to understand their socio-demographic characteristics and their real life behavior regarding energy consumption. Second, they were asked to play the NRG game for 45 min on average, in which they played 10 rounds of the game, simulating 10 years. Each player started the game with the same amount of money, which was available for buying new appliances, new thermal insulation or new devices to increase energy efficiency. The available catalogue for buying new devices contains 97 different appliances (this includes TVs, HiFi systems, washing and drying machines, movement sensors for reducing energy consumption, air conditioning, solar panels, wind turbines, different types of insulation etc.). After each round (i.e. each simulated year) players received an annual income that simulated the average annual amount of money people spend on electric appliances or energy efficiency solutions. The one and only instruction players received was to play the game as they would do it in real in life. Round by round, players had to pay their energy bills according to the energy consumption they had in that specific round. That money for paying bills was automatically deducted from the income players received after each round. Players used different strategies to manage their energy consumption in the game. Some players preferred to increase their comfort level in their virtual houses by buying luxurious appliances without taking care too much of their energy consumption, while others preferred to reduce their energy consumption by buying energy efficient appliances in order to spend less money on their energy bills after each round. All the decisions players made to manage their energy consumption were stored during the game for further analysis. The main idea was to compare how the two different groups of players (who received a house with a different initial energy efficiency) behaved throughout the rounds.

The third and final step was to answer a post-game questionnaire about their impressions of the game and the strategies they used while playing the game. From all that information (the questionnaires and the game itself) it was possible to investigate each group of players according to their decisions. If the two groups of players behaved significantly different with respect some of the defined KPI's we could infer that receiving a house with a certain initial energy efficiency affected their behavior during the game.

This experimental setup is different from a real before/after analysis in which the energy efficiency would have been improved at a certain point in the game and we investigate the behavior of players after it has been improved. The reason for this setup is rooted in the duration of the experiments. If one player is exposed to efficiency improvements in the middle of the game, there may not be enough time left in the game to properly analyze the impact of the efficiency improvement. If we can analyze the impact of this stimulus from the beginning of the game, the results may be richer and more conclusions may be obtained.

The low efficiency house group is used as a control group for the analysis, since they did not start with an "improved" energy efficiency house. The actual savings consist of the difference between the consumption of the low efficiency group and the high efficiency group (as this is what the high efficiency group saved).

The two types of houses have the same appliances at the beginning of the game and the only difference is the efficiency level of those appliances, resulting in a different energy consumption. Since the NRG game also gives an indication about the comfort level of players, this index must initially be equal in both types of houses. In doing so, the possible differences in the energy consumption of the two types of houses throughout the game is caused uniquely by a different initial energy efficiency level.

Fifty participants took part in the experiments of which 65% were students and 35% were (self) employed, 64% of the participants were male and 36% female, 15% were home owners and 85% lived in rented accommodation. These socio-demographic characteristics may have influenced the way participants behaved when consuming energy, which may limit the representativeness of the results.

3 Results

3.1 Presence of the Rebound Effect

Over the course of the game, the energy consumption of the two groups showed that the low efficiency houses group decreased their average energy consumption more than the other group, up to the point that in round 10 they consumed, on average, less than the high efficiency houses group (see Fig. 4), although the difference at the end is not statistically significant.

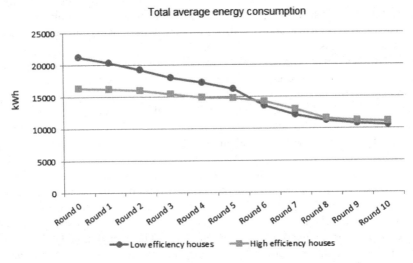

Fig. 4. Total average energy consumption per group per round.

The comfort level (Fig. 5) did not show significant differences between the two groups from round 1 to round 5 (both groups started at the same comfort level). However, from round 6 onwards, the comfort level showed significant differences between both groups. After finishing the game in round 10, the high efficiency houses group had increased their total comfort level by 16% on average, whereas the low efficiency houses group had increased their total comfort level by 4% on average.

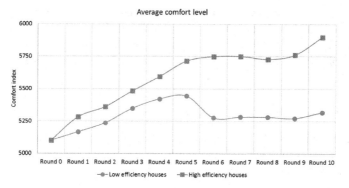

Fig. 5. Average comfort level per group.

Different patterns are observed for different types of decisions that can be made by players. With regard to purchasing energy management devices (any device that can reduce the overall consumption of a house, such as smart meters, movement sensors, stand-by-killers, or insulation), the average reduction of the total energy consumption can be seen in Fig. 6.

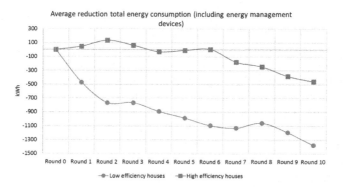

Fig. 6. Reduction of total energy consumption by including energy management devices.

The group with the low efficiency houses reduced their energy consumption more by including energy management devices than the high efficiency houses group. There is a significant difference in terms of the reduction of energy consumption between the two groups.

In Ref. [9] other decisions players made are analyzed in order to investigate if both groups significantly differ in taking one action more than the other group. For example, both groups did not show any significant difference in the decision to buy energy production devices (wind turbines/solar panels). However, when the decision of selling or getting rid of appliances was analyzed, the behavior showed that the low efficiency group got rid of more appliances than the high efficiency group, in a way to reduce their initially high energy consumption.

It is also interesting to note that from the post-game questionnaire it became clear that in the game significantly more people invested in energy production devices than in energy management devices, whereas energy management devices are more economically profitable. The latter shows that participants were more influenced by their own previous knowledge of the appliances than the information given in the game, somehow replicating what may happen in real life when consumers show irrational behavior when making a decision.

3.2 Calculation of the Rebound Effect

The differences between the two groups of players can be used to estimate the size of the rebound effect, which we do according to Eq. (1), which follows directly from our definition of the rebound effect [8].

$$r = ((e - a)/e) * 100 \tag{1}$$

Where r is the rebound effect, e represents the expected savings and a represents the actual savings.

However, we first need to determine actual and expected 'savings' in order to be able to apply the equation. The actual savings consist of the difference between the consumption of the low efficiency group and the high efficiency group (as this is what the high efficiency group saved).

In order to determine the expected savings we need a base case scenario. The base case scenario represents the behavior of the high efficiency houses group if the rebound effect was zero (note that this is not the same as the control group which is the low efficiency group). In other words, the base case scenario can be interpreted as the lowest energy consumption the high efficiency houses group could have had (the situation in which no energy savings are lost due to the rebound effect). Two different ways to define the base case scenario were implemented, one taking into account that that the high efficiency houses group has less opportunity to improve their energy efficiency since they are already highly efficient, and one without considering this difference in the opportunities to improve energy efficiency. Calculations using both approaches are discussed in [9]. The two approaches to calculate the base case scenarios showed similar behavior. The results for the (simplest) approach in which they have the same possibilities for reduction are shown in Fig. 7.

The dotted (green) line is the base case scenario and shows what reductions the high efficiency group could have achieved if they had reduced their consumption in the same way as the low efficiency group. For this reason the dotted line is parallel to the low efficiency (blue/top) line. We can see that the high efficiency houses (orange line/line which starts at same point as dotted line) in the game do not decrease their energy consumption to the same extent as could have been expected (dotted line). For each round the rebound effect (Eq. 1) may be calculated and the results are shown in the black line in Fig. 7, with the related axis on the right hand side.

When we regard individual rebound effects of the most energy consuming appliances in households, e.g. central heating, shower, refrigerator, the results differ from the overall rebound effect and also show differences between the two approaches to calculate the base case scenario [9]. The results show that the way the base case scenario is calculated is crucial for the final calculation of the rebound effect.

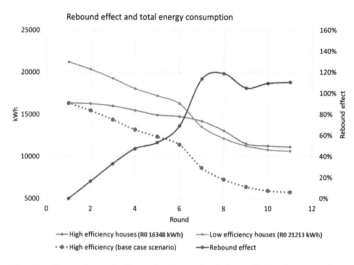

Fig. 7. Illustration of rebound effect calculation. (Color figure online)

With regard to Fig. 7, we conclude that the game enables us to calculate a rebound effect, but the number as such is very sensitive to the approach to determine the expected effect (base case).

4 Conclusions and Discussion

The results of the experiments allow us to draw some initial conclusions about the presence of the rebound effect in the game. If we take a look at the total energy consumption, we can see that the initial difference between the groups diminished over time. The low energy efficiency houses group managed to reduce their energy consumption more than the high efficiency houses group. With respect to the comfort level, we saw that in the later rounds, the high efficiency houses show a significantly higher comfort level than the low efficiency houses. This is explained by the fact that the high efficiency group had more money to spend due to their lower initial consumption, and thus lower energy bills. As a result, this group had the opportunity to buy more appliances that increased their overall comfort level than the other group. We also found that the group with the low efficiency houses reduced their energy consumption more by including energy management devices than the high efficiency houses group. Calculations of the size of the rebound effect depend on the definition of a base case and showed differences between appliances, confirming that the existence of one single rebound effect size should not be the focus of a study aiming to assess the rebound effect.

The objective of this study was to investigate the potential of a game to investigate the rebound effect. Using the game, we were able to conduct an ex-ante analysis and compare groups in a controlled setting. However, there were also some limitations which could be addressed in future research. The modified before/after setup may have influenced the outcome, since there was no change in efficiency within groups during the game. The post-game questionnaire also indicated that the realism of the game still requires some attention, partially because the way the game is set up does not allow players to change the real usage of appliances and it is assumed that appliances have a constant energy consumption.

References

1. Herring, H., Roy, R.: Technological innovation, energy efficient design and the rebound effect. Technovation **27**, 194–203 (2007). https://doi.org/10.1016/j.technovation.2006.11.004
2. Ouyang, J., Long, E., Hokao, K.: Rebound effect in Chinese household energy efficiency and solution for mitigating it. Energy **35**, 5269–5276 (2010). https://doi.org/10.1016/j.energy.2010.07.038
3. Greening, L.A., Greene, D.L., Difiglio, C.: Energy efficiency and consumption - the rebound effect - a survey. Energy Policy **28**, 389–401 (2000). https://doi.org/10.1016/S0301-4215(00)00021-5
4. Binswanger, M.: Technological progress and sustainable development: what about the rebound effect? Ecol. Econ. **36**, 119–132 (2001). https://doi.org/10.1016/S0921-8009(00)00214-7
5. Sorrell, S., Dimitropoulos, J., Sommerville, M.: Empirical estimates of the direct rebound effect: a review. Energy Policy **37**, 1356–1371 (2009). https://doi.org/10.1016/j.enpol.2008.11.026
6. Dimitroupoulos, J.: Energy productivity improvements and the rebound effect: an overview of the state of knowledge. Energy Policy **35**, 6354–6363 (2007). https://doi.org/10.1016/j.enpol.2007.07.028
7. Aydin, E., Kok, N., Brounen, D.: Energy efficiency and household behavior: the rebound effect in the residential sector. RAND J. Econ. **48**, 749–782 (2015)
8. Sorrell, S., Dimitropoulos, J.: The rebound effect: microeconomic definitions, limitations and extensions. Ecol. Econ. **65**, 636–649 (2008). https://doi.org/10.1016/j.ecolecon.2007.08.013
9. Garay Garcia, O.: Residential energy rebound effect assessment by using serious games. M.Sc. thesis, Delft University of Technology (2016). https://repository.tudelft.nl

A Model for the Development of Stealth Serious Games

Victor A. Cuesta Aguiar[(⊠)] and Masaru Nakano

Graduate School of System Design and Management, Keio University, Kyosei Building 4-1-1, Hiyoshi, Kohoku-ku, Yokohama, Kanagawa 223-8526, Japan
vcuesta@keio.jp, m.nakano@sdm.keio.ac.jp

Abstract. In this paper, a model for serious game (SG) development is presented and explained along with a definition of stealth serious games (SSG). A systemic review on existing models is performed; based on the existing model's deficiencies and the researchers' previous experience in the development of SG the SSG model is created and explained. To observe how a SSG developed with the SSG Model would behave, "Chain of Command: A Sustainable Supply Chain Management Stealth Serious Game" is developed and tested. The developed SG is tested on 4 metrics: replay value, education, fun and simple vs realistic. The SSG model is successful in helping to develop a SSG that performs acceptably. Further validation of the SSG model is still required.

Keywords: Serious game model · Sustainable supply chain management
Stealth serious games · Replay value · Stealth learning

1 Introduction

Any serious game (SG) starts with an idea, how the idea of the specific serious game is further developed is the responsibility of the SG designer. Serious game designers have several tools at their disposal, such as models, to help them along the creative process. In this paper, a model is a simplified version of a system to facilitate understanding by eliminating unnecessary components and presenting only the most important features that should be considered when developing SG. The use of models help ensure quality work.

Mechanics Dynamics Aesthetics (MDA) [1] is a model whose limitation is primarily that is was not conceived as a model to help in the design of SG, MDA's primary concern is the design of entertainment games. This issue was partially solved by Design Play Experience (DPE) [2] which is an extension of MDA. The player is presented with what he/she must learn from the SG. The Educational Games (EG) Design Framework [3], provides a model that focuses on Game Design, Pedagogy and Learning Content Modelling. This model/framework leans towards the design of highly educational SG that clearly show the user what he or she should be learning. The EG Design Framework generates SG that remove from the player the opportunity to experiment and build his/her own knowledge without him/her being aware of it. This paper presents an alternative model for SG development and a definition for stealth serious games (SSG).

H. K. Lukosch et al. (Eds.): ISAGA 2017, LNCS 10825, pp. 139–147, 2018.
https://doi.org/10.1007/978-3-319-91902-7_14

A novel model for SG design is presented in this paper, the SSG model (SSG). The purpose of the SSG model is to bridge the gap between game design and serious game design, to create experiences that are educational, nevertheless, the player is not fully aware the he or she is learning, known as "stealth learning" [4] and that possess a high replay value. Replay value is the property of the SG to be played repeatedly, providing new experiences, and learning to the player every time the SG is played. Additional to presenting a model to develop SG, a definition of what SSG should be is presented. SSG have a high replay value coupled with an equal ratio of fun to educational content, the player is not aware that he or she is learning when playing and can be played for amusement or education. SSG are primarily designed with education as a goal, thus, SSG differ from conventional games acquired at toy shops. Games acquired at toy shops have not been designed with any educational purpose into consideration.

2   Background Research

A systemic review of models available for SG development is performed to identify what current models may lack. Systematic review has its origins in the medical field [5] but has also been adopted to education [6]. This study's approach entailed extensive searches using a meta search engine (Google scholar). Words used for performing the search were: Serious, Game, Model, Framework, Education. The previous keywords are later combined into several strings. The strings used in the search are:

(1) Serious Game Model
(2) Serious Game Framework
(3) Serious Game Model Education
(4) Serious Game Framework Education

The intention is to create a search that will yield the most relevant examples. A 12-year limitation is set as to encompass all possible modern SG models. The results of the search are categorized as follows:

Models taking into consideration Fun: Educational Games Design Framework [3], MDA [1], Design Play Experience (DPE) [2], P-III Framework [7], SGSID [8], Theoretical Framework for Serious Game Design [9], Robert L. Appelman Model [10], Six Facets of Serious Game Design [11] Serious Game Constructivist Framework for Children [12], SGameFlow Framework [13].

Models taking into consideration replay value: Key Criteria for Game Design [14].

Models taking into consideration stealth learning: Design Play Experience (DPE) [2], Theoretical Framework for Serious Game Design [9], Serious Game Constructivist Framework for Children [12].

Models not including fun, replay value or stealth learning: Simport [15], HABS +ISIS [16], Model Driven Framework to Support Development of SG [17], DODDEL [18], 4 Dimensional Framework [19], CMX Design Framework [20], Digital Game Based Training Systems [21], ARCS [22].

19 models were analyzed and categorized; based on the limitations that these models possessed the SSG model was developed. Stealth learning and replay value were 2 important concepts that the previous models do not address in conjunction.

3   Stealth Serious Games Model

3.1   Replay Value

Replay value is the property of the SG to be played repeatedly, providing a new experience, and learning to the player every time the SG is played. Replay value has a direct interaction with the Gaming aspect of the model and is profoundly dependent on mechanics and dynamics. SG often make the mistake of not emphasizing replay value. After playing the SG once, there is no need to replay the SG again, as all learning has already been achieved.

Replay value has three main aspects:

No game is the same: The SG should have several mechanics and dynamics that can generate multiple scenarios and situations.

Allow for different approaches: The SG should permit the player the freedom to approach any situation the game simulates in any way he/she wants.

New learning happens every time the game is played: Not all learning should be achieved if the game is played once.

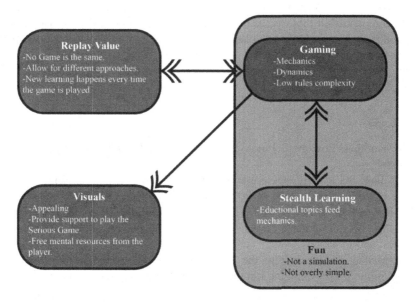

Fig. 1. SSG model components.

3.2   Gaming

Low Rule Complexity: This aspect is extremely important, if the rules are too complex the barrier to play the game becomes too high and some players might lose motivation to learn how to play. Rules directly affect mechanics and dynamics; simple rules that allow for deep mechanics and dynamics are necessary.

Mechanics: Describe the components of the SG, at the level of data representation and algorithms [1].

Dynamics: Describes the run-time behavior of the mechanics acting on player inputs and each other's outputs over time [1].

3.3 Stealth Learning

Stealth learning: Eventuates when "players are focused not on learning but on playing" [23]

Educational topics feed mechanics: The mechanics in the SG must be generated using the topics the designer wants the player to learn. It is important to state that the topics must be presented in such a way that the player does not fully realize he/she is learning.

3.4 Fun

Fun is a combination of simulation, simplicity, and the gaming and stealth facet.

Not a simulation: If the game is a simulation the SG becomes too complex for non-professionals and can potentially lead to boredom for those who are not professionals. Complexity in this case is defined as giving the player several variables and interdependencies to control when playing the SG, the ability to control every aspect of the game is not always met with joy by players.

Not overly simple: If the game is too simple, professionals will not take the game seriously.

3.5 Visuals

Visuals encompass how the SG looks and must emerge from the Gaming aspect of the SSG model.

Appealing: SG usually lack enthralling visuals; good visual representations allow for more player immersion and make the player feel excited about playing the SG.

Provide support to play the SG: The player does not need to remember everything in the game. It is the game's responsibility to remind players about important rules, mechanics, and dynamics.

Free Mental resources from the player: Well implemented visuals free mental resources in the player allowing him/her to focus on the strategic layer of playing the SG.

4 Method

The SSG model and the five dimensions it encompasses are developed based on the gap current models exhibit and from the lessons learned from previous SG development and testing [24].

Chain of Command: A Sustainable Supply Chain Management Stealth Serious Game (CoC) Fig. 1 is the SSG developed to test the SSG model. CoC is a board game

(2 to 4 players) where players need to optimize their supply chain to meet environmental needs, achieve economic success, uphold ethical behavior in dealings with other players and manage risk as they try to outperform rival supply chains to be the only player left in the game. Players must make decisions to go green, invest in technology, establish partnerships with other players, build close loop supply chains, optimize their supply chain to meet their needs and choose which products to manufacture to have an edge over the competition. The game uses event cards to introduce penalties and bonuses as well as a dice mechanic for the strategic combat mechanic in the SG.

CoC manages each of the SSG model dimensions in the following way:

Replay Value: Adversarial multiplayer SSG with a strategic layer giving players control over where they produce, deploy units, and how to invest his/her cash. Depending on how the players chooses to invest cash and interact with other players he/she will learn different aspects of sustainability in supply chains.

Gaming: In CoC the game manual is designed to have many visuals and as few text as possible. Rules are simple to understand yet the mechanics and dynamics allow for multiple scenarios to develop.

Stealth Learning: Focus is not placed on definitions of supply chains or sustainability. It is not desired to portray CoC as a SG in the mind of the player. The player acquires knowledge by exercising the mechanics and dynamics of CoC.

Fun: The player is given just enough controllable parameters to not overburden his/her decision process. Relevant parameters for sustainability and supply chains are chosen, such parameters include lead time, investment in newer technologies, human relationships etc.

Visuals: CoC is made to be visually appealing and present the player with relevant information that helps the player focus on controlling the parameters that are important for sustainability and supply chain management (Fig. 2).

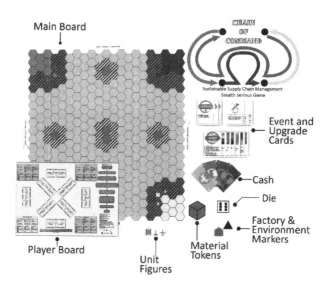

Fig. 2. Chain of command a sustainable supply chain stealth serious game

To observe how SSG developed with the SSG model perform, CoC is tested with a sample of 30 people. A total of 8 tests are performed, each testing session lasting an average of 3.5 h and having 4 to 2 players per test. Test participants are graduate students with no background knowledge on sustainable supply chain management, 50% engineers and 50% other disciplines. The participants were given the game manual to read, the facilitator was present during the time the participants were reading the manual to answer any questions regarding the rules. There was no further interaction with the facilitator after the game rules were read by the participants. The game facilitator was present during the whole game session. At the end of each test, players are required to evaluate the SSG CoC on the following four important metrics: Fun, Simple vs Realistic, Replay Value and Educational. Prior to each session players were briefed on how to play the SG CoC. Sessions were photographed. No explanation regarding sustainable supply chain management was given to the players before or after the game session. Users rated the game on a 0 to 100 scale on the following metrics: simple vs realistic (closer to 0 means the SG is simple closer to 100 means the SG is realistic), fun (closer to 0 means not fun and closer to 100 means significantly fun), replay value (closer to 0 means low replay value and closer to 100 means high replay value) and educational (closer to 0 means less educational and closer to 100 means highly educational). The average rating for each metric is then calculated and reported in Fig. 3.

5 Results

In Fig. 3 the results of the evaluation of CoC can be observed. In the "Simple vs Realistic" metric, CoC was rated 67.25 points. CoC, as based on the SSG model was designed to not be overly simple or overly realistic. The perfect score for CoC, from the researchers and developer's viewpoint, would have been a 50. It is important to clarify that CoC was rated by non-experts in SSCM. CoC could come across as simple when rated by experts in the field of sustainable supply chain management. The rating of 67.25 as rated by non-expert users is an acceptable rating. "Replay value", the game was given an average score of 64.75. It is important to mention that participants did not play CoC more than once, hence, the rating in this category represents the potential replay value as perceived by the players. The game was rated a 62 in the "Fun" metric. While the game is fun to play, there is still a considerable amount of player downtime which negatively impacts the fun factor of the game. The "Educational" metric had an average rating of 57.5 points. A possible explanation for the low rating in this area can be the way the tests were conducted. Participants were never briefed on SSCM; participants were only instructed to play the game. It is conceivable that a structured SSCM discussion before playing CoC can further enhance the rating given on the "Educational" metric. The fact that CoC manages to have an average rating in education above 50 with no discussion of SSCM indicates that stealth learning is being achieved.

Chain of Command Evaluation

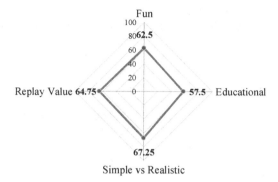

Fig. 3. Results of chain of command evaluation

6   Discussion and Conclusion

Using the SSG model could lead to more compelling SG that can make players learn without them realizing and also provide enjoyment. The next generation of SG should aim to educate and entertain in equal shares. The difficulty lies in balancing the previous two dimensions. Failing to do so, results in games that are too serious or games that are not serious enough, and therefore, not useful for learning. By bringing an emphasis on visuals, the SSG model can help create more compelling experiences that should be able to rival conventional board games or video games. The significance of having a high replay value is that the player must play the SSG several times to potentially experience everything the SSG has to offer. The SSG model aim is to develop SG in which no facilitator is required, at the same time, the SG is able to teach players regarding the topic for which it was designed.

This paper presented a systemic review of current models and tested the SSG model with the development and testing of CoC. Further validation of the SSG model is still required. Additional SSG using the SSG model need to be developed and tested. The concept of SSG requires additional empirical evidence.

Acknowledgments. This work was supported in part by Keio University Doctorate Student Grant-in-Aid Program.

References

1. Hunicke, R., LeBlanc, M., Zubek, R.: MDA: a formal approach to game design and game research. In: Proceedings of the AAAI Workshop on Challenges in Game AI (2004)
2. Winn, B.: The design, play, and experience framework. In: Handbook of Research on Effective Electronic Gaming in Education, vol. 3, pp. 1010–1024 (2008)

3. Ibrahim, R., Jaafar, A.: Educational games (EG) design framework: combination of game design, pedagogy and content modeling. In: International Conference on Electrical Engineering and Informatics 2009. ICEEI 2009, pp. 293–298 (2009)
4. Sharp, L.: Stealth learning: unexpected learning opportunities through games. J. Instr. Res. **1**, 42–48 (2012)
5. Sheldon, T., Chalmers, I.: The UK cochrane centre and the NHS Centre for reviews and dissemination: respective roles within the information systems strategy of the NHS R&D programme, coordination and principles underlying collaboration. Health Econ. **3**(3), 201–203 (1994)
6. Hemsley-Brown, J., Sharp, C.: The use of research to improve professional practice: a systematic review of the literature. Oxford Rev. Educ. **29**(4), 449–471 (2003)
7. Vanden Abeele, V., et al.: P-III: a player-centered, iterative, interdisciplinary and integrated framework for serious game design and development. In: De Wannemacker, S., Vandercruysse, S., Clarebout, G. (eds.) ITEC/CIP/T 2011. CCIS, vol. 280, pp. 82–86. Springer, Heidelberg (2012). https://doi.org/10.1007/978-3-642-33814-4_14
8. Kirkley, S.E., Tomblin, S., Kirkley, J.: Instructional design authoring support for the development of serious games and mixed reality training. In: Interservice/Industry Training, Simulation and Education Conference (I/ITSEC) (2005)
9. Rooney, P.: A theoretical framework for serious game design: exploring pedagogy, play and fidelity and their implications for the design process. Int. J. Game Lear. **2**, 41–60 (2012)
10. Appelman, R.L.: Serious game design: balancing cognitive and affective engagement. In: Proceedings of ISAGA, Nijmegen, The Netherlands, pp. 1–10 (2007)
11. Marne, B., Wisdom, J., Huynh-Kim-Bang, B., Labat, J.-M.: The six facets of serious game design: a methodology enhanced by our design pattern library. In: Ravenscroft, A., Lindstaedt, S., Kloos, C.D., Hernández-Leo, D. (eds.) EC-TEL 2012. LNCS, vol. 7563, pp. 208–221. Springer, Heidelberg (2012). https://doi.org/10.1007/978-3-642-33263-0_17
12. Obikwelu, C., Read, J.C.: The serious game constructivist framework for children's learning. Procedia Comput. Sci. **15**, 32–37 (2012)
13. Zain, N.H.M., Jaafar, A., Razak, F.H.A.: SGameFlow framework: how to experience enjoyment in serious game (SG) for motor impaired users (MIU). In: 2012 International Conference on Computer & Information Science (ICCIS), pp. 1020–1024 (2012)
14. Sanchez, E.: Key Criteria for Game Design. A Framework (2011)
15. Warmerdam, J., et al.: SimPort: a multiplayer management game framework. In: 9th International Conference on Computer Games (CGAMES06), Dublin, Ireland (2006)
16. Marsh, T., Yang, K., Shahabi, C.: Game development for experience through staying there. In: Proceedings of the 2006 ACM SIGGRAPH Symposium on Videogames, pp. 83–89 (2006)
17. Tang, S., Hanneghan, M.: A model-driven framework to support development of serious games for game-based learning. In: Developments in E-Systems Engineering (DESE), pp. 95–100 (2010)
18. McMahon, M.: Using the DODDEL model to teach serious game design to novice designers. In: Ascilite 2009, pp. 646–653 (2009)
19. De Freitas, S., Oliver, M.: How can exploratory learning with games and simulations within the curriculum be most effectively evaluated? Comput. Educ. **46**(3), 249–264 (2006)
20. Malliarakis, C., Satratzemi, M., Xinogalos, S.: A holistic framework for the development of an educational game aiming to teach computer programming. In: European Conference on Games Based Learning, p. 359 (2013)
21. Brennecke, A., Schumann, H.: A general framework for digital game-based training systems. University of Rostock (2009)

22. Bulander, R.: A conceptual framework of serious games for higher education: conceptual framework of the game INNOV8 to train students in business process modelling. In: Proceedings of the 2010 International Conference on E-Business (ICE-B), pp. 1–6 (2010)
23. Shreve, J.: Let the Games Begin. Video Games, Once Confiscated in Class, Are Now a Key Teaching Tool. If They're Done Right." George Lucas Educational Foundation (2005)
24. Cuesta, V., Nakano, M.: Appendix A: ISAGA-JASAG 2015 program "the use of origami in serious games". Simul. Gaming Netw. Soc. **9**, 463 (2016)

Attitude Measurement with Board Games in Transportation Nodes

Shalini Kurapati[1(✉)], Maria Freese[2], Ioanna Kourounioti[1],
Heide Lukosch[1], Geertje Bekebrede[1], Thijs Smit[3],
Jaco van Meijeren[3], Bas van Nuland[4], and Linda van Veen[5]

[1] Faculty of Technology Policy and Management,
Delft University of Technology, Jaffalaan 5, 2628 BX Delft, The Netherlands
S.Kurapati@tudelft.nl
[2] German Aerospace Center (DLR), Institute of Flight Guidance,
Lilienthalplatz 7, 38108 Braunschweig, Germany
[3] Netherlands Organisation for Applied Scientific Research,
Anna van Buerenplein 1, 2595 DA The Hague, The Netherlands
[4] The Barn, Frederik Matthesstraat 45, 2613 ZX Delft, The Netherlands
[5] TU Delft Gamelab, Jaffalaan 5, 2628 BX Delft, The Netherlands

Abstract. Transportation systems are complex yet vital infrastructures. Different stakeholders have to work together to guarantee the most efficient traffic of humans and goods. Challenges that stakeholders face in such infrastructure systems, like divergent interests and attitudes, make it hard to predict behaviour. To understand the complex systems including the behaviour of the stakeholders, it is relevant to model decision-making processes. For this reason, simulation games were developed. The present article focuses on two different case studies. Both are studies in which board games were used. After explaining each case study, a comparative section follows to give an overview about advantages and disadvantages of the use of board games in the transportation sector.

Keywords: Airport management · Freight transport · Simulation games
Board games · Digital games

1 Introduction

Transport systems are critical infrastructures that facilitate the mobility of humans and freight, which are imperative for the functioning of economical and societal well-being [1]. These systems are complex because they represent limited resources and at the same time consist of a network of interdependent stakeholders who have to work together to ensure the functioning of such systems [1]. Given the different stakeholders with varied power, divergent interests and attitude it is hard to predict or assess the behavior when changes or new ways of working are introduced within the systems. In particular, when government agencies, think tanks or research bodies study the effects of an innovative transport concept theoretically, another challenge is to visualize its effects or consequences when applied in practice [2]. Therefore, we used simulation games to introduce innovative ideas that have a potential to streamline and optimize

© Springer International Publishing AG, part of Springer Nature 2018
H. K. Lukosch et al. (Eds.): ISAGA 2017, LNCS 10825, pp. 148–157, 2018.
https://doi.org/10.1007/978-3-319-91902-7_15

transport systems to stakeholders. The main objective of this paper is to evaluate the value of two board games in the complex system of transportation. In this paper two case studies are presented: freight bundling in rail transport (simulation game "Rail Cargo Challenge") and planning activities in airport management (simulation game D-CITE[1]). Both games are played with professionals having a background respectively in the rail and the airport system. This paper explains the design of the games and the experiences of using these games in the design process to optimize the performance of the rail and airport system. The comparative approach enabled us to explore board game characteristics that are useful for attitude measurement and changes on a more general level than when only one game would have been addressed. In this case, some of the results could have been relate top the distinct context of the game. In a comparison, we were able to better identify the shared characteristics of board games.

2 Case Study 1: Freight Bundling with Rail Transport

Freight bundling describes the process of consolidating shipments in one vehicle (like truck or train) during a common part of their journey from their origin to the destination [3]. Operators opt for the bundling solution to decrease the number of empty or half full loads achieving better economies of scale and higher environmental advantages. Bundling can have disadvantages such as longer routes, longer travel times and in many cases extra handling of transport units when they are loaded/ unloaded to the different modes [4]. Bundling freight, especially in rail transport and between the different terminals of a seaport, is a complex process that requires a good understanding of the challenges faced by stakeholders, like the pre-planning of transport capacities, or the coordination of different modalities of transportation. A game was designed that aims at illustrating these challenges to the stakeholders and raise their awareness of the importance of sharing information and good communication, defined as attitude change towards these aspects of transportation.

2.1 Description of the Rail Cargo Challenge Game

The key objective of the Rail Cargo Challenge (RCC) was to assess the attitudes and behaviour of stakeholders in the freight transportation domain with respect to efficient transportation of containers through rail. The RCC is a multiplayer board game, set in the ambience of a seaport corridor connecting the port to several destinations in Europe. The roles in the game are two competing rail operators who can transport freight using rail by charging a price to shippers, who are played by the other participants. The shippers have to organize the transport of the containers from various container terminals in the port. In the first round of the game, there are three terminals A, B and C and three shippers in the game. Each shipper has order cards that denote the number of containers that need to be transported, the terminal in which they are stored, their destination and the time limit for transporting them. The rail operators have to pick up

---

[1] Decisions based on Collaborative Interactions in TEams.

freight from different terminals in the port at a pre-defined or a negotiated price. However, rail operators have only a limited capacity of picking up containers from different terminals. By throwing a dice, the number of terminals that can be visited is determined. All rail operators and shippers start with 50 tokens, each one representing a certain amount of money. The rail operators can arrange trains, each with a capacity of 10 containers for 10 tokens. The shippers can make arrangements with the rail operators to pick up their containers from a certain terminal at a specific price. If they can ship their containers successfully through rail they receive four tokens per shipment. If they fail to reach an agreement they have to send their containers through trucks to higher costs. The rail operators will benefit most if they can manage to fill up all their trains up to full capacity and make sure they can pick up shipments from the terminals as agreed with the shippers. If the dice is in their favour, and they are able to transport all containers as planned on time, they receive four tokens per shipment. If they fail to do so, they are responsible to ship the cargo using trucks that will cost them additional tokens. Additionally, the competitiveness of the port will drastically reduce if many containers are shipped using trucks instead of rail. In the subsequent rounds, two new terminals open up in the port. This makes the starting position of the containers more scattered across the port, while the rail services and frequency remain the same. The challenge of the game is to efficiently transport the dispersed freight through rail. At the end of the game play session, a de-briefing discussion is held to allow participants for reflection on the opportunities and challenges of rail transportation. The de-briefing includes a conversation on how innovative solutions like freight bundling help in increasing the efficiency and favourability of rail as a transport option for shippers, representing one alternative for freight bundling.

2.2   Participants and Experimental Set-Up

We organized a game session with 20 participants who were professionals in the Dutch logistics industry at a transport conference held at Tilburg, Netherlands. The session comprised three parts:

1. *Briefing and pre-survey* - The game master gave a brief introduction on the background of the game together with the game rules for about 10 min. He also mentioned the research aspect of the game and requested the participants to fill in a pre-game survey. In this survey, the participants were asked about their attitudes towards freight bundling together with their demographic information.
2. *Game-play* - The game play lasted one hour, and we only played two rounds of the game due to time limitations (see Fig. 1). We took observation notes during the game play related to the player decisions.
3. *De-briefing and post-survey* - The game master concluded the session by inviting the participants for a discussion on their game playing experience. We administered a post-game survey to measure the change in attitude of the players related to freight bundling using rail.

Fig. 1. Impression of the game board and play session of RCC.

2.3   Results

Pre-survey. On beforehand, the majority of the respondents agreed that rail bundling would increase rail efficiency by decreasing the amount of trains traveling empty or half empty. They also believed it could lead to lower costs and overall improvement of the sustainability of freight transport. The design of an efficient rail network, with optimized and synchronized schedules that permitted the consolidation of freight could increase the benefit of train modal share. According to the respondents, the promotion of collaboration between the different stakeholders had been a critical point.

On the other hand, professionals highlighted the challenges they expect to face when consolidating freight. For them, information and data sharing is one of the biggest hindrances in freight bundling together with legal issues that are expected to rise. Bundling is complex because it will require mode coordination, capacity availability and synchronization of modes and services to align transport containers within the time constraints given.

Post-survey. After the participants played the game they completed a post-game survey. Specifically they were asked to state their level of agreement in a scale where 1 = totally disagree and 7 = totally agree. Figure 2 shows the opinions on the game play. The figure shows five aspects that have been addressed by the game. The participants had to rate in how far they thought the game was able to illustrate the respective topics. In general, the participants agreed that the game gave them an insight on rail bundling and helped to reflect on the challenges and opportunities related to freight consolidation.

We then asked them to reconsider the opportunities and challenges and tried to observed modifications in their attitudes towards those. The generalized reflection is that we did not observe significant modifications in the replies of the stakeholders before and after the game session. They continued to believe that cost reduction, environmental benefits and higher rail efficiency are amongst the most important advantages of rail bundling. On the other hand, the majority of respondents highlighted the importance of designing e-solutions to enhance the provision of essential information for the scheduling of services. In addition, the adoption of profit-loss models is considered as one of the essential challenges that should be solved along with the related legal issues.

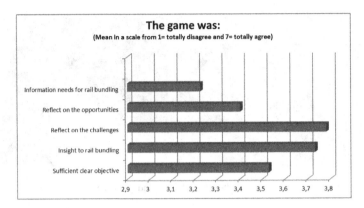

Fig. 2. The opinion of the participants about the game.

2.4   Discussion on the Rail Cargo Challenge Board Game

Positive Aspects of the Game Play. The participants were very enthusiastic to play the RCC. They were very playful with the tokens, cards and pawns of the game. Many participants requested to organize another session to play further rounds of the game play. Many critical points related to the challenges and opportunities of freight bundling were part of the de-briefing discussion. The design of the game is such that after inserting more terminals the players will fail because they will gradually decrease the reputation of the port and lose the cargo to the rival port. Shippers understand the importance of cooperating with the terminal operator because a low reputation port will impact their operations.

Challenges in the Game Play. The key challenges in the game play were to maintain the time for decision making in every round. The game was heavily dependent on the game master; therefore he had to explain several rules to the participants who often interrupted the game play. It was also challenging to keep track of all the decisions made by the players regarding price agreements and rail dispatching.

3   Case Study 2: Decision-Making in Airport Management

Air traffic is nowadays pressed by high demands on safety, punctuality, and economy. Therefore, it is necessary to use all capacities efficiently. To guarantee this, different stakeholders (e.g., airlines, air navigation service providers, airport authorities, ground handlers) have to work together. Particularly during disturbances all involved stakeholders must be included in the decision-making process to mitigate negative effects. As a result most European airports have already implemented the Airport Collaborative Decision-Making (A-CDM) [5, 6]. This concept allows the involved stakeholders to use a common database and share useful information with each other. But there are challenges, like divergent interests and goals, which make it hard to find a common solution. Because of this, it is relevant to model decision-making processes and find factors, which have an influence on the process in the area of airport management. With the help of the simulation games it is possible to analyze complex human decision-making processes.

3.1 Description of D-CITE

The simulation game D-CITE was initially developed as a research instrument with focus on human decision-making processes [7]. It exists as a digital and paper-based version. In the present paper the focus will be on the paper-based version (see Fig. 3). D-CITE is a round-based multi-player simulation game, which can be playable with four people. The roles are two airlines agents (it is possible to add more airline agents), one ground-handler agent and one airport agent. Moreover, a game master moderates the game play.

Fig. 3. Overview on the paper-based version of D-CITE.

The overall goal of all players is to optimize the business of an airport while playing the game. D-CITE consists of two phases for each round. The first phase is the planning phase, in which the players have the task of collaboratively optimizing a flight plan, taking critical events (e.g. thunderstorm) into consideration. These critical events lead to limited resources (e.g., a closed runway in one step). After finishing the planning phase, the simulation phase starts. In this phase the simulation of all planning activities is conducted. All players have to pay attention to and maximize their individual financial incomes and expenses. Each player has individual tasks to fulfill, which have an influence on the financial situation. Furthermore, there is a team score, which consists of the financial parameters of each player. The team score is an indicator of how good the team worked together. The higher the team score is, the better the whole team worked in collaboration. More details about the game mechanics can be found in [8] and an overview about the financial aspects of one paper-based version of D-CITE can be found in [9].

Studies [8, 10] have already shown that it is possible to transform D-CITE from a research instrument to a training environment. For example showed [10] already how playing D-CITE influences the attitude of airport managers towards A-CDM in a positive way. This study has been conducted to analyze a possible attitude change towards simulation games in general after playing D-CITE as well as to discuss pros and cons of paper-based games in contrast to digital ones.

3.2 Participants and Experimental Set-Up

A workshop was conducted with four participants from the Institute of Flight Guidance ($N = 4$, w = 1; M = 28.50 yrs., SD = 5.32 yrs., R = 23–34). One team was testing consisting of four players (airline red, airline yellow, airport agent, ground-handler agent). They already knew and played the digital version of D-CITE. No special training was necessary. The experimental set-up took about 90 min and consisted of three phases:

1. *Briefing and pre-survey* - After some minutes where the players had the chance to get to know each other, an introduction about the structure of the session was given. Then, D-CITE was introduced, whereas the focus was on changes in contrast to the digital version. After this, a demographic questionnaire and a questionnaire about simulation games were distributed. This phase lasted 15 min.
2. *Game-play* - During this phase all players took part in a round of D-CITE. This phase lasted 30 min. Observations during the game-play were noted.
3. *De-briefing and post-survey* - In the discussion phase the participants were asked about pros and cons of paper-based games. In addition to this, a post-survey was conducted.

In this study only four participants participated. Therefore, the data will only be analyzed descriptively. For more generalizable statements it is necessary to test more people.

3.3 Results

Attitude Measurement. Before actual game-play started, the familiarity (1 = familiar, 5 = not familiar) and thoughts about the use of simulation games (1 = positive, 5 = negative) were measured. The participants were familiar with simulation games (M = 2.25, SD = 0.96). Furthermore, they felt positive towards the use of simulation games (M = 2.25, SD = 0.50). The main focus is on the attitude change of the participants. Therefore, their attitude towards simulation games was measured before and after playing D-CITE. The attitude toward simulation gaming has changed slightly in a positive direction (1 = very positive, 5 = very negative, $M_{pre} = 2.25$, $SD_{pre} = 0.50$; $M_{post} = 2.00$, $SD_{post} = 0.00$).

Post-survey. During the post-survey, the participants had the task of fulfilling questions about the game, the role and design aspects of D-CITE and the abstracted degree of reality. The game is especially for the game-based learning approach relevant. The players should feel engaged and be motivated to learn (see Fig. 4). The results indicate that D-CITE is a well-designed game with focus on decision-making.

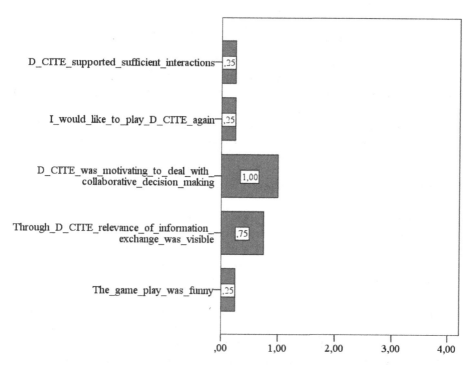

Fig. 4. The opinion of the participants about D-CITE (selected questions): mean scores (five-point scale from 0 = I agree through 4 = did not agree).

Observations. During the game play it was visible that all participants worked collaboratively until the end. Their primary goal was to maximize the team score. Furthermore, each player considered his or her own targets.

3.4   Discussion on the D-CITE Game Results

D-CITE is a simulation game to analyze human decision-making in the environment of airport management. In a first step it had been developed as a research instrument and was already successfully evaluated. The next step will be to transform D-CITE to a training environment. In the area of game-based learning it is necessary to have a positive attitude towards simulation games. It is easier to conduct a simulation game session if the players are open to simulation games. The results of the participants have shown that the attitude towards simulation games in general can be positively changed. It could be possible that the collected experience during the game-play can influence real-life attitudes.

Positive Aspects of the Game Play. The participants enjoyed the higher number of social interactions during the game play in contrast to the digital version of D-CITE. This led to a better understanding for the other players, their particular tasks, and to a higher situational awareness. All participants had a better understanding of the gameplay from the paper-based game cards, game board, and tokens. The closer cooperation in contrast to the digital version was fun for all participants.

Challenges in the Game Play. One of the main challenges is that playing the paper-based version of D-CITE took more time than the digital version. One reason for this is that one must move the tokens by yourself. This can result in mistakes or in accidental movements of the tokens.

The limited number of participants has to be discussed. It is not possible to derive generalizable statements. To do this more participants have to be analyzed.

4 Discussion and Conclusion

The main objective of this paper is to understand the value and limitations of board game to conduct research in the transportation domain despite the availability of digital tools in today's technological society. Therefore, two case studies were conducted. In the first study, attitudes towards and solutions in the field of synchromodal hinterland transportation were addressed. The second study considered attitude change in the area of airport management. Before and after playing rounds of D-CITE, attitude questionnaires were distributed. The results have shown a slightly positive attitude change towards serious games in general. Moreover, based on our experience with the Rail Cargo Challenge and D-CITE we will present the advantages and disadvantages of board games. The principle advantages of the board game are the social cohesion and interaction offered by the board game environment. Participants have a shared view of the game environment and can interact naturally. The physical elements of the board game such as tokens, cards and pawns increase the fun element of an otherwise serious play. It is relatively inexpensive to create prototypes of the board games. Board games also produce rich qualitative data. [11] also shares our view on the ease of prototyping and the social and flexible environment of the board games. On the flip side, we observed that data collection was very difficult during a board game session. It was not possible to collect sufficient quantitative data from the session. [11] also acknowledges this disadvantage. The presence of the game master, while adding to the social environment to the game, poses a challenge with respect to scalability and portability of board games to conduct extensive research studies. The issues of scalability of board games are also highlighted in [12] work on transferring board games to digital games. We can conclude that, despite the limitations related to data collection and portability, board games offer a valuable social environment to observe the behaviour of participants in their natural form. Therefore board games are valuable research instruments even in today's digital era.

In future studies, we will include more participants to generate more generalizable results. To make more comparable statements, it is furthermore necessary to focus on identical research instruments in different experimental set-ups. This makes an objective comparison challenging. However, the focus of the present paper was not only on attitude change via different methods, but on the advantages and disadvantages of board games. As D-CITE exists as both physical and digital version, we would like to conduct sessions with both versions, to find out more on the advantages and disadvantages of both technologies. It's also very interesting to investigate how expert players value the fidelity, or level of realism that can only be limited in physical games. The fidelity might affect the results of the game sessions, and how these can influence the attitudes of the players. This will also be subject of future studies.

References

1. Taylor, M.A.P., D'Este, G.M.: Transport network vulnerability a method for diagnosis of critical locations in transport infrastructure systems. In: Murray, A.T., Grubesic, T.H. (eds.) Critical Infrastructure, pp. 9–30. Springer, Heidelberg (2007). https://doi.org/10.1007/978-3-540-68056-7_2
2. Van Os, M.: Using gaming as a data collection tool to design rules for agents in agent-based models. Delft University of Technology (2012)
3. Bontekoning, Y.M.: The importance of new generation freight terminals for intermodal transport. J. Adv. Transp. **34**(3), 391–413 (2000)
4. Kreutzberger, E.: Lowest cost intermodal rail freight transport bundling networks: conceptual structuring and identification. EJITR **10**(2), 158–180 (2010)
5. EUROCONTROL: Airport CDM Operational Concept Document (2006). http://www.euro-cdm.org/library/cdm_ocd.pdf. Accessed 10 Mar 2017
6. Günther, Y., Inard, A., Werther, B., Bonnier, M., Spies, G., Marsden, A., Temme, M., Böhme, D., Lane, R., Niederstrasser, H.: Total Airport Management (2006). http://www.bs.dlr.de/tam/Dokuments/TAM-OCD-public.pdf. Accessed 10 Mar 2017
7. Freese, M., Drees, S., Meinecke, M.: Between game and reality: using serious games to analyze complex interaction processes in air traffic management. In: Kaneda, T., Kanegae, H., Toyoda, Y., Rizzi, P. (eds.) Simulation and Gaming in the Network Society. TSS, vol. 9, pp. 275–289. Springer, Singapore (2016). https://doi.org/10.1007/978-981-10-0575-6_20
8. Schier, S., Freese, M., Mühlhausen, T.: Serious gaming in airport management: transformation from a validation tool to a learning environment. In: Bottino, R., Jeuring, J., Veltkamp, Remco C. (eds.) GALA 2016. LNCS, vol. 10056, pp. 187–196. Springer, Cham (2016). https://doi.org/10.1007/978-3-319-50182-6_17
9. Metz, I., Freese, M., Schier, S.: Integrating bird strike risk information into the airport management system. In: Proceedings of the Deutscher Luft- und Raumfahrtkongress (2016)
10. Freese, M.: Game-based learning – an approach for improving collaborative airport management. In: Proceedings of the 10th European Conference on Games Based Learning (2016)
11. Meijer, S.: The power of sponges: comparing high-tech and low-tech gaming for innovation. Simul. Gaming **46**(5), 512–535 (2015)
12. Lukosch, H., Kurapati, S., Bekebrede, G., Tiemersma, S., Groen, D., van Veen, L., Verbraeck, A.: Design considerations for building a scalable digital version of a multi-player educational board game for a MOOC in logistics and transportation. In: Bottino, R., Jeuring, J., Veltkamp, R.C. (eds.) GALA 2016. LNCS, vol. 10056, pp. 167–176. Springer, Cham (2016). https://doi.org/10.1007/978-3-319-50182-6_15

Learning

Assessment of Hybrid Board Game-Based Learning Outcomes Using the Beatty Theoretical Framework

Abby Muricho Onencan[(⊠)]

Multi-Actor Systems (MAS) Department, Faculty of Technology,
Policy, and Management, Delft University of Technology,
P.O. Box 5015, 2600 GA Delft, The Netherlands
a.m.onencan@tudelft.nl

Abstract. Hybrid board games draw benefits from both the digital and physical worlds. They increase social interaction and provide an enjoyable, seamless experience. Nevertheless, hybrid artefacts do not fit snugly into established game genres, leading to ambiguity regarding the selection of measurement tools. To address this challenge, a video game assessment framework, as outlined in Beatty (2014), was selected. It has a generic template, four dimensions with their respective templates (macro-level, micro-level, builder meta-level and social meta-level) and two feedback loops. This framework was applied from April to August 2016 in Kenya, to assess the learning outcomes of the Nzoia WeShareIt game. Results indicate that the framework could provide a solution for assessing hybrid board games, subject to some adjustments, as outlined in this paper. Future work may entail application of the framework, in other drainage basins.

Keywords: Assessment · Game-based learning · Complexity science
Board games · Digital games · Hybrid games · Theoretical framework

1 Introduction

The global game market is rapidly growing, with an estimated revenue of 108.9 billion in 2017 [1]. As new hybrid games emerge, corresponding assessment frameworks are being developed or customized. With this massive growth, should there be generic "multi-purpose frameworks for evaluating games" [2 p. 233], or are games too diverse to fall into straight-jackets? This complicated question is not the focus of this paper. However, it triggers discourse and enhances learning.

Klabbers (2009) defines a game as "any contest or effort (play) among adversaries or teammates (players) operating under constraints (rules and resources) for an objective (winning, victory, prestige, status, or pay-off)" [3 p. 33]. A hybrid game is one that is designed for players to experience both the virtual and physical realities, simultaneously. An assessment is "the process of using data to demonstrate that stated goals and objectives are being met" [4 p. 2]. Assessment of game-based learning is the use of data to establish whether a particular game has facilitated the attainment of teaching and learning objectives [5].

© Springer International Publishing AG, part of Springer Nature 2018
H. K. Lukosch et al. (Eds.): ISAGA 2017, LNCS 10825, pp. 161–172, 2018.
https://doi.org/10.1007/978-3-319-91902-7_16

Assessments are vital in establishing a niche for game-based learning, in diverse fields and sectors [6, 7]. Examples include, games assessing: situation awareness in a logistics value chain [8]; upper extremity motor dysfunctions [9]; cooperative learning in design studios [9]; values in the design of socially-oriented games [10]; pain application for adolescents with cancer [11]; content validity for ICT managers [12]; influence on sustainable behaviour in higher education institutions [13]; effectiveness of blended e-learning in secondary schools [14]; residents preparedness for emergencies [15]; and patients' dynamic balance when undergoing rehabilitation [16]. Therefore, assessments are diverse and span multiple sectors and fields.

Since assessments mainly influence the creation of niche markets, many game design applications have custom-made assessments, as part of the game design. Examples of assessment frameworks designed for specific games are: the three dialogs [17], designed for the Gamestar mechanic [18]; the post-test assessment framework for second language acquisition [19]; the PACE framework, for a localised iterative language learning game [20]; the game-based stealth assessment to assess skills and abilities through learners interactions [21]; and the C-VAT 2.0 assessment tool for a game that clinically tests disorders [22]. Harteveld's (2011) triadic game design [23] also supports game assessment. Thus, custom-made assessments are useful, if there are no time and budget constraints, and especially when the game is new in the market, with no corresponding tools.

Alternatively, some scholars argue that there exists untapped potential, due to the absence of a formalized approach or overarching methodology to game evaluations [2, 24, 25]. In response, game experts designed some generic frameworks. These include: (1) Beatty (2014) "video games as a theoretical framework for instructional design" [26]; (2) Mitgutsch (2012) "serious game design assessment framework" [25]; (3) Annetta et. al (2011) "serious educational game assessment" [27]; (4) Winn (2009) "design, play and experience" framework [24]; (5) Sanchez (2011) key game design criteria through "a framework" [28]; and (6) Mayer (2012) "comprehensive methodology for the research and evaluation of serious games" [2].

In deciding which framework to select for the Nzoia WeShareIt game, we preferred the generic frameworks over custom-made assessment frameworks. There is a danger of not maintaining internal consistency, reliability, and validity when further adopting custom-made tools. The frameworks of Annetta et al. (2011), Winn (2009) and Sanchez (2011), were not selected because the Nzoia WeShareIt game assessment purpose was different from their respective assessment purposes. The Nzoia WeShareIt assessment framework seeks to assess more than the game content and whether the design, play, and interactions between players contribute to the game purpose. Beatty (2014) was selected instead of Mitgutsch (2012) and Mayer (2012) because it is easy to design and contained all the sought game assessment framework components. The paper seeks to assess whether the Beatty framework, designed for video games, applies to hybrid board games. The paper concludes that the framework applies to hybrid board games, subject to certain limitations, as explained in the discussion section.

2 Background

2.1 Nzoia WeShareIt Game

Nzoia WeShareIt is a hybrid board game designed to enhance water partnerships between policymakers through harnessing their respective comparative advantages, in the Nzoia catchment [29]. We designed the game to address the challenges of weak cooperation and low trust, as identified during the Nile Basin by 2050 scenario development process [30–34]. Nzoia catchment comprises of six local governments (Trans-Nzoia, Uasin-Gishu, Kakamega, Bungoma, Siaya, and Busia). Water partnerships between these governments were weak, leading to unsustainable management of the catchment area [31]. Strengthened water partnerships would lead to increased water access, food production, and energy.

The game comprises of two parts; a trading and water allocation part. In the trading part, the countries trade in food, energy and wood fuel. In the allocation part, they make water allocation decisions aimed at increasing productivity and ensuring that their citizens are happy. A climate change round (fourth) is introduced to increase trust, situation awareness, and collaborative actions. In this round, all their resources are halved, encouraging governments to manage the food and energy crises, jointly.

2.2 The Beatty (2014) Framework

Beatty framework (see Fig. 1), is designed to address complex multi-actor system challenges through multiple layers [35]. The multi-layer phenomena, facilitates systematic mastery of specific skills, through iteration and leveling up. Beatty designed the framework based on learning principles from various research professional [35], including McGonigal (2011), [36] Gee (2005, 2007) [37, 38], Squire (2006) [39] and Steinkuehler (2006) [40].

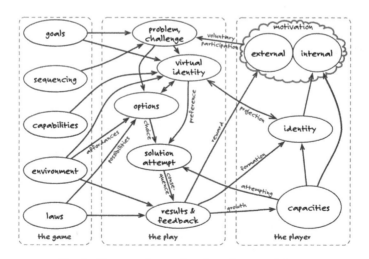

Fig. 1. The generic template for a framework layer.

The Beatty framework comprises of the generic template, four core templates, and two feedback loops. The generic template is the basic template that guides the overall design of the other templates and assessment tools. The micro-level game layer focuses on problem-solving and learning (both facts and skills). The macro-level game layer is designed to assess players experience of the world, storyline, and learning (professional attitudes and identity). The builder, meta-level game layer, assesses whether the players were part of the game development. The social meta-level game layer evaluates social experiences within the group and the extent that social identity is developed. The Intrinsic motivation and exploratory learning loop measure the quality of the learning environment and player motivation. Finally, we did not exclusively integrate the identity loop, into the feedback form. We incorporated this loop into the in-game data collection tool and in-game questionnaire.

3   Methods

3.1   Participants

Beatty framework was applied from April to August 2016 in Kenya, to assess the learning outcomes of the Nzoia WeShareIt game. 35 (23 male and 12 female) policymakers, between the ages of eighteen and sixty-four, participated in the game sessions. We conducted seven-game sessions on different days, in four of the six county governments (Trans-Nzoia, Bungoma, Kakamega, and Busia). All the participants were Kenyans from the public sector, water companies, and other private institutions.

3.2   Procedures

The assessment of the game is through pre-game, in-game, post-game questionnaires, debriefing sessions, observations and rough-cut videos clips. The theoretical framework was used to design the post-game questionnaire (Fig. 2).

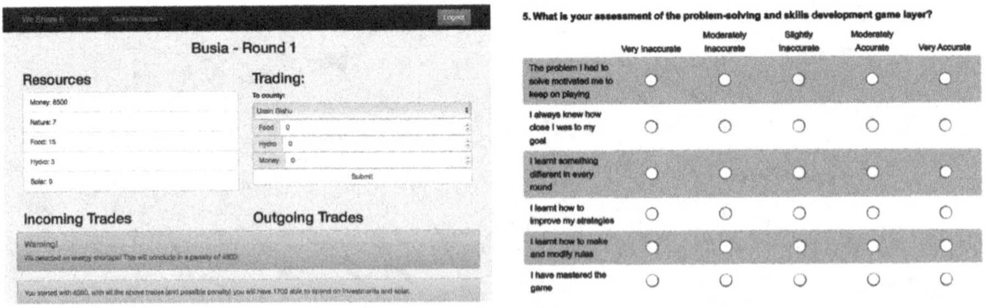

Fig. 2. Screenshots of the (a) first screen of the Nzoia WeShareIt game with a button on the top left that enables the players to access both the pre-game and post-game questionnaires; and (b) the Survey-monkey post-game questionnaire with the microgame layer questions.

3.3   Statistical Analysis

The paper's purpose is to consider whether the Beatty theoretical framework applies to hybrid board games. This sub-section seeks to answer two procedural questions: (1) does the Nzoia WeShareIt post-game questionnaire demonstrate content validity? Moreover, (2) does the modified Beatty framework maintain internal reliability, when applied in a hybrid board game, in the form of questionnaires? In this section, we discuss these procedural questions in detail and make conclusions.

3.3.1   Content Validity Analysis

Before adopting the designed post-game questionnaire, we undertook a content validity analysis, through an iterative process. We assessed whether the questionnaire: (1) measured the Beatty framework elements; (2) incorporated all the essentials; (3) had no overlaps and (4) and is replicable. Several drafts were developed and mirrored against the framework to remove overlaps, add content that was not captured and reword questions to ensure critical components are measured and guarantee replicability (see Fig. 3). The final questionnaire was found to demonstrate content validity.

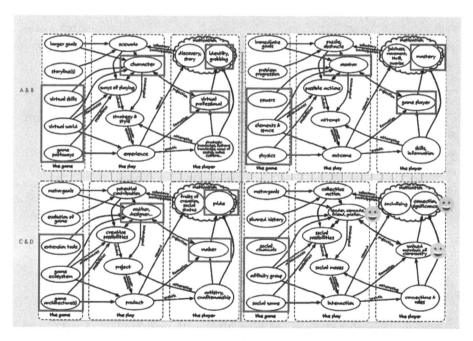

Fig. 3. The outcome of the content validity analysis. (a) micro-level; (b) macro-level; (c) builder meta-level; and (d) social meta-level. The red rectangles represent elements that were not adequately measured by the post-game questionnaire. Place consistency between missing elements in the various templates was an important outcome of the analysis. The same place where elements were not sufficiently measured in template A was replicated in subsequent templates, though the content changed. Nevertheless, some elements were addressed in the game design and measured by the in-game assessment tool. The drought round increased player interaction and compensated for the missing elements in the questionnaire (Color figure online).

3.3.2   Chi-Square Goodness of Fit Analysis

The test was conducted to check whether the modified Beatty framework maintained internal reliability when applied in a hybrid board game, in the form of questionnaires. Chi-square goodness of fit test was applied because n was above 5 and the variables are categorical. Since n = 35, the specified distribution is an equal distribution on a five-point Likert scale (35/5 = 7). The null hypothesis provides that the data is consistent with the specified distribution (equal distribution of 7 in all the responses). The alternative hypothesis provides that the data is not consistent with a specified distribution. The p-value is calculated using the CHISQ.TEST function. Alternatively, the level of significance (α) is calculated using the CHISQ.INV.RT function. As illustrated in Fig. 4, $p \leq \alpha$, in all the responses. Therefore we rejected the null hypothesis, and the alternative hypothesis is adopted. Based on the findings of the chi-square goodness of fit test, the survey monkey data is considered reliable.

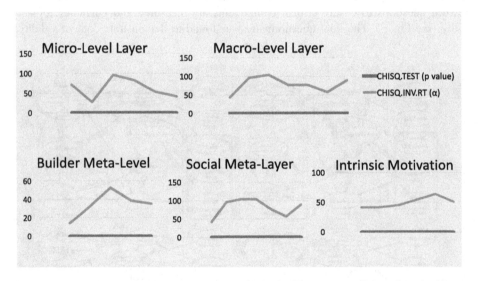

Fig. 4. Results of the reliability assessment. In all the findings $p < \alpha$ and there is a significant difference between p and α, which increases the reliability of the findings.

4   Results

A significant proportion of the results is positive, as illustrated in Figs. 5 and 6, with a few areas that need improvement. Majority of the responses fall between the "very accurate" and "moderately accurate" range. The highest number of responses, in all the categories, is the "very accurate" response. In addition to the positive outcomes, the results indicate essential areas that need further development.

The findings identified several critical areas that need further development. First, the builder's meta-level should be adjusted to provide more room for players to co-design, change rules and make rules. Second, missing or weak links between the primary goal, actions leading to a mastery of skills and the player's strategies, needs to be strengthened. Third, the macro-level layer's storyline was not clear. The players preferred a simulated game that reflects the actual circumstances in the watershed. Fourth, the players recommended improvement of the user interface to increase players' interaction with two worlds, three identities, and three interfaces.

The rating average function provided vital information that we could not derive directly from the survey monkey feedback (Figs. 5 and 6).

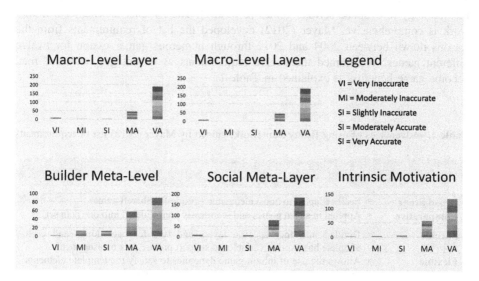

Fig. 5. Results from implementation of the Beatty framework in Nzoia Basin

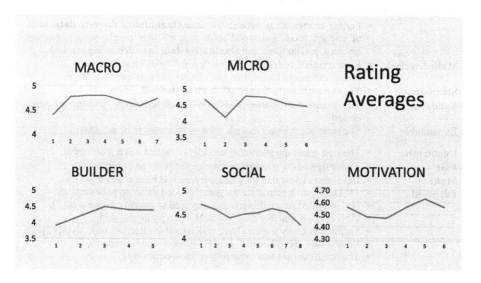

Fig. 6. Rating averages for all the responses.

5   Discussion

This section will critically discuss the advantages and limitations of using the Beatty framework and examine whether the framework applies to hybrid board games.

5.1   Advantages of Using the Theoretical Framework

This discussion is guided by Mayer (2012) list of requirements and comprehensive methodology to evaluate serious games [2 p. 237]. The list checks whether a framework is comprehensive. Mayer (2012) developed the list of requirements from the lessons drawn between 2004 and 2012 through numerous game session for twelve different games. We framed the twelve requirements as advantages, which if met, become game benefits, as explained in Table 1.

Table 1. Advantages of using Beatty framework, guided by Mayer (2012) list of requirements

ADVANTAGE	HOW THE FRAMEWORK MEETS REQUIREMENTS
Broad Scope	▪ Easily adapted to non-video game - Nzoia WeShareIt game.
Comparative	▪ Applied in seven games and seamlessly consolidated into one data set.
Specific	▪ Divided into four specific layers and two feedback loops and each template has explicit variables to support precise data measurement
Flexible	▪ Allows the use of inbuilt game dynamics to satisfy the template elements that were eliminated when designing the questionnaire.
Triangulated	▪ **Quantitative: Continuous:** time and money. ▪ **Qualitative: (1) Categorical:** gender, education, country, local authority, industry, knowledge of gaming; and (2) **Ordinal:** Rankings, survey monkey questions on a five-point Likert scale. ▪ Further triangulation through in-game **Quantitative discrete data:** units of energy, food, and wood sold, unit of solar panels bought, amount invested, and so forth, and **Qualitative data** from debriefing sessions.
Multi-Levelled	▪ Each template is divided into the "game," "play" and "player." ▪ Micro and macro layers, two meta-layers and two feedback loops.
Standardised	▪ The comprehensive framework leads to standardization.
Validated	▪ The inclusion of "game" and "play" in all templates validates the game design.
Expandable	▪ The template is broad enough for new measures to be added.
Unobtrusive	▪ The post-game questionnaire was highly ranked and not obtrusive.
Fast	▪ The design of the questionnaires was fast, easy and economical.
Multi-Purposed	▪ Developers know that the game purpose had been attained [41]. ▪ TU Delft can demonstrate the game's added value, to policymakers. ▪ Has informed future designs and may lead to improved upgrades [7]. ▪ Players know whether they had mastered a particular skill. ▪ Facilitators know learners have understood the learning objectives[42]. ▪ Results can strengthen the niche for game-based learning [6, 7]. ▪ The results ensure accountability and responsibility [2].

5.2   Limitations of Using the Theoretical Framework

Beatty framework's application resulted in many benefits, as outlined in the previous sub-section and also limitations. We grouped the limitations into three main groups, namely: the framing of the words, the challenge of undertaking comparative and longitudinal research and practical/technical limitations of adopting a video game assessment framework for a hybrid board game.

Framing is a critical issue when adopting an assessment framework from a different genre of games. The framing of words in video games and hybrid board games is different. Examples of words used in the Beatty framework that are common in video games and though known by hybrid board game developers, are rarely used, include powers, elements, space, avatar, thrill, identity grokking, virtual professional, virtual skills, virtual world, affinity group and virtual identity. Some words may not be appropriate, due to the nature of the game. Some may be applicable but may eventually not have a comfortable resting place in the customized assessment framework. Some of these words are applicable but need to be reframed to reflect or communicate the same meaning to a different audience. Since these words form a critical part of the assessment, accurate framing and reframing are essential to the success of the customized framework. If we missed the meanings, then customization will not be an accurate reflection of the original framework. We addressed this major challenge by research and consultation. Eventually, based on the research and consultation outcomes, we left some parts out of the customized framework.

Challenges that accompany comparative and longitudinal research was also another limitation. WeShareIt game is a hybrid board game. The stand-alone game transverses two game genres, digital games, and board games. Also, the game seeks to simulate a drainage basin in Kenya. Additionally, simulation and trans-boundary water management are complex fields. We heightened the complexity when we adopted the video game assessment framework for a hybrid board game. To address this, we conducted in-depth research to understand the framework and the context it is embedded. Also, the process of designing the assessment framework underwent several iterations, while synchronizing with the Nzoia policymakers and other stakeholders, to ensure that the final product met framework requirements, was replicable, comparable and met the game goals and the needs of the beneficiaries.

Finally, there were practical/technical limitations to adopting the Beatty framework. Beatty framework was preferred to other known frameworks because it was not a high-level model. It specifies what needs to be assessed, in great detail. However, since Beatty designed the framework for video games, we made some adjustments to the measured elements, as illustrated in Fig. 3. As a consequence, some elements were not measured in the post-game questionnaire, as planned, but incorporated in the in-game assessments. Moreover, time and resource constraints led to the design of the assessment tool separate from the game and after that linking it to the game. Thus limiting the number of elements that could be measured. Measuring all the elements would make the assessment long and tedious and would affect the final results.

These trade-offs had definite effects on the quality of the assessment. However, according to Fig. 3, it was evident that the non-measured elements in the first two templates were compensated by the in-game assessment, leading to a positive outcome.

The flexibility of the framework was a positive indication of applicability outside the realm of video games. Based on the findings, we safely concluded that despite the challenges, we overcame all the three limitations.

5.3   Applicability of the Beatty Theoretical Framework

The Beatty framework holds a promise for future assessment of hybrid board games because of the positive findings from its application. Additionally, the benefits derived from the game outcomes outweigh the three limitations, as explained in Sect. 5.2. Moreover, the process of addressing the challenges increases knowledge and builds synergies between different disciplines.

Importantly, the pressing questions that we seek to address are: why should this framework be applied to hybrid board games, since it belongs to a different field of game development? Why should the framework be selected, if it augments complexity, increases framing issues, involves extensive comparative and longitudinal research and leads to practical/technical limitation challenges?

The global game market is rapidly growing, and we are at a critical point when game experts are constructing the game layer. Undoubtedly, the construction of a game layer is more critical than the current Facebook social layer. Games use dynamics that are consciously or unconsciously incorporated to influence behavior. Since games influence behavior, they affect people acutely and mostly, unconsciously. To build efficient game dynamics requires persons who are willing to span through the already established boundaries and strengthen collaboration between critical game developer groups.

Video game developers are at the forefront of generating most of the games that influence our day to day lives. These developers have mastered the skill of drawing large groups to play games for extended periods of time. Game-based learning experts have mastered the skills of developing games that enhance learning for the social good, in specialized fields. A mix of these two skills and a combination of these two game developer worlds is a necessity. However, since most of these developers are busy designing more games, in their respective fields, we need a practical approach to bring these groups together. Sharing frameworks is one of the practical ways to learn and get into another game developer world and experience it.

Admittedly, the Beatty framework is not only applicable because the results were beneficial and outweighed the limitations, but also because it is a baby-step towards bridging two game-worlds to solve global challenges, together. Future work may entail applying the WeShareIt game and its assessment framework in other drainage basins, in Kenya.

References

1. Newzoo: The Global Games Market Will Reach $108.9 Billion in 2017 With Mobile Taking 42%. Newzoo, Amsterdam (2017)
2. Mayer, I.: Towards a comprehensive methodology for the research and evaluation of serious games. Proc. Comput. Sci. **15**, 233–247 (2012)

3. Klabbers, J.H.: The Magic Circle: Principles of Gaming and Simulation. Sense Publishers, Rotterdam (2009)
4. Chin, J., Dukes, R., Gamson, W.: Assessment in simulation and gaming a review of the last 40 years. Simul. Gaming **40**(4), 553–568 (2009)
5. Ifenthaler, D., Eseryel, D., Ge, X.: Assessment for game-based learning. In: Ifenthaler, D., Eseryel, D., Ge, X. (eds.) Assessment in game-based learning, pp. 1–8. Springer, New York (2012). https://doi.org/10.1007/978-1-4614-3546-4_1
6. Connolly, T., Stansfield, M., Hainey, T.: Towards the development of a games-based learning evaluation framework. In: Games-Based Learning Advancements for Multisensory Human Computer Interfaces: Techniques and Effective Practices. IGI Global, Hershey (2009)
7. Loh, C.S., Sheng, Y., Ifenthaler, D.: Serious games analytics: theoretical framework. In: Loh, C.S., Sheng, Y., Ifenthaler, D. (eds.) Serious Games Analytics. AGL, pp. 3–29. Springer, Cham (2015). https://doi.org/10.1007/978-3-319-05834-4_1
8. Klemke, R., Kurapati, S., Lukosch, H., Specht, M.: Lessons learned from creating a mobile version of an educational board game to increase situational awareness. In: Conole, G., Klobučar, T., Rensing, C., Konert, J., Lavoué, É. (eds.) EC-TEL 2015. LNCS, vol. 9307, pp. 183–196. Springer, Cham (2015). https://doi.org/10.1007/978-3-319-24258-3_14
9. Shih, S.-G., Hu, T.-P., Chen, C.-N.: A game theory-based approach to the analysis of cooperative learning in design studios. Des. Stud. **27**(6), 711–722 (2006)
10. Flanagan, M., Howe, D.C., Nissenbaum, H.: Values at play: design tradeoffs in socially-oriented game design. In: Proceedings of the SIGCHI Conference on Human Factors in Computing Systems. ACM (2005)
11. Stinson, J.N., et al.: Development and testing of a multidimensional iPhone pain assessment application for adolescents with cancer. J. Med. Internet Res. **15**(3), e51 (2013)
12. Hummel, H.G., et al.: Content validity of game-based assessment: case study of a serious game for ICT managers in training. Technol. Pedagog. Educ. **26**(2), 225–240 (2017)
13. Mercer, T.G., et al.: The use of educational game design and play in higher education to influence sustainable behaviour. Int. J. Sustain. High. Educ. **18**(3), 359–384 (2017)
14. Reynolds, R., Leeder, C.: Information uses and learning outcomes during guided discovery in a blended e-learning game design program for secondary computer science education. In: Proceedings of the 50th Hawaii International Conference on System Sciences (2017)
15. Dankbaar, M.E., et al.: Preparing residents effectively in emergency skills training with a serious game. Simul. Healthc. **12**(1), 9 (2017)
16. Lange, B., et al.: Development of an interactive game-based rehabilitation tool for dynamic balance training. Top. Stroke Rehabil. **17**(5), 345–352 (2010)
17. Games, I.A.: Three dialogs: a framework for the analysis and assessment of twenty-first-century literacy practices, and its use in the context of game design within gamestar mechanic. E-Learn. Digital Media **5**(4), 396–417 (2008)
18. Salen, K.: Gaming literacies: a game design study in action. J. Educ. Multimedia Hypermedia **16**(3), 301 (2007)
19. Rankin, Y.A., et al.: User centered game design: evaluating massive multiplayer online role playing games for second language acquisition. In: Proceedings of the 2008 ACM SIGGRAPH Symposium on Video Games. ACM (2008)
20. Kam, M., et al.: Localized iterative design for language learning in underdeveloped regions: the PACE framework. In: Proceedings of the SIGCHI Conference on Human Factors in Computing Systems. ACM (2007)
21. Shute, V.J., Moore, G.R.: Consistency and validity in game-based stealth assessment. In: Technology enhanced innovative assessment: development, modeling, and scoring from an interdisciplinary perspective. Information Age Publisher, Charlotte (2017)

22. Van Rooij, A.J., Schoenmakers, T.M., Van De Mheen, D.: Clinical validation of the C-VAT 2.0 assessment tool for gaming disorder: a sensitivity analysis of the proposed DSM-5 criteria and the clinical characteristics of young patients with 'video game addiction'. Addict. Behav. **64**, 269–274 (2017)
23. Harteveld, C.: Triadic game design: balancing reality, meaning and play. Springer Science & Business Media, Heidelberg (2011). https://doi.org/10.1007/978-1-84996-157-8
24. Winn, B.M.: The design, play, and experience framework. In: Handbook of Research on Effective Electronic Gaming in Education, pp. 1010–1024. IGI Global (2009)
25. Mitgutsch, K., Alvarado, N.: Purposeful by design?: a serious game design assessment framework. In: Proceedings of the International Conference on the Foundations of Digital Games. ACM (2012)
26. Beatty, I.D.: Gaming the system: video games as a theoretical framework for instructional design (2014)
27. Annetta, L.A., Bronack, S.: Serious educational game assessment: practical methods and models for educational games, simulations and virtual worlds. Springer Science & Business Media, Heidelberg (2011). https://doi.org/10.1007/978-94-6091-329-7
28. Sanchez, E.: Key criteria for game design. A framework (2011)
29. Onencan, A., et al.: WeShareIt game: strategic foresight for climate-change induced disaster risk reduction. Proc. Eng. **159**, 307–315 (2016)
30. Enserink, B., Onencan, A.: Nile Basin Scenario Construction (2017)
31. Onencan, A.: TU Delft serious game elevates Nzoia (2017). uuid:91914ae3-453b-458a-ab58-555789a4533c
32. Onencan, A., et al.: Weshareit: a nexus approach to Nile basin water resources management. Decis. Making Under Deep Uncertain. (2015). uuid:13043885-19e2-44dc-adef-2155 db774832
33. Onencan, A., et al.: Coupling Nile basin 2050 scenarios with the IPCC 2100 projections for climate-induced risk reduction. In: Humanitarian Technology: Science, Systems and Global Impact 2016, HumTech2016, Boston, USA (2016)
34. Onencan, A.M., Enserink, B.: The Nile Basin By 2050: Strategic Foresight on the Nile Basin Water Governance, 28 February 2014
35. Onencan, A., et al.: MAFURIKO: design of Nzoia basin location based flood game. Proc. Eng. **159**, 133–140 (2016)
36. McGonigal, J.: Reality Is Broken: Why Games Make Us Better and How They Can Change the World. Penguin Group, New York (2011)
37. Gee, J.P.: What Video Games Have to Teach Us About Learning and Literacy, 2nd edn. Palgrave MacMillan, Basingstoke (2007)
38. Gee, J.P.: What would a state of the art instructional video game look like. Innovate **7**(6), 1–6 (2005)
39. Squire, K.: From content to context: videogames as designed experience. Educ. Res. **55**(8), 19–29 (2006)
40. Steinkuehler, C.A.C.: Fostering scientific habits of mind in the context of online play. In: Presented at the Proceedings of the 7th International Conference on Learning Sciences. International Society of the Learning Sciences (2006)
41. Emmerich, K., Bockholt, M.: Serious games evaluation: processes, models, and concepts. In: Dörner, R., Göbel, S., Kickmeier-Rust, M., Masuch, M., Zweig, K. (eds.) Entertainment Computing and Serious Games. LNCS, vol. 9970, pp. 265–283. Springer, Cham (2016). https://doi.org/10.1007/978-3-319-46152-6_11
42. Michael, D.R., Chen, S.L.: Serious Games: Games that Educate, Train, and Inform. Muska & Lipman/Premier-Trade, Roseville (2005)

The Effects of Debriefing on the Performance and Attitude of Japanese University Students

Toshiko Kikkawa[1(✉)], Junkichi Sugiura[1], and Willy Christian Kriz[2]

[1] Keio University, 2-15-45, Mita, Minato-Ku, 108-8345 Tokyo, Japan
tompei22@keio.jp
[2] FHV University Vorarlberg, Hochschulstrasse 1, 6850 Dornbirn, Austria

Abstract. The present study examined the effects of debriefing on 171 Japanese university students as part of an international collaboration between Austria and Japan. There were eight experimental conditions, as follows: control group without treatment, fun game with no debriefing, Prisoner's Dilemma (PD) game with no debriefing, PD game with self-completed debriefing, PD game with guided written debriefing, PD game with guided written debriefing and a conceptual frame, no game but reading of a text, and no game but study of a picture. Following completion of these activities, groups of four participants then played the Highway Planning Game [1], which deals with cooperation and conflict. Although performance during the Highway Planning Game did not significantly differ among the groups (probably because of the small number of groups), there were interesting differences in terms of performance and attitudes that will stimulate further research.

Keywords: Debriefing · Learning · Engagement · Cooperation
Conflict

1 Introduction

The effects of debriefing are of primary interest in the field of simulation and gaming. Because gaming simulations represent various aspects of reality, the question arises as to how the experiences and results of games for a given participant are related back to their own reality and context. The term "debriefing" refers to a method used to combine participants' reflections on their experiences with the assessment of mental (cognition, emotion, etc.), social (action, communication, etc.), and reference systems (change of resources, structures, etc.) processes to deduce applications for real situations beyond the gaming simulation experience [2]. The use of gaming simulations that allow for experiential learning, in conjunction with debriefing, has a long history of creating active and engaging learning opportunities [3]. Debriefing can be defined as "the process in which people who have had an experience are led through a purposive discussion of that experience" [p. 146; 4]. Gaming simulations without adequate debriefing are often considered to be ineffective, and it is widely understood that effective learning is dependent on reflection during the debriefing process [5–7]. In terms of debriefing in educational gaming simulations, learning stems from the debriefing rather than from the

© Springer International Publishing AG, part of Springer Nature 2018
H. K. Lukosch et al. (Eds.): ISAGA 2017, LNCS 10825, pp. 173–180, 2018.
https://doi.org/10.1007/978-3-319-91902-7_17

game itself [8]. In fact, Crookall proposed a formula to this effect, as follows: "[(Simulation/game + proper debriefing) × engagement] = learning" [p. 419; 9].

Although many good arguments have been derived from theories of learning and instruction regarding why and how debriefing is an important factor in learning during gaming, remarkably few studies have attempted to research this crucial element empirically. For example, Crookall's formula has never been supported by empirical data. Additionally, a review of the literature reveals two major weaknesses of past research. First, few systematic studies with sound methodologies have been conducted. Second, many studies utilized only questionnaire data to measure the outcomes of gaming and, as a result, performance data are lacking.

The aim of the present study was to address these gaps in the literature and overcome the weaknesses of previous studies. Our group began a research project to this end in 2016 and performed the first experiments in 2017; as a result, a large amount of performance data remains to be produced. Thus, the primary aim of the present paper was to describe our research approach and to discuss the initial pre-post questionnaire and group performance data. More specifically, the present study examined the effects of different types of debriefing, using a no debriefing condition as a control. Because several experimental conditions were run simultaneously including large numbers of students (i.e., up to 140 students per class), all debriefing sessions employed a written answer sheet. In other words, the debriefing process was performed by the participants themselves, by following written instructions, to remove the possibility of experimenter effects.

2   Method

Participants The present study included 171 university students from Tokyo, Japan aged between 19 and 25 years (mean age = 20.39 ± .89 years); there were 114 females and 57 males.

Procedure The procedure was identical in all experimental conditions. First, the participants filled out a questionnaire (hereafter referred to as the pre-test questionnaire), completed the activity for their condition, and then were either debriefed or not debriefed. Next, as a test scenario, the participants played the Highway Planning Game in groups of four and individual and group performances were measured. Finally, the participants filled out another questionnaire (hereafter referred to as the post-test questionnaire). The overall length of the experiment was 90 min, which included the briefing and debriefing procedures.

Experimental Design and Manipulations. The present study utilized a between-subjects design with eight experimental conditions (Table 1).

Treatments. In our opinion, it is not sufficient to only assess the effects of different types of debriefing, because it is possible that the gaming experience itself could generate a positive mood among the participants, thus encouraging learning even without debriefing. To examine this possibility, a "fun game" condition with no debriefing element– the Footsteps game [10] – was included in the present study and

Table 1. Summary of the experimental design

Condition	(5) Pre-test-questionnaire	(15) Treatment	(5) Debriefing	(30) Test-scenario game	(5) Post-test-questionnaire
1	yes	Fun game	no	yes	yes
2	yes	PD game	no	yes	yes
3	yes	PD game	self-completed	yes	yes
4	yes	PD game	written guidelines	yes	yes
5	yes	PD game	written guidelines + conceptual frame	yes	yes
6	yes	Text	no	yes	yes
7	yes	Picture (comic)	no	yes	yes
8	yes	no	no	yes	yes

Note: Numbers in parentheses indicate time in minutes.

played in pairs. The study also included the Prisoner's Dilemma (PD) game, which is a modified version of the Baregg Tunnel game [11]; this educational game concerns conflict and cooperation and was also played in pairs.

To precisely measure the effects of gaming, it is necessary to compare gaming with other learning activities. Thus, the present study included three conditions without games. The first of these conditions involved pairs of participants reading a text about cooperation and conflict, extracted and translated into Japanese [p. 362–367; 12]; the text comprised approximately 1,000 Japanese characters and the participants were asked to underline the most important points. The second non-game condition involved pairs of participants looking at an image relating to cooperation and conflict. The image contained a small number of sequential pictures (i.e., a comic strip), portraying two donkeys, which began with a conflict situation and ended in cooperation. The comics were taken from a book [p. 349; 11] and did not include an explanation. The third condition was the "control group without treatment" condition.

Debriefing. The study included four debriefing categories. The first category did not involve a debriefing (no debriefing); the second involved self-completed debriefing; the third involved debriefing with written guidance; and the fourth involved debriefing with written guidance and a conceptual frame.

In the self-completed debriefing condition, the participants were asked to discuss the gaming experience freely in pairs. In the debriefing condition with written guidance, pairs of participants discussed the following four subsets of questions that were written on an instruction sheet: (1) "How did you feel during the game?" and "Describe your feelings during the game."; (2) "What happened during the game?" and "Talk about your perceptions, observations, and current thoughts about the game"; (3) "In what respects are aspects of the game connected with reality?" and "What are the commonalities between the game and reality?" (e.g., behaviors used both in the game and in society); and (4) "What did you learn?" and "What are the main conclusions you can draw from the gaming experience?".

The debriefing condition with written guidance and a conceptual frame aimed to explore the effects of debriefing that provided the participants with an opportunity to more deeply reflect on the gaming experience. According to Kolb's learning cycle [13], a gaming experience can be conceptualized as including a "concrete experience" and "observations and reflections" as the first and second steps. Although debriefing after the gaming session could accelerate the reflection process, the third and fourth steps (i.e., "formation of abstract concepts and generalizations" and "testing implications of concepts in new situations") are essentially for participants to complete by themselves. It seems somewhat difficult for participants to derive abstract concepts from concrete experiences. However, if at least the third debriefing step is included, this would facilitate more effective and deeper learning. In the presently described condition, the participants were given a conceptual frame, or theory, with which to interpret their experience of the game in addition to the four abovementioned questions.

All of the debriefing conditions had written instructions and did not include verbal debriefing from an experimenter (facilitator).

Test-Scenario-game (The Freeway Planning game). Groups of four participants played the Highway Planning Game, which involves communication, teamwork, cooperation, and conflict [1]. Typically, the Highway Planning Game is played by groups of six players with different roles, but only four roles were used in the present experiment; i.e., Archeologist, Resident, Storekeeper, and City Engineer. Each participant in the groups of four students assumed one of the roles during the game, the ultimate goal of which was to agree on a common route for the highway that, at the same time, was advantageous for each individual. Each participant received a map featuring hexagons (representing land) and symbols (representing houses, shops, mountains, and cultural and archeological sites). Each student were required to pay different penalties, according to their assumed role, for building the highway through hexagons with symbols that were relatively more or less important from their particular perspective.

Dependent variables. The study measured two types of dependent variable to evaluate the effects of both the games and the debriefing. The first type of dependent variable encompassed performance indices that were calculated according to the number of hexagons that the highway passed through (each consumption of a hexagon of land causes penalties), the route used and the penalties (for destroying objects situated on the land) that were incurred. The second type of dependent variable encompassed the questionnaires assessing cooperation and leadership that were completed before and after the activity; i.e., a pre- and post-test questionnaire. Attitudes toward cooperation were indexed by five items (e.g., "It is important to cooperate to achieve a goal", "I prioritize my own interests over helping others" (reverse item), and "I like to actively cooperate when necessary"). Leadership was assessed by one item, as follows: "When working in a team, I prefer to take a leadership role rather than be a follower".

The study also measured learning effects, teamwork behaviors, and satisfaction regarding the results of the game using 5-point Likert scales ranging from 1 (*strongly disagree*) to 5 (*strongly agree*). These items included the following: "I am satisfied with the results of the game", "I told the others what the most important result was for us", and "Through playing the game, I know more about the factors involved in effective teamwork". Additionally, items assessing the game playing experience, experience of the group work, and several demographic variables were included in the post-test questionnaire.

3   Results

3.1   Performance

There were no statistically significant performance differences among the experimental conditions. This was likely due to there being an insufficient amount of data to conduct an analysis of variance (ANOVA) including all eight conditions; there were only 3–6 groups (of four students) per condition. Therefore, to provide a rough initial look at this study, the data were merged into two conditions: Condition A, in which the participants either did not play an educational game (PD game) or played a game without debriefing (original conditions 1, 2, 6, 7, and 8), and Condition B, in which the participants played an educational game and received some form of debriefing (original conditions 3, 4, and 5).

The group results are shown in Table 2. Groups that played a game and received a debriefing exhibited better performance compared to those that either did not play a game or played a game without debriefing. Better performance was indexed by the following:

- less total use of land (i.e., less hexagons used on the game board);
- lower total cost to the group (calculated by summing the costs incurred by all four participants in the group); and
- smaller standard deviation between individual costs (taking into account the sum of the costs incurred by all four participants in the group).

Lower scores denoted greater social equality; i.e., all group members made sacrifices of equal magnitude when deciding on the joint route compared with the egoistic optimum for each individual role.

3.2   Changes in Attitudes Toward Cooperation and Leadership

A two-way ANOVA with experimental condition as the between-subjects factor and pre- and post-test questionnaire results as within-subject factors was conducted. The analysis revealed that attitudes toward cooperation significantly decreased after playing the Highway Planning Game ($F_{(1,157)} = 1102.67$, $p < .001$; Table 3) but the main effect of experimental condition and the interaction effect were not significant ($F_{(7,157)} < 1$ and $F_{(7,157)} = 1.09$, respectively; n.s.). On the other hand, leadership significantly increased after playing the Highway Planning Game ($F_{(1,158)} = 5.77$, $p < .05$; Table 4). The main effect of experimental condition ($F_{(7,157)} = 2.05$, $0.05 < p < .10$) and the interaction effect ($F_{(7,158)} = 1.82$, $0.05 < p < .10$) were marginally significant.

Table 2. Means of performance indices

Performance indices	A: No game or no debriefing (N = 25)	B: Game with debriefing (N = 18)
Number of hexagons	17.00 (2.92)	16.22 (.88)
Total cost	464.12 (53.39)	445.17 (22.45)
Equality of costs	19.65 (7. 85)	19.07 (7.85)

Note: numbers in parentheses show standard deviation.

Table 3. Means of attitude toward cooperation

Condition	Before	After	N
Fun game with no debriefing	3.91 (.23)	3.08 (.28)	18
PD-game with no debriefing	3.95 (.30)	3.17 (.32)	12
PD-game, self-organized debriefing	3.82 (.40)	2.93 (.32)	24
PD-game, written guided debriefing	3.81 (.35)	2.99 (.37)	23
PD-game, guided and conceptual frame	3.80 (.32)	2.95 (.29)	24
Text	3.85 (.38)	2.97 (.30)	30
Picture	3.96 (.37)	2.91 (.46)	18
Control	3.88 (.42)	3.06 (.32)	16
Total	3.86 (.35)	3.00 (.33)	165

Note: Numbers in parentheses show standard deviation.

Table 4. Means of attitude toward leadership

Condition	Before	After	N
Fun game with no debriefing	2.56 (.92)	2.89 (.96)	18
PD-game with no debriefing	2.41 (.90)	2.50 (1.09)	12
PD-game, self-organized debriefing	3.29 (.95)	3.29 (1.12)	24
PD-game, written guided debriefing	2.52 (.95)	3.22 (.74)	23
PD-game, guided and conceptual frame	3.12 (.94)	3.25 (.85)	24
Text	2.60 (1.00)	2.80 (1.00)	30
Picture	2.79 (.63)	2.89 (.88)	18
Control	3.06 (.93)	2.85 (1.02)	16
Total	2.81 (.95)	3.00 (.97)	165

Note: Numbers in parentheses show standard deviation.

4 Discussion

Task performance in the present study did not significantly differ among conditions, but this was likely due to the small number of groups that were assessed. However, the results were as expected (as shown by the mean scores) in indicating that the groups that played a game and then received a debriefing exhibited better performance than did the groups that either did not play a game or played a game but did not receive a debriefing. Future research with a larger number of participants and groups in each of the eight conditions will be necessary to validate the hypothesis that completion of educational games results in better performance in a subsequent test scenario compared to conditions that do not include a game. Additionally, our research group intends to investigate the hypothesis that games including debriefing lead to better performance. It was hypothesized that the condition that included debriefing with written guidance and a conceptual frame would produce the best performance, followed by the debriefing with written guidance only condition and the self-completed (unstructured) debriefing condition.

The present study found significant differences in questionnaire data among conditions, probably because these data were in the form of individual responses. The test scenario game can also be interpreted as being an experimental condition in the context of the differences between the pre- and post-questionnaire data. All participants in all conditions played the Highway Planning Game and, overall, attitudes towards taking a leadership role after playing the game got significantly stronger after playing the game. This was interpreted to mean that the study participants were more involved and engaged in the game, and were trying to contribute to resolving the predetermined role/conflict scenario. However, the degree of cooperation significantly decreased from a very high level (pre-game) to a medium level, or even to a medium level of conflict (post-game).

This finding is in accordance with the leadership results. After playing the Highway Planning Game, the individual players (and groups) were more engaged in negotiation and bargaining, and actively attempted to solve conflicts. In trying to solve conflicts, engage in different forms of cooperative behavior, and ensure equality among group members in terms of penalties, the participants had to deal with conflict in an authentic way and leave their comfort zone. Therefore, the decrease from unrealistically high levels of cooperation to a more realistic level of conflict during the game is actually a positive sign with respect to maintaining harmony within the group (i.e., "cozy" team behavior as seen prior to playing the game). According to previous research on conflict levels and group performance [p. 409; 14], very high and very low levels of conflict are both signs of dysfunction that lead to low group performance. Thus, a medium level of conflict may be optimal, because such functional conflict can lead to higher group performance. In the present study, there was a significant shift towards this functional level of conflict within the groups, but at the same time the conflict level did not become too high. Nevertheless, additional data will be necessary to explore the differences in conflict levels among the eight conditions in more detail.

Our group has several plans for future research. First, the number of participants and groups in the experiments will be increased to detect the effects of different debriefing methods more precisely. Second, additional methods of debriefing will be assessed. For example, at least two forms of standardized oral debriefing supervised by a moderating facilitator (with and without a conceptual frame) will be included, because this is more common in the debriefing sessions of studies on games and simulations. Third, the present study was originally designed as an international collaboration between Austria and Japan, and the Austrian branch of the study will begin soon. Based on the present data, several inferences regarding the characteristics of our Japanese cohort, with respect to cooperation and conflict resolution, can be drawn, particularly regarding consensus-making; the results could be different in the Austrian population. Additionally, cultural influences on the effectiveness of different forms of debriefing will be investigated. These data should produce interesting results regarding cultural differences in cooperation and negotiation that will contribute to gaming and simulation research, as well as the field of conflict resolution. Finally, future studies could also include participants from countries other than Japan and Austria.

Acknowledgments. Part of this work was supported by JSPS KAKENHI Grant Number JP15K0436.

References

1. Meadows, D., Seif, A.: Creating high performance teams for sustainable development: 58 initiatives. The Institute for Policy and Social Science Research, University of New Hampshire, Durham, NH (1995)
2. Kriz, W.C.: A Systems-oriented Constructivism Approach to the Facilitation and Debriefing of Simulations and Games. Simulation & Gaming **41**(5), 663–680 (2010)
3. Peters, V.A.M., Vissers, G.A.N.: A simple classification model for debriefing simulation games. Simul. Gaming **35**(1), 70–84 (2004)
4. Lederman, L.C.: Debriefing: toward a systematic assessment of theory and practice. Simul. Gaming **23**, 145–160 (1992)
5. Decker, S., Fey, M., Sideras, S., Caballero, S., Rockstraw, L., Boese, T., Borum, J.C.: Standards of best practice: simulation standard VI: the debriefing process. Clin. Simul. Nurs. **9**(6), S26–S29 (2013)
6. Pavlov, O.V., Saeed, K., Robinson, L.W.: Improving instructional simulation with structural debriefing. Simul. Gaming **46**(3–4), 383–403 (2015)
7. Van den Hoogen, J., Lo, J., Meijer, S.: Debriefing research games: context, substance and method. Simul. Gaming **47**(3), 368–388 (2016)
8. Crookall, D.: Serious games, debriefing, and simulation/gaming as a discipline. Simul. Gaming **41**, 898–920 (2010)
9. Crookall, D.: Engaging (in) gameplay and (in) debriefing. Simul. Gaming **45**(4–5), 416–427 (2014)
10. Footsteps (Author unknown). http://www.gamecabinet.com/rules/Footsteps.html
11. Capaul, R., Ulrich, M.: Planspiele: Simulationsspiele für Unterricht und Training mit Kurztheorie: Simulations- und Planspielmethodik. Tobler Verlag AG, Altstätten (2003)
12. Johnson, D.W., Johnson, F.P.: Joining Together: Group Theory and Group Skills, 5th edn. Allyn and Bacon, Needham Heights (1994)
13. Kolb, D.A.: Experiential Learning: Experience as the Source of Learning and Development. Prentice Hall, Englewood (1984)
14. Furnham, A.: The Psychology of Behavior at Work. Psychology Press, New York (2005)

Transitions – From Deterministic
to Probabilistic Learning Conditions -
Managing Simulations in Complex Conditions

Elyssebeth Leigh$^{(\boxtimes)}$ and Elizabeth Tipton

University of Technology Sydney, Ultimo, Australia
elyssebeth.leigh@icloud.com

Abstract. When human beings congregate – whether in meetings, public pla-
ces, urban environments or learning contexts – there is a need for management
of the emotional content of the milieu. In many situations this is a personal and
private task and its enactment does not intrude on others. In simulations this task
is – to varying degrees – deferred to the facilitator. When simulations and
game-based activities are used for social change purposes a specific set of
(usually) unspoken assumptions must be identified and controlled for. This
paper explores the role of the facilitator in regard to the knowledge and capabilities required to successfully engage the diversity of interests and embedded
assumptions which shape and inform the actions of all those present (including
themselves).

Keywords: Innovation diffusion barriers · Environmental conditions
Power relationships · Skill and attitude development

1 Introduction

Why do people resist change? What causes perfectly acceptable and achievable change
to be stalled, even undone? How do individuals justify their opposition to new concepts? Why do 'good ideas' become mired in delay and denial? What would cause
sensible adults to flee from beneficial new concepts? Understanding how to identify
and address factors behind such resistance to 'good ideas' is an essential first step for
anyone hoping to see their ideas embedded in future developments. We are concerned
here with the role and requirements of individuals given the task of managing public
events intended to achieve 'buy-in' from those affected by change in regard to community engagement projects. The merits of such changes are acknowledged as having
an ongoing impact on all activity, and are usually subject to intense scrutiny. We want
to highlight expectations about the person/s tasked with managing those public events,
and how hidden assumptions may affect their capacity to operate effectively.

We suggest that 'resistance' is logical, practical and familiar and that even great
ideas are opposed when they first emerge as alternatives to current practices and beliefs,
especially when they seem likely to alter social and power relationships.

Apart from the emotions raised by the nature of proposed physical and
community-based changes responses to ideas promulgated in public meetings are often

© Springer International Publishing AG, part of Springer Nature 2018
H. K. Lukosch et al. (Eds.): ISAGA 2017, LNCS 10825, pp. 181–190, 2018.
https://doi.org/10.1007/978-3-319-91902-7_18

based on challengeable - but widely accepted – assumptions. Such assumptions also shape beliefs about what is appropriate when constructing and managing meeting formats, as well as concern for who is 'in control' of the process. Facilitators championing use of simulations and games for such engagements, can quickly become mired in diverse – and often diffuse – forms of resistance to, and denial of, their efficacy. Such opposition may come from employers as well as those present and involved, and can severely limit the options available for achieving positive engagement with urban change projects. When the process is not well managed this may ensure ongoing opposition as long as emotionally charged issues remain unresolved.

2 Assumptions and Beliefs

We all have embedded, hidden, assumptions about 'how things work' which shape and inform our responses to events and conditions. One way of thinking about where and how they are embedded in human thinking is to consider the formation and basic tenets of educational curricula and how these influence our responses. In her work on the formation and sources of educational curricula, Wilson [9] lists eleven different ways of thinking about them, and describes assumptions and beliefs underlying each one. Community engagement activities, insofar as they are educationally oriented, encounter similar assumptions and beliefs, making her work a useful tool for exploring the 'world views' or mental models held by individuals likely to engage in community engagement projects.

Each of the perspectives informing these curricula have their own stakeholders and driving forces. A wise facilitator facing the task of managing public communication events will give close attention to addressing as many of these assumptions and sets of beliefs as possible, well before engaging with their audience.

They remain constantly aware that not everything can be anticipated, so that reserves of energy must be withheld for unexpected emergences. This paper (i) explores barriers to implementing innovation, (ii) suggests how Wilson's list of explanatory frameworks can inform planning and management of public communication events, (iii) offers a knowledge management approach with which to address emerging conflicts, and (iv) proposes use of knowledge management tools as a way to prepare for unknown uncertainties and emergent opposition. Change champions must navigate these perspectives, while they help resistors to sustain the status quo. Thus a problem for those hoping to create and sustain change may be too many forces are arrayed against them. Their own enthusiasm may be their own worst enemy (Table 1).

Overstepping, even unintentionally, the mark of advocacy for change frequently generates stakeholder opposition, influencing and shaping one or more of Wilson's curricula. This is seldom clearly defined and can be passed by, easily and quickly.

Motivated by curiosity, pleasure in working with what is 'new', and enjoyment of the challenge of being at the leading edge, early enthusiasts may not even realise that they have moved beyond the 'known' into unknown territory. In a major educational change strategy, Jerome Bruner and his supporters discovered this in the 1970's as they strove to implement a celebrated – and reviled – educational program called "Man: A Course Of Study" (MACOS). The initially enthusiastic uptake was worn away by a

Table 1. Forms of curricula compared across domains of activity

Forms of educational curricula	Community engagement concepts
Overt, explicit, or written curriculum	
That written as part of formal instruction of schooling experiences.	Documents and guides for community development/urban renewal projects.
Societal curriculum	
Informal curriculum of socializing forces "educating" all of us throughout our lives.	Informal forces at work shaping social perspectives on planned actions.
Hidden or covert curriculum	
Derived from the nature and organizational design of school, as well as the behaviors and attitudes of teachers and administrators.	Factors so familiar, in a context, as to be hidden - e.g. side of the road on which we drive; shape and operation of traffic lights
Null curriculum	
What we **do not teach**, giving a message that it is not important in education or in society.	Things we **do not talk about**: inequities in access to housing; accessible public transport, etc.
Phantom curriculum	
Messages given in/through exposure to media.	What/how media sources speak about our context.
Concomitant curriculum	
Taught/emphasized at home; experiences *as* a family, or sanctioned *by* the family.	Messages from family through use/non-use of relevant public spaces and facilities.
Rhetorical curriculum	
Ideas from policymakers, school officials, administrators, or professionals involved in concept formation and content changes	What we hear politicians and public figures tell us about our environment.
Curriculum-in-use	
As delivered and presented by each teacher.	Evident in facilitators' work and actions.
Received curriculum	
Concepts and content that are truly learned and remembered.	What we take from all we hear/encounter about environmental needs/purposes/values.
Internal curriculum	
Educators have little control over an internal curriculum - it is unique to each student.	We individually make sense of what we hear, receive and remember
Electronic curriculum	
Lessons from searching the Internet for information, and e-forms of communication.	The same for community engagement and urban development as for schooling.

campaign of opposition from conservative Christians who perceived it to be a means of indoctrinating young students into a kind of 'secular humanism' or 'cultural relativism' [4] thus challenging beliefs embedded in powerful societal thinking frameworks. Proposed curricula-in-use changes, championed by MACOS supporters, was seen to have such beneficial potential, that its advocates found it hard to conceive of anyone denying the validity of their work. One key difference between proponents of change, and those who resist, may be that the former sees obstacles as barriers to be overcome on the way to new understanding, while the latter simply regard change as defeat, desolation and loss. For enthusiasts, 'societal' resistance comes as an unpleasant surprise. And unless they prepare and develop sustainable arguments, it will continue to do so for modern evangelists of change – including, in this context – the use of simulations and games as learning strategies.

Given this perspective two key questions emerge –

1. How can those who prefer the safe and familiar learn to appreciate the benefits of loosening their grip on the 'known' and step into new challenges with hope?
2. How can enthusiasts learn to walk alongside those who cannot yet see the benefits and provide insight and guidance appropriate to their concerns, rather than relying on insistent claims of 'value' and 'rightness'?

Addressing these questions requires analysis of both perspectives, and a clear and dispassionate understanding of *why* there is resistance to change. This helps in preparation and accurate application of advocacy strategies. Understanding both the espoused and in-action [1] positions of resisters assist achievement of outcomes that contribute to sustainably improved practices and environments which are also acceptable to all stakeholders who claim an interest in the matter. The causes for opposition and resistance must be addressed - not denied or denigrated.

3   Who 'Consumes' Innovation?

So who are the 'consumers' in settings where the use of 'play' (simulations and games) in change management contexts? Analysis shows there are four identifiable 'consumer groups' in all social change settings. The first, most obvious, consumer-group is participants involved in the process of 'playing to learn' about change. The other three groups may not be obvious 'consumers' but addressing their needs and concerns is vital, because the use of games and simulations for community engagement must pass through their 'gateways' before reaching the players.

- The first 'gateway' is defended by those who are unfamiliar with such communication strategies and yet are asked to use them to achieve pre-determined goals. They are conscious of demands for consistency and conformity, and concerned about their own insecurities in regard to using such strategies. They believe they know what has worked with relevant target groups before, and are hesitant to stray from the 'tried and true'.
- The second 'gateway' is watched over by administrators who believe they must control what happens in public meetings within their context. They want outcomes and progress, yet are reluctant to try anything that may not guarantee desired outcomes. They are conscious of other measures of performance, especially ones used by those controlling the final gateway.
- This final 'gateway' is safeguarded by external groups – parents, social groups, professional and government bodies who are certain of their right to intervene. Members of this group may be unaware of the paradoxical nature of their demands

on all the other consumers. These external groups, may – at any time – emerge to drive opposition to many proposed changes.

While we respect the power of this final group and are concerned by the frequently paradoxical nature of their opposition, this chapter offers facilitators and administrators resources for addressing such opposition to good ideas.

Observed from enough distance, all these groups can be seen as engaged in a formal 'dance' with pre-determined steps timeframes and rules. As long as everyone performs the steps in an agreed manner the dance continues. Disturbing the steps of the dance challenges everything. Introducing change strategies that may unsettle the 'rhythm of the dance', can be disturbing and will generate opposition.

4   Deterministic and Probabilistic Environments

Reducing the impact of such opposition needs focused attention on identifying and resolving the causes for both overt and covert (unexpressed) reservations. This section introduces two ways of thinking about how to manage and set up the environments for public engagement. These are described as deterministic and probabilistic environments which each has characteristics, benefits and drawbacks.

Deterministic environments
Deterministic environments are familiar to everyone. Human beings have been establishing and using them for centuries. While they enable us to impart vast quantities of information they do not always accurately address the immediate needs of those being 'informed'. A 'deterministic environment' is one where conditions are completely predictable [10] which is exactly what many are led to believe is the best setting for achieving information transfer. In the world of artificial intelligence – where this term is frequently found – this may be true. However, it can seldom be applied to effective information sharing among human beings in the 21st century where the goal is achieving satisfactory transitions to new and different conditions. Deterministic environments are comfortable but unchallenging.

While human organisations are not 'completely' predictable environments, working to achieve predictability is often considered desirable. In this context, challenges to its validity are considered traitorous denials of the validity of the 'ideal'.

4.1   Probabilistic Environments

Probabilistic environments are the common state of most simulations and games. As Klayman [6] notes -

A great deal of what people know about the world is handed to us from learners of the past, through books, schools, and social interaction. But if knowledge is to be advanced, or new problems mastered, we must of necessity learn from experience in probabilistic environments.

Using simulation or game-based activities affect all the factors which support stable relationships in deterministic educational settings. They do so in ways that individuals, who like certainty and order, will inevitably find hard to accept. Games introduce uncertainty and alter relationships, shift perceptions of power and authority and redefine disruption. Outcomes will 'probably' be as predicted – but are never certain to be so. The uncertainty of 'probabilistic' environments is unlikely to be attractive to individuals who prefer stability and order and keeping control. Sensibly enough, they do not welcome efforts to destabilize things, especially when a tenuous goal of 'advancing knowledge/living conditions/etc.' in some unknown future context, is not equivalent to maintaining control now.

4.2   Resisting the Transition

Failure to address real and immediate concerns about loss of control is a sure fire way to generate resistance to change. Relying on enthusiasm for 'new' ideas while not providing adequate support or rationale for thoughtful transitions from order to uncertainty is not an effective way to generate enthusiasm for change. As Machiavelli (quoted in Watford, 2006) noted succinctly

> there is nothing more difficult to take in hand, more perilous to conduct, or more uncertain of success, than to take the lead in the introduction of a new order of things. Because the innovator has for enemies all those who have done well under the old conditions, and lukewarm defenders in those who may do well under the new.

And in this regard Dewey [3] noted that

> Man is not logical and his intellectual history is a record of mental reserves and compromises. He hangs on to what he can in his old beliefs even when he is compelled to surrender their logical basis.

So we should not be surprised if over-enthusiastic promotion of new ideas, that seem to come with attendant denial of the value of current efforts, generates a hardening of resistance, and not unalloyed joy. Committed enthusiasts do not have a clear view of the problems anticipated by resistors, considering them simply to be 'challenges to be overcome' bypassing deeper implications. Those who are not fearful of challenges are prepared for occasional failures relishing the delights of new, original and engaging learning. However, they are regularly surprised by the vehemence of resistance, asking in surprise *"can't you see the delights to be enjoyed?"* and are unable to accept the legitimacy of the response *"No! No I can't"*.

5   Encouraging Uptake

If enthusiasm and clear sighted awareness of the value of games and simulations for learning is not sufficient to help resistors consider adopting them – what will be enough to make new ideas acceptable? We propose nine key actions to help 'early adopters of games for learning' assist colleagues in making a shift in their thinking and practices. Four of these are "always do", three are "never do's" while the last three are "backup options" to keep in mind.

5.1   Strategies to Encourage Uptake

Listen
The first logical, but often difficult, action involves simply listening to objections and seeking out the 'question behind the question' [8] that is shaping a speaker's concerns and objections.

Understand the constraints in the wider context
The second strategy requires allowing time to understand a speaker's wider context. It will often be that they are – or believe themselves to be - in a place that is not supportive of innovation. Give them credit for understanding the limitations imposed on them, and seek ways to help them expand their horizons by walking alongside them instead of rushing at them front on.

Acknowledge all efforts
Thirdly, acknowledge and admire all efforts to be good at what they do and how they do it. Remember, no one deliberately set out to be a 'poor performer', and educators, more than most, value quality performance.

Listening, understanding and acknowledging the present situation, will also generate resources and insights to assist in addressing resistance to change. This helps create an atmosphere of mutual admiration rather than shared dislike.

At all times - Exercise restraint
The first – and most constant – action to take when working to achieve uptake of new ideas is the exercise of restraint in regard to displays of enthusiasm and engagement. Enthusiasts too easily forget their own first tentative steps, the failures and setbacks that contributed to their present engagement with new ideas. The rush of excitement when something works – and then continues to deliver on its promise - obscures early doubts and deletes memories of those initial hesitations.

5.2   Actions and Beliefs to Avoid

These all involve conscious effort and require rigid avoidance of criticism.

Never claim to have the 'right' answer
Never insist that you possess 'the right answer' to a problem. Claims of 'rightness' are seldom a winning argument when working with resistors uncertain of their own fallibility and certainly unconvinced by your enthusiasm. Halfman et al. [5] noted -

> *Difficulties of Change. .... to suggest an alternative [to my well-practiced actions] is, by definition, to attack me.*

Avoid rushing in - "Angels" have a special wisdom
The saying that "fools rush in where angels fear to tread" is vital when promoting change. Never push pass resistance. Stop and consider its origins and causes; and accept that it has a validity which may initially escape you.

Promote slow change
Never demand swift replacement of existing practices with new ones. Invite engagement, seek adaptation, encourage small tests, support small steps, celebrate minor

changes and resist the impulse to rush to change. The hare and the tortoise show the problem of using speed to get to a difficult goal.

5.3 Backup Options – Strategies to Consider

Tackle projects collaboratively
Work with 'like minds' who have a capacity to influence resistors. Offer to do some of the work in tandem with the person/team you are engaged with. This help with handing on ideas and skills in a collaborative atmosphere and enacts the mantra of "teaching a man to fish gives him a lifetime of skills, rather than giving him a fish, which only feeds him today and leaves him to starve again tomorrow".

Publicise indicators of change
Ensure that achievements are widely advertised remembering that 'nothing succeeds so well as obvious success'. This takes longer – but then again everything that is worth doing does so.

Provide resources – do not impose their use
Make resources available but do not inflict them on others. Make them easy to read, and use. Help others find the fun in new activities – the WIIFM[1] factor is a powerful motivator. And make yourself available when someone is ready to ask about the new ideas you are proposing!

6 Why Games and Simulations Unsettle Stability

Regardless of the care with which a game or simulation is chosen to achieve specific communication goals, it is vital to remember that intended learning outcomes can be affected by circumstances – and may be unknown until they emerge during the action. Sometimes this may be simply a small shift sideways into topics not usually touched on in similar conditions; however, on some occasions the shift can be so dramatic that a planned lesson does not occur.

For a facilitator, decisions about choosing – or not choosing – to use simulations and games for communication activities will determine much of what happens next. In effect, pre-conditions shape mindsets. A factor limiting acceptance of games and simulations for community engagement is the tendency to imagine things going wrong, this is often coupled with an emotional state of unease generated by such thoughts. To call experienced group facilitators 'novices' may seem discourteous. However being skilled at 'session management' is not the same as being skilled in managing environments where things will be un-ordered for much of the time. Such conditions require a particular set of skills, since effective actions for probabilistic working conditions involves abstaining from any move to impose 'order'.

---

[1] WIIFM – what's in it for me?

A real and continuing problem facing those promoting change, is the question of how to demonstrate that richer, deeper, yet totally unplanned benefits may emerge during probabilistic conditions and that these may have a profound impact on participants' ultimate success. While such unplanned learning may disrupt a short term plan, the long term gains are well worth the deviation.

7   Perspectives, Theories, Frameworks

In summary, we know that the innovation/diffusion problem is not new. In fact, its impact affects every facet of change, yet enthusiasts committed to achieving social/political/economic change often overlook it as a factor requiring sustained attention. Personal security, emotional inhibitions (e.g. 'locus of control' personal preferences, group dynamics) and organizational/structural factors all influence the capacity of any individual to willingly adopt anything new.

Knowledge Management provides frameworks for deciphering some aspects of the situation, and the psychotherapeutic work of researchers including Wilfred Bion, Carl Rogers, Lev Vygotsky, Ivan Illich, and Karen Horney, provides insights and strategies to address actual and anticipated resistance.

The scope of that work is too broad to be explored here, however the general message from such work is that learning is a complex, multivariate process unique to each individual. While orderliness can impart facts and data and enable one person to maintain control of a situation, it cannot guarantee that the data will be understood, absorbed or made personal or enacted in any future time. In truth nothing can guarantee that.

8   Future Needs

In 1930s the author of the "Saber Tooth Curriculum" - J Abner Pettiwell [2] - pointed out that a particularly vital 'future need' is to eradicate the belief -

> ... that the essence of true education is timelessness. It is something that endures through changing conditions like a solid rock standing squarely and firmly in the middle of a raging torrent. You must know that there are some eternal verities, and the saber-tooth curriculum is one of them!"

in the 21st century awareness of the fact that education must accept change is slowly being accepted - although accompanied by continuing resistance. Facilitators involved in community engagement contexts must accept that this is a dance of two partners – change and resistance - and that their key task is to manage the music so as to allow each partner to remain engaged while moving the whole in a direction most likely to achieve positive outcomes for all – whether these are recognised at once or over a longer period of time.

References

1. Argyris, C.: The Executive Mind, and Double Loop Thinking in Organisational Dynamics. In: Autumn 1982 AMACOM (1982)
2. Benjamin, H.R.W.: Saber-tooth Curriculum, Including Other Lectures in the History of Paleolithic Education. McGraw-Hill, New York City (1939)
3. Dewey, J.: Human Nature and Conduct: An Introduction to Social Psychology. Kessinger Publishing, Whitefish (2005). First published in 1922 by Henry Holt & Co., New York, and G. Allen & Unwin, London
4. First Baptist Church, Perryville, MD. http://www.perryville.org/2013/06/28/clash-of-worldviews%E2%80%94man-a-course-of-study/. Accessed 16 Oct 2012
5. Halfman, R., MacVicar, M., Martin, W., Taylor, E., Zacharias, J.: "Tactics for Change", MIT Occasional Paper No. 11 (1977). http://web.mit.edu/jbelcher/www/TacticsForChange/
6. Klayman, J.: Learning from feedback in probabilistic environments. Acta Psychol. **56**, 81–92 (1984)
7. Metafilter. http://www.metafilter.com/107770/Man-A-Course-of-Study. Accessed 16 Oct 2013
8. Miller, J.: The Question behind the Question (2013). http://qbq.com/. Accessed 8 Aug 2013
9. Wilson, L. http://www4.uwsp.edu/education/lwilson/curric/curtyp.htm. Accessed 16 Oct 2013
10. Xu, X.: EECS 492 Discussion #2 (2010). http://april.eecs.umich.edu/courses/eecs492_w10/wiki/images/4/4f/Disc2_xueyang.pdf. Accessed 6 Aug 2013

A Framework for Developing Multi-Layered Networks of Active Neurons for Simulation Experiments and Model-Based Business Games Using Self-Organizing Data Mining with the Group Method of Data Handling

Mihail Motzev$^{(\boxtimes)}$

School of Business, Walla Walla University, College Place, WA 99324, USA
mihail.motzev@wallawalla.edu

Abstract. Artificial Neural Networks make it possible to develop faster model-based business games, but in general, they are neither easy to develop nor easy to understand. This paper presents a highly automated framework for developing Multi-Layered Networks of Active Neurons for simulation experiments and model-based business games using self-organizing data mining with the Group Method of Data Handling. It discusses some of the results from international research done in Europe, Australia, and most recently at Walla Walla University in College Place, Washington, USA.

Keywords: Business simulations · Model-based business games
Artificial Neural Networks (ANNs)
Multi-Layered Networks of Active Neurons (MLNAN)
Group Method of Data Handling (GMDH)

1 Introduction

Business simulation is described, in general, as a sequential decision-making exercise structure around a model of a business operation, in which participants assume the role of managing the simulated operation [1]. Management and business games are defined as a simplified simulated experiential environment that contains enough verisimilitude, or illusion of reality, to include real world-like responses by those participating in the exercise [2]. Consequently, a simulation game contains a mixture of skills, chance, and strategy to simulate an aspect of reality, such as a stock exchange, with rules that refer to an empirical model of reality. It combines the features of a game (competition, cooperation, rules, participants, roles) with those of a simulation (i.e. incorporation of critical features of reality).

A properly designed simulation game for business training would closely follow the assumptions and rules of the theoretical models within this discipline. In the model-based games, especially, if the game does not accurately represent a real system, then the knowledge that the students receive about real-life business is questionable. Therefore, if the game model is not accurate and the predictions made by students are not close enough to the real-life business case, then learning will be minimal.

© Springer International Publishing AG, part of Springer Nature 2018
H. K. Lukosch et al. (Eds.): ISAGA 2017, LNCS 10825, pp. 191–199, 2018.
https://doi.org/10.1007/978-3-319-91902-7_19

Artificial Neural Networks (ANNs) make it possible to develop faster and more accurate model-based business games, but in general, they are neither easy to develop nor easy to understand. The difficulties with ease of development and use stem mainly from the extensive data preparation required to get good results from a neural network model. The results are difficult to understand because an ANN is a complex nonlinear model that does not produce rules.

This paper presents a highly automated framework for developing *Multi-Layered Networks of Active Neurons (MLNANs)* for simulation experiments and model-based business games using self-organizing data mining with the *Group Method of Data Handling (GMDH)*. It discusses some of the results from international research done in Europe, Australia, and most recently at Walla Walla University in College Place, Washington, USA.

2 Artificial Neural Networks for Business Games and Simulations

The basic objective of *Artificial Neural Networks (ANNs)*, according to Berry and Linoff [3], and many other authors (Zhang et al. [4]) is to construct a model for mimicking the intelligence of the human brain into machine. Similar to the work of a human brain, ANNs try to recognize regularities and patterns in the input data, *"learn"* from experience, and then provide generalized results based on their known previous knowledge.

In neural network terminology, a *neural network* (*NN*) can be thought of as a network of *"neurons"* organized in *layers* as shown on Fig. 1. The factors form the *input layer* (the first layer), and the projections form the *output layer* (the last layer). Each of the inputs gets its own unit, or *network node*. In general, it is not the actual values of the input variables that are *fed* into the input layer, but some transformation of those values. Each input unit is connected to the output unit with a *weight*. Inside the output unit, the input weights are combined using a *combination function* and then passed to a *transfer function*, the result of which is the output of the network. Together, the *combination function* and the *transfer function* make up the unit's *activation function*. The value produced by the output node's activation function is usually some transformation of the actual desired output.

Figure 1(a) contains no hidden layers and can be considered a neural network version of a linear regression with four predictors. The coefficients attached to these predictors are the *weights*. The projections are calculated by a linear combination of the inputs. The weights are selected in the neural network framework using a *learning algorithm* that minimizes a *cost function* such as *Mean Squared Error (MSE)*. Usually, most ANNs have one or more additional layers (called *hidden layers*) of *hidden units* between the input and output layers (Fig. 1b).

If the model, cost function, and learning algorithm are selected appropriately, the resulting ANNs can be extremely robust. ANNs are data-driven and self-adaptive in nature [3, 4] (i.e. there is no need to specify a particular model form or to make any *a priori* assumption about the statistical distribution of the data). Perhaps the greatest advantage of ANNs is their ability to be used as an arbitrary function approximation

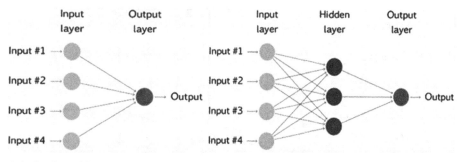

a) A simple Artificial Neural Network   b) Multilayer Feed-Forward Network

Fig. 1. Examples of Artificial Neural Networks

mechanism that *"learns"* from observed data. As mentioned by Hornik and Stinch-combe [5], ANNs are universal functional approximators and can deal with situations where the input data are erroneous, incomplete, or fuzzy, as shown in [6, 7].

ANNs are a good choice for most classification and prediction tasks when the results of the model are more important than understanding how the model works. At the same time, there are many issues that should be addressed during the major steps in ANN model building [8]. For example, in data selection and pre-processing, how can secondary series be inferred for the network generating process, or what forms of data treatment such as scaling, smoothing, interpolation should be applied to training data? Other questions include, given selected and treated data, how should data be segmented for network training? What should the number of input nodes for the NN be (i.e. what is the order of the model)? In ANNs architecture, what should the number of hidden nodes be, and/or which is the best activation function in any given instance, and what bias does it introduce? Concerning learning rule and style, what rule should be used to control the weight update during training? Finally, once all of the above have been completed, how should the network be validated?

3   Group Method of Data Handling ANN Algorithms

The *Group Method of Data Handling (GMDH)*[1] was introduced in 1968 by Alexy Ivakhnenko as a *heuristic self-organizing modeling method* [9]. In GMDH-based self-organizing modeling algorithms, models are generated adaptively from data in the form of *networks of active neurons* in a repetitive generation of populations of competing models of growing complexity, corresponding *cross-validation*, and model selection until an optimal complex model is finalized (Fig. 2).

In ANNs, the user estimates its structure by choosing the number of layers and the number and transfer functions of nodes. This requires not only knowledge about the

---

[1] Group Method of Data Handling (GMDH) is a method of inductive statistical learning. See: www.gmdh.net.

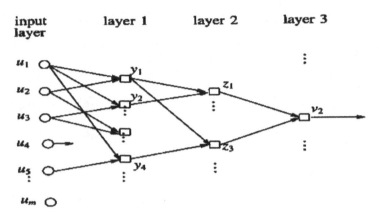

Fig. 2. General scheme of GMDH self-organizing modeling algorithm [9]

theory of ANNs, but also knowledge of the modeled object's nature. In addition, the knowledge from systems theory about the object is not applicable without transformation in the NN world, and the rules of translation are usually unknown.

GMDH ANNs can overcome these problems – they can pick out knowledge about object directly from data sampling. GMDH is an *inductive sorting-out method*, which has advantages in case of rather complex objects and/or when there is no explicit theory.

Comparisons [10] show that, in distinction to neural networks, the results of GMDH algorithms are explicit mathematical models generated in a relatively short time on the basis of even small samples. The well-known problems of an optimal (subjective) choice of the neural network architecture are addressed in the GMDH algorithms by means of an adaptive synthesis (objective choice) of the architecture. GMDH algorithms could be used to estimate networks of the right size with a structure evolved during the estimation process to provide a parsimonious model for the particular desired function. Such algorithms, combining in a powerful way the best features of neural nets and statistical techniques, identify the entire model structure in the form of a network of polynomial functions, differential equations and others. Models are selected automatically based on their ability to solve a given task such as approximation, identification, prediction, or classification.

4   A Framework for Developing Multi-Layered Networks of Active Neurons for Simulation Experiments and Model-Based Business Games with the Group Method of Data Handling

The self-organizing GMDH ANNs are similar in many respects to the NN of active neurons. The goal in combining many neurons into a network is to enhance the accuracy in achieving the assigned task through a better use of input data. The exhaustive search is first applied to determine the number of neuron layers and the sets of input and output variables for each neuron. The minimum of the external criterion suggests the variables for which it is advantageous to build a neural network, as well as how many neuron layers should be used. Active neurons are able, during the self-organizing process, to estimate which inputs are necessary to minimize the given objective function of the neuron.

The framework proposed here for developing a *Multi-Layer Net of Active Neurons (MLNAN)* is a hybrid GMDH algorithm. It works both for multi-input to single-output model identification (for example, different types of regression models) and for building complex models of simultaneous equations (i.e. multi-input to multi-output). The net of complex active neurons identifies the effective inputs and their corresponding coefficients in a process of highly automated self-organization.

The MLNAN model with multiple inputs (x_j) and one output (Y) is a subset of components of the base function (1):

$$Y(x_1, \ldots, x_n) = a_0 + \sum_{i=1}^{m} a_i f_i \qquad (1)$$

- where f_i are functions dependent on different sets of inputs (i = 1, 2 ... m);
- x_j (j = 1, 2 ...n) are the inputs at the first layer (predictors)
- a_0 is the constant term;
- a_i are the unknown coefficients and
- m is the number of the base function components.

In order to find the best solution, MLNAN considers various component subsets of the base function (1) known as *partial models*. Unknown coefficients a_i in these models are estimated by the *Least Squares* (*LS*) method. MLNAN algorithms gradually increase the number of partial model components as shown on Fig. 3 and find a model structure with optimal complexity indicated by the minimum value of an external criterion. For multi-input to single-output model identification task, the framework follows the typical *Multilayered Iterative* (*MIA*) procedure [9], similar to the general scheme of GMDH self-organizing modeling algorithm (Fig. 2). At first, the partial models on a lower layer are estimated and the corresponding intermediate outputs are computed. These outputs become inputs of the next layer where the new partial models are estimated, and so on. Estimation of the coefficients in each partial model is performed using LS and cross validated by MSE criterion [11].

At the first layer, all possible pairs of the inputs are considered as potential factors, and only some of the best (in the sense of the selection criteria – here coefficient of correlation) intermediate partial models are used as inputs for the next layer(s). In the succeeding layers, all possible pairs of the intermediate models from the preceding layer(s) are connected as inputs to the partial models of the next layer(s). This means that the output of a partial model at a given layer is or may become an input (depending on a local threshold value for the selection criterion, which here is the coefficient of determination of the partial model) to one or more partial models at the next layer

(Fig. 3). Finally, if additional layers provide no further improvements to the models' accuracy, the network self-organization stops.

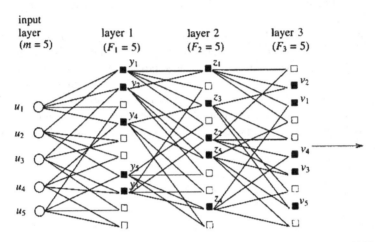

Fig. 3. General scheme of multilayered active neuron neural network (MLNAN) [9]

At the end, a certain predefined number of partial models with similar accuracy from the last layer are selected and the base function (1) for each of them is restored using an automated backward tracking algorithm, providing "*freedom of choice*" (i.e. the user has a set of alternative good models).

In case of synthesizing complex multi-input to multi-output models in the form of *simultaneous equations (SE)*, there is an additional layer where the framework is similar to the *Combinatorial (COMBI) algorithm* [9]. Here:

- Similar to the combinatorial algorithm, the partial models are generated combining already chosen outputs (i.e. equations) from the last layer of multi-input to single-output procedure;
- Each new input represents a hypothesis about the significance of entering a given version of a single equation into the system of SE;
- Each generated system of SE is considered as a potential final model, which competes with other potential models "*fighting for survival*";
- The evaluation of these competing models is performed, using a complex set of criteria – MSE, coefficient of determination, MAPE, and others.
- If the results are unsatisfactory after solving the structural form of the SE (biased values of the coefficients and/or low accuracy of the SE model), the procedure returns to the first step.
- Now, the decision maker can apply new, *a priori* knowledge and/or add fresh data observations (if available), or change the selection criteria. MLNAN begins again, and with the so-updated new set of equations, the final part is repeated. The iterations end when satisfactory results are achieved. In the end, the user has a set of alternative SE models with similar accuracy.

The final choice of the best model is made by the decision maker, who has the option to apply additional insights, qualitative information, or knowledge, but after having the guarantee that a large number of possible models have been evaluated and the final choice is based on a small number of good ones.

The main advantages of MLNAN over structural identification, genetic and best regression selection algorithms are as follows:

- *Use of external criteria*, which are based on cross-validation and are adequate to model building with low volume of initial information;
- It provides *more diversity of structure identification* than in regression algorithms through full/reduced sorting out of structure variants in multi layered procedures;
- *Higher level of automation* – it has a multi layered structure which allows parallel computing, and it is only necessary to enter the initial data sample and the type of external criterion – no need of data preprocessing at all;
- *Provides additional definition and automatic adaptation* of optimal model complexity and the external criteria to the level of noise or statistical variation – effect of noise immunity causes robustness of the approach;
- *Applies the principle of inconclusive decisions and freedom of choice* in the process of gradual models complication.

Of course, there are limitations of such algorithms based on data fitting. For example, the future cannot always be predicted based on history; using relations derived from historical data to predict the future implicitly assumes certain steady-state conditions or constants in the complex system.

Another issue is the "*unknown unknowns*". In all data collection, the researcher first defines the set of variables for which data is collected. However, no matter how extensive the researcher considers his selection of the variables, there is always the possibility of new variables that have not been considered or even defined, yet that are critical to the outcome.

5 Applications

The MLNAN presented above provides processed data that are needed in the business context. The researcher has to decide the relative importance of the facts generated within the framework. The extracted information is useful to a business in making decisions that create value or that predict market behavior in a way that provide a competitive advantage.

MLNAN algorithms have been used successfully in many different areas, including simulation experiments and model-based business games for training and education. The first working prototype of the MLNAN described above was used to improve an existing business game [12]. The "National Economy" game has been used for many years at the Economic University in Sofia, Bulgaria. The original version contains a model developed with the general multiple regression analysis. The same data and set of variables were used to build a new model using the MLNAN algorithm. The new model has much better accuracy (more than five times smaller MSE%) and thus provides a more reliable base for simulations and what-if analysis. Increasing model accuracy also provides many other benefits [6].

More recently, the MLNAN was used in the process of developing the "NEW PRODUCT" game series at the Walla Walla University in College Place, USA [13] – an integrated, role-playing, model-based, simulation game designed for the purposes of business training and education. The latest versions of the game cover all major stages in the process of new product planning and development, production and operations management, sales and marketing. It could be used not only as an educational tool for teaching business, but it may also be carried out for business training in general management, production management, inventory and stock control, and small business management.

Another area of application of the MLNAN is the predictive modeling. A series of increasingly complex simulation models of the Bulgarian economy was developed with a very high level of accuracy [11, 12]. It is worth mentioning that a similar algorithm is used [10] successfully in developing a simulation model of the National Economy of Germany. Simulations and predictions made with both models show almost insignificant difference in their errors and similar high level of accuracy [12].

6   Conclusions

The proposed framework helps researchers by making business simulations and model-based business games development more cost-effective. All results so far show that it is able to develop even complex models reliably with better overall error rates than state-of-the-art methods.

The framework makes it possible to develop faster model-based business games and to improve the decisions that students make during the games. It provides opportunities to shorten time and reduce the cost and efforts in game model building and at the same time to develop reliable complex models with low overall error rates. Increasing model accuracy helps users to analyze problems more precisely, which leads to deeper and better understanding. Finally, models with increased accuracy generate better predictions and support managers in making better decisions that more closely relate to real-life business problems.

References

1. Greenlaw, P., Herron, L., Rawdon, R.: Business Simulation in Industrial and University Education. Prentice-Hall, Englewood Cliffs (1962)
2. Keys, B., Wolfe, J.: The role of management games and simulations in education and research. J. Manage. **16**(1), 307–336 (1990)
3. Berry, M., Linoff, G.: Mastering Data Mining. Wiley, Hoboken (2000)
4. Zhang, G., Patuwo, B., Hu, M.: Forecasting with artificial neural networks: The state of the art. Int. J. Forecast. **14**, 35–62 (1998)
5. Hornik, K., Stinchcombe, M., White, H.: Multilayer feed-forward networks are universal approximators. Neural Networks **2**, 359–366 (1989)
6. Mueller, J.-A., Lemke, F.: Self-Organizing Data Mining: An Intelligent Approach to Extract Knowledge from Data. Trafford Publishing, Victoria (2003)

7. Onwubolu, G. (ed.): Hybrid Self-Organizing Modeling Systems. Springer, Heidelberg (2009). https://doi.org/10.1007/978-3-642-01530-4
8. Kingdon, J.: Intelligent Systems and Financial Forecasting. Springer, Heidelberg (1997). https://doi.org/10.1007/978-1-4471-0949-5
9. Madala, H., Ivakhnenko, A.G.: Inductive Learning Algorithms for Complex Systems Modelling. CRC Press Inc., Boca Raton (1994)
10. Müller, J-A., Lemke, F. Self-organizing modelling and decision support in economics. In: Proceedings of The IMACS Symposium on Systems Analysis and Simulation, pp. 135–138. Gordon and Breach Publishers (1995)
11. Motzev, M., Marchev, A.: Multi-Stage Selection Algorithms in Simulation. In: Proceedings of XII IMACS World Congress, Paris, vol. 4, pp. 533–535 (1988)
12. Motzev, M., Lemke, F. Self-organizing data mining techniques in model based simulation games for business training and education. In: Vanguard Sci. Instrum. Manag. 11 (2016)
13. Motzev, M.: New product – an integrated simulation game in business education. In: Bonds and Bridges. Proceedings of the World Conference of the ISAGA, pp. 63–75 (2012)

Author Index

Printed in the United States
By Bookmasters